*Studies in Economic Transition*

*General Editors*: **Jens Hölscher**, Senior Lecturer in Economics, University of Brighton; and **Horst Tomann**, Professor of Economics, Free University Berlin

This new series has been established in response to a growing demand for a greater understanding of the transformation of economic systems. It brings together theoretical and empirical studies on economic transition and economic development. The post-communist transition from planned to market economies is one of the main areas of applied theory because in this field the most dramatic examples of change and economic dynamics can be found. The series aims to contribute to the understanding of specific major economic changes as well as to advance the theory of economic development. The implications of economic policy will be a major point of focus.

*Titles include*:

Lucian Cernat
EUROPEANIZATION, VARIETIES OF CAPITALISM AND ECONOMIC PERFORMANCE IN CENTRAL AND EASTERN EUROPE

Irwin Collier, Herwig Roggemann, Oliver Scholz and Horst Tomann (*editors*)
WELFARE STATES IN TRANSITION
East and West

Bruno Dallago (*editor*)
TRANSFORMATION AND EUROPEAN INTEGRATION
The Local Dimension

Hella Engerer
PRIVATIZATION AND ITS LIMITS IN CENTRAL AND EASTERN EUROPE
Property Rights in Transition

Hubert Gabrisch and Rüdiger Pohl (*editors*)
EU ENLARGEMENT AND ITS MACROECONOMIC EFFECTS IN EASTERN EUROPE
Currencies, Prices, Investment and Competitiveness

Oleh Havrylyshyn
DIVERGENT PATHS IN POST-COMMUNIST TRANSFORMATION
Capitalism for All or Capitalism for the Few?

Jens Hölscher (*editor*)
FINANCIAL TURBULENCE AND CAPITAL MARKETS IN TRANSITION COUNTRIES

Jens Hölscher and Anja Hochberg (*editors*)
EAST GERMANY'S ECONOMIC DEVELOPMENT SINCE UNIFICATION
Domestic and Global Aspects

Mihaela Kelemen and Monika Kostera (*editors*)
CRITICAL MANAGEMENT RESEARCH IN EASTERN EUROPE
Managing the Transition

Emil J. Kirchner (*editor*)
DECENTRALIZATION AND TRANSITION IN THE VISEGRAD
Poland, Hungary, the Czech Republic and Slovakia

Tomasz Mickiewicz
ECONOMIC TRANSITION IN CENTRAL EUROPE AND THE CIS COUNTRIES

Julie Pellegrin
THE POLITICAL ECONOMY OF COMPETITIVENESS IN AN ENLARGED EUROPE

Stanislav Poloucek (*editor*)
REFORMING THE FINANCIAL SECTOR IN CENTRAL EUROPEAN COUNTRIES

Gregg S. Robins
BANKING IN TRANSITION
East Germany after Unification

Johannes Stephan
ECONOMIC TRANSITION IN HUNGARY AND EAST GERMANY
Gradualism and Shock Therapy in Catch-up Development

Johannes Stephan (*editor*)
TECHNOLOGY TRANSFER VIA FOREIGN DIRECT INVESTMENT IN CENTRAL AND EASTERN EUROPE

Hans van Zon
THE POLITICAL ECONOMY OF INDEPENDENT UKRAINE

Adalbert Winkler (*editor*)
FINANCIAL DEVELOPMENT IN EASTERN EUROPE
The First Ten Years

---

**Studies in Economic Transition**
**Series Standing Order ISBN 0–333–73353–3**
(*outside North America only*)

You can receive future titles in this series as they are published by placing a standing order. Please contact your bookseller or, in case of difficulty, write to us at the address below with your name and address, the title of the series and the ISBN quoted above.

Customer Services Department, Macmillan Distribution Ltd, Houndmills, Basingstoke, Hampshire RG21 6XS, England

---

# Transformation and European Integration

## The Local Dimension

Edited by Bruno Dallago

palgrave
macmillan

First published 2006 by
PALGRAVE MACMILLAN
Houndmills, Basingstoke, Hampshire RG21 6XS and
175 Fifth Avenue, New York, N.Y. 10010
Companies and representatives throughout the world

PALGRAVE MACMILLAN is the global academic imprint of the Palgrave Macmillan division of St. Martin's Press, LLC and of Palgrave Macmillan Ltd. Macmillan® is a registered trademark in the United States, United Kingdom and other countries. Palgrave is a registered trademark in the European Union and other countries.

ISBN-13: 978-1-4039-4781-9
ISBN-10: 1-4039-4781-3

This book is printed on paper suitable for recycling and made from fully managed and sustained forest sources.

A catalogue record for this book is available from the British Library.

Library of Congress Cataloging-in-Publication Data

Transformation and European integration : the local dimension / edited by Bruno Dallago.
p. cm. — (Studies in economic transition)
Includes bibliographical references and index.
ISBN 1-4039-4781-3 (cloth)
1. Balkan Peninsula—Economic conditions. 2. Balkan Peninsula—Economic policy. 3. European Union—Balkan Peninsula. 4. Europe—Economic Integration. I. Dallago, Bruno, 1950– II. Series.

HC401.T68 2006
338.9496′009′0511—dc22 2005044517

10 9 8 7 6 5 4 3 2 1
15 14 13 12 11 10 09 08 07 06

Printed and bound in Great Britain by
Antony Rowe Ltd, Chippenham and Eastbourne

# Contents

# List of Tables and Figures

## Tables

## Figures

Figures

# Preface

The Balkan countries have acquired a particular importance since the nineties due to their domestic destabilization that had, or threatened to have, important negative external effects, particularly in Western Europe. They have consequently attracted great attention, pointing at finding ways to control negative external effects; stop domestic destabilization; rebuild their economic, political, and social fabric; and foster economic and social development within new circumstances. This has been a huge enterprise combining various forms of stabilization with transformation and domestic and international integration.

In pursuing these goals both the international community and the Balkan countries have been looking eagerly for inspiration, ideas and positive examples in order to pursue these goals in destabilized and ethnically complex and conflicting areas. The few successful examples point at the relevant role for local development. This perspective is also supported by both theory and the final goal of integration within the EU.

Based on these theoretical and practical considerations, a group of scholars at the University of Trento in Italy elaborated the idea of analysing these issues more deeply, also considering the experiences of the multi-ethnic region of the University of Trento – Trentino-Alto Adige/Südtirol. Their aim was to see whether, in which sense, and how far these could offer inspiration for the Balkan situation. The region is home to three major linguistic groups: Italian, German, and Romance speaking people, who have witnessed serious social and political tensions up to the early 1970s. Thanks to an internationally supported local political agreement, which led to the settlement of those tensions, and also to important external support, mainly by the Italian state, the region became one of the richest in Italy after having been one of the poorest.

The group's predominant aim was to give a central role to local development as a critical device to stabilize a tension- and war-torn society and polity first, and then build upon it a new process of economic and social development. This had to be done in comparative perspective, to evaluate the different solutions that have been experienced against different economic, institutional, political, and social backgrounds and international circumstances.

From these considerations the idea of organizing an international conference on 'Organising Co-habitation' was developed and implemented in Trento in 2001 (http://www.regione.taa.it/giunta/conv/balcani/inglese/Balcani_pag_ing.htm). The success of the conference (part of the papers presented have been published in English in Skurbaty, 2005) prompted the organizers to organize a Joint European Master in comparative local development, addressed particularly to students coming from South-Eastern Europe (SEE) (http://www.didatticaonline.unitn.it/master.asp) and an international research project on 'Actors and change in local development: a comparative approach applied to the Balkan area'. The research project was sponsored by the Autonomous Province of Trento and the University of Trento and included a number of scholars at the University of Trento and also other scholars from different countries.

The present book includes a substantial number of the papers that have been developed within the research project. Previous versions of the papers were presented at two international conferences that took place in Trento in May 2003 and January 2004 and another one in Belgrade in September 2004. The book, therefore, is the result of a joint effort that has tried to combine the experiences from the Balkan situation with those from around the world, with particular reference to Western Europe.

The approach of the book is comparative and interdisciplinary because the research group is convinced that local development is a multi-faceted and complex issue that needs to be treated from different and coordinated perspectives in order to be successful. The book also places particular emphasis on institutions as the critical device that, when properly defined and managed, address actors to make use of their energies and capabilities to find and implement a positive solution to their problems.

*Bruno Dallago*

# Acknowledgements

This study has been prepared within a research project on 'Actors and change in local development: A comparative approach applied to the Balkan area', directed by Bruno Dallago and sponsored by the University of Trento and the Autonomous Province of Trento. A number of people made this book possible. Martina Cvajner offered precious and skilful organizational support. Daniela Mezzena prepared the manuscript for publication. Various people within the University and the Province provided administrative and organizational support. A number of colleagues offered useful comments, criticisms and corrections and the individual authors interacted to the same aim. The recently (2003) established OECD LEED Trento Centre for Local Development provided an excellent and stimulating arena to discuss some of the topics analysed in this book. A particular gratitude goes to the students of different years of the Joint European Master in comparative local development, who provided a continuous intellectual challenge and supplied the authors with better knowledge of the reality of those countries and additional information.

# Notes on the Contributors

**Milford Bateman** is an independent consultant specializing in local economic development policy and programming issues in South-East Europe and Visiting Professor of Economics at the University of Pula, Croatia.

**Will Bartlett** is Reader in Social Economics at the School for Policy Studies, University of Bristol. He is currently Vice-President of the European Association for Comparative Economic Studies. His research interests lie in the fields of economic and social development in transition economies of South-East Europe, focusing mainly on SME policies, local and regional economic development, and welfare state reform.

**Gabriella Berloffa** is a Professor of Microeconomics at the University of Trento. Her research interests and econometric analysis of households' consumption and saving choices, labour market and human capital.

**Antonio M. Chiesi** is Professor of Methodology of Social Research and of Comparative Social Systems at the University of Milano. His research interests include social capital, network analysis, ethnic entrepreneurship, social accountability, comparative social systems and quantitative methods for social research.

**Bruno Dallago** is Professor of Economics at the University of Trento and Academic Director of the Joint European Master in Comparative Local Development. He was President of the European Association for Comparative Economic Studies, Visiting Professor at the University of California at Berkeley and Hitotsubashi University, Tokyo and consultant to various international organizations. His research interests include comparative economics, transforming economies of Central and East Europe, SMEs and entrepreneurship.

**Sandro Gozi** works in the bureau of the European policy advisers to the President of the European Commission. After having worked for the Italian diplomacy, he was in the cabinet of the EC President Romano Prodi, the Directorate-General External Relations and Relations with the European Parliament. He teaches at the College of Europe in Bruges and Parma, at the Institut d'Etudes Politiques in Paris and at the University of Lecce (Italy). His research interests include the relations between the European Union and the Balkans, European law and politics.

**Bruno Grancelli** is Professor of Economic Sociology at the University of Trento, Department of Sociology and Social Research. His research interests include entrepreneurship and management in Russia, social change, comparative methods, social consequences of delocalization, EU technical and managerial assistance in the post-Soviet countries.

**Paul Marer**, PhD, is former Professor at Indiana University (Bloomington) and Professor and Academic Director at the Business School of Central European University (Budapest). He was Visiting Professor at the China Europe International Business School (Shanghai); and at the University of Trento (Italy). He has consulting experience with various international organizations. His research interests include the European Union and the transforming economies of Central and East Europe, Russia and China.

**Simona Piattoni** is Associate Professor of Political Science at the University of Trento. Her research interests include clientelism and governance with particular reference to the European Union.

**Maria Luigia Segnana** is a Professor of International Economics at the University of Trento. Her research interests are theoretical and empirical analysis of open economies and international institutions, with emphasis on intra-industry trade and trade impact on inequality, growth and poverty.

**Italo Trevisan** is Associate Professor of International Management and Marketing at the Universitá di Trento and responsible for the Economics/Business area of the Joint European Master on Comparative Local Development. Among his research interests are the internationalization of small businesses and their role in the development of less developed regions, with particular attention to Africa.

**Jens Woelk** is Lecturer and Researcher in Comparative Constitutional Law at the Law Faculty of the University of Trento (Italy) and Senior Researcher at the European Academy of Bolzano/Bozen (Institute for Studies of Federalism and Regionalism). His current research focuses on federalism/regionalism, minority-group issues, and South-East Europe.

# List of Abbreviations

| | |
|---|---|
| AAC | Administrative Absorption Capacity |
| AS | Area Sistema |
| BEEPS | Business Environment and Enterprise Performance |
| BiH | Bosnia and Herzegovina |
| CAP | Common Agricultural Policy |
| CARDS | Community Assistance for Reconstruction, Development and Stability (in the Balkans) |
| CDA | Co-operative Development Agency |
| CEE | Central and East Europe(ean) |
| CEECs | Central and East European countries |
| CFSP | Common Foreign and Security Policy |
| CLRAE | Congress of Local and Regional Authorities in Europe |
| CoE | Council of Europe |
| CoR | Committee of the Regions |
| CRDA | Community Revitalization through Democratic Action |
| CSB | Baltic Countries |
| DfID | Department for International Development |
| DPS | Democratic Party of Socialists of Montenegro |
| EAGGF | European Agricultural Guidance and Guarantee Fund |
| EAR | European Agency for Reconstruction |
| EBRD | European Bank for Reconstruction and Development |
| EC | European Community(ies) |
| ECCS | European Community for Coal and Steel |
| ECLSG | European Charter of Local Self-Government |
| ECU | European Currency Unit |
| EIB | European Investment Bank |
| EIP | European Integration Partnership |
| EPPA | Enterprise Policy Performance Assessment |
| ERDF | European Regional Development Fund |
| ESF | European Social Fund |
| EU | European Union |
| FDI | Foreign Direct Investments |
| FIFG | Financial Instrument for Fisheries Guidance |
| FTAs | Free Trade Areas |
| FYROM | Former Yugoslav Republic of Macedonia |
| GDP | Gross Domestic Product |
| GDR | German Democratic Republic |
| GLG | Good Local Governance |
| GNI | Gross National Income |

| | |
|---|---|
| GNP | Gross National Product |
| HBOR | Croatian Bank for Reconstruction and Development |
| HPZS | Croatian Agricultural Co-operative Alliance |
| HRM | Human Resource Management |
| HSS | Croatian Peasant Party |
| HSZ | Croatian Co-operative Alliance |
| HZS | Croatian Co-operative Federation |
| ICE | Istituto per il Commercio Estero |
| IFIs | International Financial Institutions |
| Ifor | Implementation Force |
| ILO | International Labour Organization |
| IMF | International Monetary Fund |
| ISPA | Instrument for Structural Policies for Pre-Accession |
| ISTAT | Istituto Italiano di Statistica |
| KfW | Kredit fuer Wiederaufbau |
| LAU | Local administrative units |
| LBCs | Local Business Centres |
| LEDAs | Local Economic Development Agencies |
| LSG | Local Self-Government |
| MARRI | Migration, Asylum and Regional Initiative for Refugees |
| MFN | Most Favourite Nation |
| MNC | Multi-national Company |
| MOU | Memorandum of Understanding |
| NATO | North Atlantic Treaty Organization |
| NDP | National Development Plan |
| NGO | Non-Governmental Organization |
| NSSED | National Strategy for Social and Economic Development |
| NUTS | (EU) Nomenclature of Territorial Units for Statistics |
| OHR | Office of the High Representative (BiH) |
| OPT | Outward Processing Traffic |
| OSCE | Organization on Security and Cooperation in Europe |
| PHARE | Poland and Hungary Assistance for the Restructuring of the Economy |
| PRSP | Poverty Reduction Strategy Papers |
| RS | Republika Srpska (BiH) |
| S&M | Serbia and Montenegro |
| SAA | Stabilization and Association Agreement |
| SAp | Stabilisation and Association Process |
| SAPARD | Special Accession Programme for Agriculture and Rural Development |
| SEA | Single European Act |
| SEE | South-East Europe |
| SEE4 | BiH, FYR Macedonia, Croatia, S&M |
| SEE5 | Albania, BiH, FYR Macedonia, Croatia, S&M |

| | |
|---|---|
| SEE7 | Albania, BiH, FYRMacedonia, Croatia, S&M, Romania, Bulgaria |
| SEE8 | SEE7 plus Moldova |
| SEEC | South East European Countries |
| Sfor | Stabilisation Force |
| SIDA | Swedish International Development Cooperation Agency |
| SME | small and medium size enterprise |
| SMEDA | Agency for Small and Medium Sized Enterprises |
| SNP | Socialist People's Party of Montenegro |
| SS | Stolper–Samuelson |
| TAIEX | Technical Assistance Information Exchange Office |
| UNDP | United Nations Development Programme |
| USAID | United States Agency for International Development |
| WB | World Bank |
| WTO | World Trade Organization |

# 1
# The Local Dimension of Transformation: an Introduction

*Bruno Dallago*[1]

## Introduction

This book is about transformation in the framework of European integration. However uncertain the latter has become after the unexpected results of the French and Dutch referendums on the European constitution, the path for the Balkans to European integration is outlined, although the exact track is admittedly uncertain, with the exception of Romania and Bulgaria.

The double challenge for the Balkan countries is to pursue transformation and integration amid difficult circumstances. Compared to the countries of Central and Eastern Europe (CEE) who became EU members on 1 May 2004, the Balkan countries have to face greater difficulties for both external and internal reasons. External factors, such as economic and political support appear, if anything, more favourable. This is due to both the experience gained by the richer countries in supporting transformation, the smaller size of the Balkan economies and societies, and the greater danger from their political and military instability. However, it is the overall environment of the European Union (EU) that has made the integration process for the Balkan countries politically much more difficult than in the case of Central and East European Countries (CEECs).

As far as internal circumstances are concerned, a critical set of difficulties result from instability, which shortens time horizons of economic, political and social actors, and increases uncertainty and transaction costs. However, another set of difficulties results from the greater institutional immaturity of the Balkan countries compared to the requirements of a competitive market economy, a pluralistic society and a democratic polity. Institutional immaturity is due to uncertain reforms as much as to more unfavourable starting conditions.

Local development is usually defined as development in a territorially, administratively, economically, legally, and socially delimited space that concerns local government, the private sector, the non-profit sectors and the local community cooperating to achieve sustainable institutional settings and pursuing social and economic growth that brings benefits and improvements in the quality of life for everyone in the locality. According to the European Charter of Local Self-Government it '. . . denotes the right and the ability of local authorities, within the limits of the law, to regulate and manage a substantial share of public affairs under their own responsibility and in the interests of the local population' (http://conventions.coe.int/Treaty/Commun/ListeTraites.asp?CM=8&CL=ENG). A locality is any component that is at sub-country or sub-state level. Therefore, a locality may be a region, a province, a county, or a municipality when discussing administrative levels. It may be a group of locally based firms, a social network or a political constituency when dealing with economic, social, or political issues.

Due to its very nature, local development encompasses different disciplines, approaches and many local government and private-sector functions including planning, infrastructure provision, finance, entrepreneurship, governance, environmental management, and culture. Local development is, therefore, about communities continually upgrading their institutional setting, improving their internal coordination and the cooperation with the outside world, upgrading the investment climate to improve their competitiveness, creating jobs and improving incomes.

In short, it is development in a limited part of a country. But how limited? Is it the development of a region of a country, perhaps of a republic in a federal country, or is it the development of a municipality, a village or a group of people? Clearly, these cases differ in the nature of the problems involved and the policies that can be implemented.

Societies and economies at a sub-national level – whatever their actual level is – share at least two important features. First, in neither case are 'local' problems self-sufficient and local policies (implemented by local authorities) really sufficient. A multilevel hierarchy of problems, policies and governments exists and the different levels are intertwined so, to form a system of multi-level governance (Bache and Flinders, 2004). The concept of multi-level governance has been defined as 'a system of continuous negotiation among nested governments at several territorial tiers – supranational, national, regional, and local – as the result of a broad process of institutional creation and decisional re-allocation' (Marks, 1993: 392). It stresses that, although conflicts should not be disregarded, these different levels are complementary and each one produces spillovers that other levels can appropriate. This point is particularly important and clear in legal and administrative issues. Yet it is also important in economic and social issues, for example, under the heading of transportation costs, the costs and problems of transacting cross-border, and costs and complexities of the (local) organization of production.

Secondly, social and political capital and also the various forms of economic capital, that are so important for supporting local development, are locally based and even success in international trade and in globalization depend largely on local development. Economists have long shown that '[a]ctivities concentrate close to their needed inputs, and this generates greater locational concentration and hence, specialization of regional economies' (Storper, 2000). The dramatic decrease in transportation costs[2] did not diminish the importance of localization of economic activities. As a result of the above reasons there is a rationale in dealing with local development in an unspecified, simply sub-national manner. Moreover, this local development has to be part of a broader national, international and supranational perspective: one adopted in this book.

The basic hypothesis of this book is that local development is a particularly useful device to overcome the difficult transformation in the Balkans, provided that it is in harmony with national and international processes. Why should it be so? Does local development show particularly useful features in any circumstances or is it so only in the Balkans? Or does local development in the Balkans require particular features, given the difficult circumstances among which it takes place?

I am going to propose a general framework for studying local development in the Balkans, and introduce the different contributions in this book by many distinguished authors. I shall first outline in the next section the issue of local development, listing its features and the reasons why it is considered generally to be a useful device for development and stability. This section will introduce Chapter 2 by Marer. The following section will describe the starting conditions in the Balkans, with particular reference to the state of transformational reforms. This section is intended to complement the chapters by Gozi (11) and Berloffa and Segnana (4) and to provide a useful background for the remaining chapters. The penultimate section is intended to assess some important aspects of institutions in the perspective of local development. The final section provides same conclusions.

## Local development

Central governments have important records of local policies as parts of the main policies in countries characterized with significant territorial differences. Other countries have used local approaches to solve problems linked with poverty. However, these approaches have been traditionally seen and managed as exceptions and prompted by particularly important, yet localized problems. Local development has been considered not as an important part of general development, but as a necessary detour.

Indeed, until recently, central policies were largely uniform and addressed to the whole country, without particular concern for its constituent parts, with some notable exceptions (e.g. central policies for the Italian South). This was typical especially of economic policies, but also of institutional and social policies, and political, legal and administrative implementation. The so-called neo-liberal wave that has been dominant in most countries and international agencies in the last two decades has remarkably strengthened this undifferentiated approach relying as it does on the mobility and substitutability of resources, price flexibility, and the goal of unifying countries and markets in the frame of the nation-state. It is interesting to note that central planning that was prevalent in Eastern Europe until the late eighties had a similar attitude in this sense.

An important reason for this approach lies in the confidence that the factors that lead or push development are universal and independent of the peculiarities of individual localities – and perhaps even of individual countries. Local assets and processes have meaning only as components of general processes. The model of the free market approach extends to most fields of social life, such as political, social and legal issues (e.g. the case of minority rights treated as – individual – human rights), whereby the individual is the principal and original depository of rights and the best interpreter and arbiter of her or his own preferences and objectives and, therefore, the only sovereign actor.

However, this mechanism needs certain conditions to work, including self-interested, rational, and profit-maximizing actors, and full knowledge and information by means of free prices, perfect mobility and substitutability of resources. However, this book deals with countries where the 'imperfections' that prevent the smooth working of the mechanism are important, evident, and resilient. They have not been removed so far either by the working of a free market mechanism or the inability of authorities to remove the obstacles to its optimal working.

Under these circumstances various questions arise. First, why is it so? Is it because free markets require special conditions to develop and work smoothly, conditions that do not hold in the Balkans which are 'abnormal' countries (Rosefielde, 2005)? Was the (economic, political, and social) action against the 'imperfections' preventing the proper working of the virtuous mechanism insufficient? Are actors self-interested in a more complex and less virtuous way than the mechanism envisages or do they pursue different kinds of rationality? Should we look for an explanation in the role of institutions or in that of knowledge and information that actors use in strategic ways or that cannot be transmitted and circulated, for instance because much of it is tacit and non-transmittable? Or is it because of a mix of these and other reasons?

Secondly, what can be done under these circumstances? Should we analyse the reasons why in the Balkans, as in so many other countries the free market mechanism has not worked properly so far and look for different, more reliable and realistic general explanations? Although the authors in this book offer different opinions on this issue, they agree that idiosyncrasies in Balkan local processes are embedded in broader and general processes.

In reality, policies are often pragmatic and proceed by trial and error. In this pragmatic perspective, policies for fostering and supporting local development and solving the problems derived from ethnic diversity have been implemented and have gone through an important process of evolution prompted by previous failures and limited successes.

In general, three waves of local development and related policies can be identified (http://www.worldbank.org/html/fpd/urban/led/defining.html). During the first wave, which lasted from the sixties until the early 1980s, the focus was on the attraction of crucial factors into the local area by means of direct intervention and direct finance by public, often central authorities. The second wave lasted from the 1980s until the mid-1990s: its focus moved towards broadening the area of public intervention, targeting specific sectors or certain geographic areas, and the means utilized to reach the objectives, including a broad set of real services. Also, local authorities took over a more active role in policy implementation.

The third wave started in the late nineties and is still continuing. The focus of analysis and policy intervention shifted to make the environment more conducive to business, with particular concern for soft infrastructure investments, public/private partnerships, networking and the leveraging of private sector investments for the public good, and targeting inward investment to add to the competitive advantages of local areas. The success of communities depends on their ability to adapt to the changing and increasingly competitive environment. The goal is to mobilize endogenous resources and processes for local development. Therefore, what matters is that the proper economic, social, political, legal and administrative conditions are created for improving the local supply of resources, including entrepreneurship and knowledge. In this framework, policies should be mostly bottom-up in the sense that they should start from local endowments, needs and opportunities, they should have a long-term perspective and strategy, and should foster and be based upon a plurality of (economic, political and social) actors.

Dealing with local development in countries in transformation means addressing the above basic questions by dividing the issue into its three constituent parts, which are the most problematic because of the negative legacy of the old system: these are the context, the actors, and policies suitable to foster and support the development of an efficiently working democratic polity, a competitive market, and an economy, pluralistic society. Although the present book also deals with policies, it concentrates particularly on the context and actors as the most resilient features of the transformation process. Since it is clear that the starting point was not favourable, why is local development a suitable device to overcome the legacy of the past and foster transformation? Does local development (re)build a situation in which the free market mechanism works smoothly? Or is local development a critical component of an alternative kind of mechanism and general development?

There are various reasons for concentrating the attention on local development. Some reasons are traditional and based on a static perspective; some are more dynamic and often linked to remoulding the traditional policy intervention, including restructuring of the welfare state. Traditional economic reasons include economies of agglomeration and local incentives to the accumulation of capital. These, by creating economies of scale and scope, may decrease production costs and also transaction costs, thus supporting the competitiveness of local economies (Becattini, 1987). Other reasons include enforcing the preferences of local constituencies. This reasoning is behind much of the debate about the advantages of decentralization in terms of greater efficiency and public responsibility: in this view a local autonomous society or administration is pushed to greater efficiency because the free riding game is more difficult than in a centralized society or administration and because local inefficiencies are evident in local constituencies. To this should be added the pragmatic approach to local development as a device that compensates for local social and political idiosyncrasies and transforms them into production factors in the economic, political and social field.

In countries in transformation such a static motivation for local development, although important, is probably of secondary importance, except for social and political idiosyncrasies. Economies of scale and scope and economies of agglomeration were important in the old system, as the concentration of investments in industrial areas or the representation of regions or minorities in politics are witness. If static motivations failed, this was primarily due to the misalignment of incentives, not to the disregard of agglomeration economies or proportional representation.

The second group of reasons supporting local development include the restructuring of the welfare state and asset building, the attempt to foster innovation in any field of social life, and the consequences of decentralization of economic and administrative activity. Local development was 'discovered' as a possible solution for the spreading crisis of the welfare state and, more generally, the fiscal crisis of the state in most countries, which promoted a drastic reduction of the direct intervention of public authorities in the economy and society. This goal is fundamental in countries in transformation, where the old paternalistic approach 'from the cradle to the grave' had to be replaced amid the disruption of the old state machine and the need to rebuild the fiscal, contributive, and social security systems (Müller, 1999).

The reaction to these problems has followed two different lines of action. First, the attempt to foster and mobilize local resources has been largely based on the concept of subsidiarity and on the provision of incentives for and support to build locally based resources, particularly through the promotion of entrepreneurship and the establishment of new businesses. This new approach required primarily setting up structures and programmes for supporting firms, for example, by means of local development agencies (World Bank, 2004). Secondly, the restructuring of the welfare state by 'lowering' the level at which the supply of services is provided and by supporting the individuals' role in providing the resources by which they can finance their own welfare. This solution is usually seen not as a substitute for the direct support to the income of poor people, but complementary to it. A good example is supporting of asset-building in poor communities, which offer a potentially important and locally based solution to the provision of social services (OECD/LEED, 2003).

In the dynamic perspective, local development may support the social stability and the economic and social utilization of locally based knowledge and information that differentiate local economies and societies and that may in turn foster locally based technical, social, institutional and economic learning and innovation, grassroots democracy and pluralistic society, and the development of new dynamic capabilities in line with the new system. It is the utilization of locally based knowledge incorporating and adapting factors external to the locality (general knowledge, techniques, information, resources) that supports the placement of local economic systems in the international division of labour (Brusco, 1994).

The creation of knowledge assumes particular importance. It is a process that results from the interaction of economic actors among themselves and within the context including the territory, a well-defined geographical entity that includes a set of agents and institutions sharing a particular culture, history and perceptions. It is the ability of people, firms, regions and countries to learn, modify, adapt and specialize that determines their long-term performance. Knowledge and information are cumulative and their growth changes progressively with the change of the accumulated stock. An important local consequence is that actors and communities who have accumulated a particular expertise have a growing advantage compared to their competitors. This is an important basis for local development, but also for inter-territorial disparities. The interaction of the actors living in a particular territory influences learning and the creation of knowledge, mainly by doing and by using – perhaps in new forms, as Grancelli and Chiesi argue in this book. Knowledge is subsequently socialized and diffused through social group interaction. Therefore, geographical proximity is important – along with decreasing transportation costs – in creating specialization and industrial concentration due to: climate of imitation/cooperation and leadership/competition, coordination of decision-making, growth and diffusion of knowledge, guarantee against risk, and uncertainty.

Although in developed areas knowledge is largely codified and is relatively easy to diffuse and acquire, in take-off circumstances productive activities are largely based on contextual knowledge, that is created, diffused and rooted in the territory. Such knowledge is usually tacit, changes through trial and error and is transferred mainly through the circulation of the knowledge holder(s) and direct experience, which prevent its diffusion outside the holding community. In a sense, transformation can be compared to a take-off process, with two important difference: first, these countries start from a complex set of codified knowledge that has lost great part of its value, since the economic, legal, political, and social systems changed; and secondly, the influx of outside knowledge (e.g. by means of Foreign Direct Investments (FDIs) or other forms of knowledge transfer) is actively pursued.

In these circumstances, external (codified) knowledge must be re-contextualized, embedded in the territory and/or organization. This may produce a *milieu* favourable to development, that is a coherent and organic system of production, institutions, culture, and history that reduces market and technological uncertainty for firms and strengthens routines. Recombination and codification produce interaction between local and global cultures, make the formation of specialization more efficacious, and influences the rate of change of organizational and technological routines.

These processes, though, cannot take place spontaneously, as many maintained in the early stage of transformation. The label of 'transition' that was used was intended to stress the nearly mechanical nature of the process. However, the Balkan countries may make use of different external supports that play an important role both directly, by supplying resources and markets, and indirectly, by creating a supportive international atmosphere.

In particular, the EU offers many devices that may support the countries in transformation in implementing local activities and recontextualizing their knowledge through its regional policies. Marer (Chapter 2 in this book) chronicles the evolution of EU regional policies, also discussing the key actors involved in regional policy decisions and the interaction among them. During this period the main regional policy instruments were the Structural Fund, the Cohesion Fund, and pre-accession assistance to the countries of CEE through Poland and Hungary Assistance for the Restructuring of the Economy (PHARE), Instrument for Structural Policies for Pre-Accession (ISPA) and Special Accession Programme for Agriculture and Rural Development (SAPARD). In 2004 the EU decided to supplement earlier aid programmes for the Western Balkans by adding pre-accession assistance to these countries as well. This chapter shows that having a favourable external context and financial resources is not enough: indeed, the main conclusion of the chapter is that the net recipients of regional aid – especially the less developed CEE and Balkan countries – should concentrate their efforts on improving the administrative absorption capacity of their public sectors.

Piattoni's chapter (3) builds on the 15-year experience with regional development policy at the European level to draw insights for the future enlargement countries, the so-called Stabilization and Association Process (SAP) countries in the Balkans. While no immediately applicable 'lesson' can be drawn, given the special nature of the problems these countries are facing, some insights can nevertheless be gleaned from the experience of the Structural Funds in the current member-states, including the ten recent enlargement countries. Apart from the obvious problems concerning the stabilization of the polities (construction of democratic institutions, rule of law, refugee repatriation, money laundering and illegal trafficking), these countries suffer from momentous structural deficits regarding insufficient infrastructure, faulty market institutions, and educational deficiencies. Even more than in the Europe of 15 and the Europe of 25, the structural problems of the SAP countries are compounded by weak and inept administrative structures. Therefore, economic catching-up is also a problem of institutional catching-up.

The relation between growth performance, income distribution and trade policies show an important problematic aspect of the external context. Berloffa and Segnana (Chapter 4) explain that trade and trade related policies are not necessarily growth-supporting. They imply significant redistributive effects that can create diffuse fears about the social and private costs of adjustments. These results are critical because, even independently of trade, growth is generating increasing inequalities in the Balkans. If trade and growth worsen the income distribution, and the speed at which poverty may be reduced in the region will be much slower, and the prospects of future growth undermined. The spatial, regional, and ethnic dimensions of poverty and inequality suggest that, if economic growth bypasses the areas where the poor are concentrated, it will further increase inequality and exacerbate spatial and social gaps in standards of living. Therefore, the local development of the poorest areas or regions becomes a strategic goal not only for the reduction of poverty and inequality but also for the long-term sustainability of growth. However, trade policy reforms will not yield the desired benefits unless there are parallel efforts to institutional upgrading, addressing the redistribution of the gains from trade and the interaction between trade openness and domestic and local redistributive policies.

## Starting conditions and reforms

Perhaps the most striking feature in SEE before transformation is that this area included the most centralized countries in Eastern Europe and also the least orthodox and most decentralized country (Table 1.1). No reform was ever attempted in Albania, except in the direction of further centralization, at least until the mid-eighties. The mild attempts at decentralizing economic management that took place in late eighties destabilized economic administration without replacing centralization with anything resembling a market mechanism. Romania and Bulgaria were also highly centralized and hardly any reform took place during the entire socialist period. In the other extreme, Yugoslavia was a self-managed economy and the state administration was substantially decentralized at a republican level.

Theoretically, the Yugoslav self-managed system resembled rather closely a market economy due to the fair autonomy of enterprises, the weak role of central planning, the wide range of free or quasi-free prices, and economic openness. However, returns to economic activity were mostly centralized, resources were allocated centrally through bargaining mechanisms with

*Table 1.1* A comparative evaluation of reforms in SEE: EBRD indices

| | *Price liberalization* | | *Foreign exchange and trade liberalization* | | *Small-scale privatization* | | *Large-scale privatization* | | *Legal extensiveness* | *Legal effectiveness* |
|---|---|---|---|---|---|---|---|---|---|---|
| | *1991* | *2003* | *1991* | *2003* | *1991* | *2003* | *1991* | *2003* | *1999* | *1999* |
| Albania | 1.0 | 4− | 1.0 | 4+ | 2.0 | 4 | 1.0 | 2+ | 2.0 | 1.7 |
| BiH | n.a. | 4 | n.a. | 4− | n.a. | 3 | n.a. | 2+ | 2.0 | 1.0 |
| Bulgaria | 3.0 | 4+ | 3.0 | 4+ | 1.0 | 4− | 1.0 | 4− | 4.0 | 3.7 |
| Croatia | 3.0 | 4 | 3.0 | 4+ | 3.0 | 4+ | 1.0 | 3+ | 4.0 | 2.7 |
| Macedonia | 3.0 | 4 | 3.0 | 4+ | 3.0 | 4 | 1.0 | 3 | 3.7 | 3.7 |
| Romania | 2.0 | 4+ | 1.0 | 4 | 1.0 | 4− | 1.7 | 3+ | 3.3 | 3.7 |
| Yu/S&M | | 4 | | 3+ | | 3 | | 2+ | | |
| *Unweighted average* | *2.4* | *4* | *2.2* | *4* | *2.0* | *4−* | *1.1* | *3* | *3+* | *3−* |

*Source*: *Transformation Report 2000*, London: EBRD. Transformation indicators go from 1 (little change compared to pre-transformation situation) to 4+ (standards and performance typical of advanced market economies).

republican governments, and wages were largely planned. Therefore, compared to a market economy institutions were distorted perhaps more than in a centrally planned economy. In fact, in the latter budget constraints were a reality, albeit mostly at political level (Kornai, 1992). Another feature of the Yugoslav system that made it unfit for an orderly and productive transformation was the distributive processes. Introduced to settle inter-ethnic and inter-republican tensions, they generated macroeconomic destabilization, which in turn exacerbated those tensions both directly and via the effect of stabilization policies (Dallago and Uvalic, 1998). However, in other fields of social life (society, polity, governments, law) the distance from a pluralistic society and democratic political regimes was actually lower in Yugoslavia than in other East European countries.

Also transformation followed different routes in different countries: '[t]he eight countries of South-East Europe (SEE8) trail their Western European neighbours in income and other measures of development, but the differences among the SEE8 are as striking as their similarities' (Broadman *et al.* 2004: xix). Looking at the European Bank for Reconstruction and Development (EBRD) evaluation, some interesting conclusions stand out (Table 1.1). First, transformation is over, or nearly so, in all countries as far as price liberalization, foreign exchange and trade liberalization and small scale privatization are concerned – with a partial exception for Serbia and Montenegro (S&M). Secondly, progress has been reached in large-scale privatization (particularly in Bulgaria, although not clearly so in Albania, Bosnia-Herzegovina (BiH), and S&M), in banking sector reform and interest rates liberalization (particularly in Croatia and also in Bulgaria, but less so in Albania, BiH, and S&M). The same holds for the coverage of legal reform, which remains mostly formal with weak legal effectiveness. Countries have roughly the same relative positions as for the previous indicator.

However, these accomplishments are only apparently positive. 'Successful' small-scale privatization means simply 'complete privatization of small companies with tradable ownership rights'. Only one country, Croatia, has reached 'standards and performance typical of advanced industrial economies: no state ownership of small enterprises; effective tradability of land'.

Looking at the two remaining 'positive' indicators in all countries, prices are liberalized in the sense that there has been 'comprehensive price liberalization; utility pricing which reflects economic costs' or that these countries have adopted 'standards and performance typical of advanced industrial economies: comprehensive price liberalization; efficiency-enhancing regulation of utility pricing'. Again, this means that prices work as informational devices, rather than pushing enterprises to productive outcomes – with perhaps the exception of utilities, which are not a particularly important field for Small and Medium size Enterprises (SMEs) and local development. Also, all this means that there are few remaining obstacles preventing SMEs from engaging in international trade despite how few actually do so or if they do, they do it in an economically productive way. For instance, SMEs may be involved in arbitraging activities, thus contributing to establish market equilibrium. However, market equilibrium is not necessarily a synonym for socially productive activity.

As to foreign exchange and trade liberalization, in some countries there was 'removal of all quantitative and administrative import and export restrictions (apart from agriculture) and all significant export tariffs; insignificant direct involvement in exports and imports by ministries and state-owned trading companies; no major no-uniformity of customs duties for non-agricultural goods and services; full current account convertibility'. Most countries, though, went further and adopted 'standards and performance norms of advanced industrial economies: removal of most tariff barriers; WTO membership'.

Other aspects of transformation – such as the spread of poverty, increasing inequalities of income and wealth distribution, SME development, the decentralization of public administration – are discussed in the different chapters of this book.

In this book three chapters deal with particularly important aspects of domestic reforms in different fields. The common goal is to assess whether these reforms have been useful in fostering democratic political regimes, efficient market economies and pluralistic societies. Woelk (Chapter 5) analyses the current process of territorial and administrative reorganization at local level in former Yugoslavia as an important aspect of reconstruction and precondition for gradual integration into the political, legal and economic space of the EU. Starting with a short exploration of the traditions of local self-government in former Yugoslavia, the European Charter of Local Self-Government (ECLSG) is introduced as the main international document of reference: the comparison concentrates on five essential issues used as parameters for a critical evaluation of the reform-process: (a) the territory (including size); (b) the position of local autonomy in the legal system; (c) the powers to be exercized by the authorities at local level and their relations with higher levels of government; (d) autonomy in financial terms; and (e) autonomy in terms of local democracy. Other issues discussed are the ethnic question, which conditions local autonomy as well as the institutional structures in a number of countries. The chapter closes with some reflections on the effects of the 'importation' of 'models' that add to the considerations of local autonomy as an important element in the process of transformation.

Entrepreneurship and its features are discussed in Dallago's chapter (6). Putting formal institutions right is fundamental if entrepreneurship is to play a productive role, i.e. producing goods and services that increase the overall economic value in the economy. Starting conditions in the Balkans were rather unfavourable in this sense and the reforms were not the most effective to streamline institutions in a productive sense. This conclusion concerns both general policies and SME specific policies. The capabilities of entrepreneurs, their origin and nature strengthen this problematic outcome. To provide a full picture the irregular economy[3] is considered: it has weakened the virtues of regular institutions and offered entrepreneurs alternative ways to survive and prosper without adhering to formal institutions. It is concluded that reforms and policies should deal carefully with the interrelationship existing between formal and informal institutions and the irregular economy.

According to Grancelli and Chiesi (Chapter 7), who concentrate on the interaction between institutions and entrepreneurial capabilities in the Balkans countries, and in the former USSR, the *Nomenklatura* is the past that largely reproduces itself in the present. But what is in need of more investigation are the reproduction and circulation mechanisms in different organizational contexts within the process of post-communist transformation. A possible analytical framework cannot but start from the fact that while the influence of experts, Western institutions, professional press and competition have changed the cognitive patterns of local key actors, this does not generally impinge much on their actual behaviour. A disparity is still apparent between the new institutions and the norms and the largely path-dependent behaviour of local elites. This chapter provides some evidence and preliminary comments on the actors who should straddle that divide, namely the elites-in-the-making that are rising in the ranks of the institutions of local development.

## Institutions in local development

Institutions in the vein of the neo-institutional economics may be defined as 'any form of constraint that human beings devise to shape human interaction' (North, 1990: 4). Institutions also define incentives and consequently determine the outcome of human activities (Baumol, 1990, 1993). Institutions may be formal, that is codified, and informal, such as conventions and codes of behaviour (Pejovich, 1998). According to the 'old' institutional economics both formal and informal institutions shape the economy by providing stability in a context of uncertainty, and provide a pattern for future development (Hodgson, 1988, 1993).

Institutions recall the issue of embeddedness, which refers to the process by which networks of inter-personal relations shape economic action beyond the assumption of the above-mentioned free market model and in ways that differ from it (Granovetter, 1985; Crosby and Stephens, 1987). Therefore, the economy is 'both an instituted process and a socially embedded activity' (Amin, 1998: 77).

The outcome of institutions also depends upon behavioural and cognitive processes in the sense that different actor rationalities produce different forms of economic behaviour (Simon, 1976). In our case, more than substantive rationality, which favours rule-bound behaviour, procedural and recursive rationality are particularly interesting. The former favours behaviour based on the accommodation of actors to the constraints posed by their environment, while recursive rationality favours strategic behaviour, because actors use their capabilities to manipulate their environment.

These perspectives are particularly useful to examine such an 'unconventional' case as that of the Balkan countries. The interplay between (changed) formal and (sticky) informal institutions is one of the key aspects of transformation. Formal institutional change at a particular moment in time may give rise to informal institutions, which may, in turn, affect the negotiation of future formal institutions (Farrell and Heritier, 2003). However, the first period of systemic change has to exist with traditional informal institutions and transformation shocks may even strengthen traditional informal institutions. The outcome of transformation is clearly determined only when formal and informal institutions change in the direction of a competitive market economy, pluralistic society and democratic political regimes, thus supporting the same kind of incentives. When this is not the case, the outcome may be path-dependence and an irregular economy, as Chiesi and Grancelli (7) and Dallago (6) show in this book respectively.

In areas in transformation, such as the Balkans, local development is particularly beneficial because it may attenuate transformational shocks, including unemployment, and because it may foster and support institutional adaptation and the mobilization of economic and social resources. In a world in which codified knowledge is becoming increasingly important, ubiquitous, tacit and uncodified knowledge, rooted in the relations of proximity of which local development is rich, may also provide advantages in the broader economic, political and social market.

Transformation, at least in CEE, has been a general process requiring a local dimension in order to support adaptation and learning and avoid excessive divergence among the constituent parts of countries. Along with this, there have been three other critical features of the process of transformation required for a strategic role of local development. The first feature relies on the centralized nature of the previous system, with the partial exception of former Yugoslavia, which required a far-reaching decentralization to support the development of a democratic political regime, a market economy and a pluralistic society. The second feature is the goal of these countries to integrate in the EU, where local development is one of the basic principles and a prominent policy goal. The third feature derives from the fragmentation in former Yugoslavia: in this case local development has been devised to support the build-up of new states and accommodate ethnic tensions.

However, local development must be of a particular type, in that it must foster and support the integration of economies, polities and societies that have lost the previous administrative glue typical of the Soviet-type system and the decentralized bargaining glue of the self-managed system. Although the required type of local development must overcome the negative effects of bureaucratization, it must also avoid the danger of secession and disintegration may follow from the disruption of a dominant system.

Recalling the three waves of local development mentioned in the second section, it will be noticed that in the Balkans:

(a) the transition to the third stage is far from fully implemented and generalized, and perhaps is still in its infancy. Policies implemented in SEE countries include important first-wave elements. Massive grants, subsidies to loans, tax breaks, subsidized hard infrastructure investment, upgrading of local governments, support to minorities, etc. are extensively used in all Balkan countries;
(b) many policies are better characterized as second-stage policies. The extensive provision with rights and protection granted to minorities, through setting up new offices or specialization of public administration sections for dealing with EU and other funds and functions, with real services, in particular, with business incubators, advice and training for SMEs, technical support, business start-up support, which are perhaps the most important components of local development policies;
(c) there are differences among countries as far as the combination of policy stages is concerned. A rather direct relation apparently exists with the level of development and economic and political openness. The countries and regions/localities that are more developed and more open also make more extensive use of second- and third-wave policies;
(d) the particular 'content' of each stage is different compared to the above summarized 'common wisdom', due particularly to differences in institutional maturity. This statement should be read in two ways: first, the relative underdevelopment of institutions and actors' capabilities in the sense of (administrative, economic, legal, political, and social) maturity requires transitorily a greater interventionist content of policies. But, secondly, those same features may allow for a wider and deeper use of an indirect approach making greater use of indirect incentives and concentrating more at each stage on creating a development friendly environment;
(e) when more mature (third-stage) policies are implemented that do not take into account the existing system and the actors' capabilities, unwanted and unforeseen consequences are widespread. These usually include the irrelevance of policies and structures, and support to rent-seeking attitudes and strategies (e.g. business incubator).

Three chapters in this book illustrate important aspects of the problematic nature of local development and show that the interaction between the external context and internal processes has been unbalanced and perhaps unilateral. Bartlett (Chapter 8) stresses that over the last decade the international community has provided enormous amounts of financial assistance to the Western Balkans. Recent literature on the effectiveness of financial aid flows has debated the influence of domestic policies on the effectiveness of financial aid. This chapter disputes the relevance of this debate in so far as it takes domestic policy as 'given'. Drawing on the recent literature on the phenomenon of policy transfer, it argues that domestic policies are likely to be endogenous factors embedded within the flow of aid, and that policies are transferred by donors to recipients alongside financial flows. This approach draws attention to the aims and purposes of the agents involved in the donor–recipient relationship, and suggests that aid effectiveness is influenced by subjective factors and incentive structures specific to each individual case. Consequently the chapter argues for a case-study approach to aid effectiveness, and to the identification of the causes of policy success and policy failure. The theme is illustrated by a detailed examination of donor interventions in the economic development of North Montenegro, the least developed region of one of the poorest countries in the Balkans. The findings point to the complexities of the relationships involved in local economic development in the region, and indicate that neither international aid nor policy transfer are likely to provide easy solutions to the problems of poverty and underdevelopment endemic to the region.

According to Bateman (Chapter 9), since the collapse of communism, the overwhelming focus of enterprise development policy in South-East Europe has been upon conventional investor-driven enterprises. Cooperative development has been largely ignored, often seen as no more than an unwelcome throwback to communism, thus pointing to institutional incompleteness. This policy choice ignores a mass of evidence from across the world that the cooperative sector can play a vital role in promoting sustainable local economic development, especially in post-conflict countries. However, the growing perception of failure surrounding the policy advice emanating from the international development agencies, such as the World Bank (WB) and International Monetary Fund (IMF), has opened up new possibilities for cooperative development in South-East Europe. As a result, many new cooperative development programmes have been started, especially in the agricultural sector. New and more pro-active policies for cooperative development are required in SEE, however, if the sector is to achieve realistic and sustainable progress against a backdrop of continued decline in most key economic and social variables.

Finally, Trevisan (Chapter 10) discusses the possibility of fostering institutional innovation in the form of SMEs networks by means of de-localization from Western market economies. The chapter analyses whether the Italian industrial districts and their most complete form, the *area sistema*, are 'reproducible' in SEE. It analyses Outward Processing Traffic (OPT) between Italy and CEECs, and presents the de-localization of Italian SMEs, using the Veronese footwear district as an example. The *area sistema* is presented as an important answer to the problems of socio-economic development in areas peripheral to the main industrial and economic centres of a country and, as such, a potential model for local development in transformation countries. Data on trade flows between CEEC and Romania, particularly OPT, are discussed and used to show the existence of an international production network between Italy and Romania in a few, SME-dominated, industries. This example shows how the attitude of many Italian *area sistema* SMEs is changing from a footloose quest for lower labour costs to a longer-term strategy of collaboration and nurturing of local capacity aimed at creating the conditions for improved strategic competitiveness of the de-localizing firms with important consequences in Romania.

## Conclusions

Local development in the Balkans shares much with local development in the most developed countries upon whose experiences the mainstream approach is based. Yet, local development in the Balkans also shows specificities that derive from the particular administrative, economic, international, legal, political, social, features of these countries and their historical and cultural experience. It is the intertwining of internal and external factors and the difficult geopolitical situation of the Balkans that create a complex situation that EU support has to take into consideration. According to Gozi, the end of the bipolar system has placed the Balkans in a new and indefensible position, showing the inability of the states of the region to realize, on their own, a new security system, and highlighting the weak territorial integrity of Yugoslavia. The Balkan conflicts started in a moment of European institutional, political and operational emptiness. With the Stabilization and Association process, the EU gave a long-term vision for integration to all the countries of the region, while the Stability Pact constitutes the greatest attempt by the international community to use economic assistance and European perspective to stabilize the entire region in a long-lasting way. Such a process represents a new political context in which the EU and the Balkan countries elaborate a real common agenda and mutually engage to complete all the necessary efforts to realize it. The Balkan region can play a multiple role: it could be the last to join the EU's enlargement process, and represent the first step within the strategy of a 'larger Europe' facilitating the implementation of a special EU relationship with all the neighbouring countries, from Russia to the Mediterranean.

The various chapters in this book offer a coherent view, that may be summarized as follows. First, the external context presents important positive elements, but also has problematic aspects. Among the former, the role and the resources of the EU stand out. Among the latter, inequality and poverty and some consequences of international trade stand out.

Secondly, reforms have been uneven and incomplete throughout the region. This refers to all fields of administrative, economic, legal, political, and social life. It refers to both institutional reform and their consequences for social actors. The general outcome is that, while on paper the most important general reforms are either completed or apparently quite close to those existing in developed market economies, pluralistic societies and democratic polities, in reality their effect is still largely formal and not particularly effective.

Thirdly, as a consequence of the contradictory external context and of reforms, the economic, legal, political, and social systems are either incomplete or their working is ineffective. This has important and often negative consequences for economic, political and social actors, who find contradictory and ineffective guides to their activity, weak and blurred constraints, and conflicting incentives. This, when added to the relatively undeveloped configuration of the actors' capabilities in terms of competitive market economy, pluralistic society and democratic polity, explains why the situation is still unstable and unsatisfactory in most fields. However, this conclusion does not apply in the same way and with the same force to each country. Intercountry differences are significant and important.

Although much has been done in difficult circumstances, much remains to be done. This is the duty of policies. Since many internal and external elements exist that may support a virtuous outcome, the duty should not be prohibitive. Unfortunately, the recent turn in the process of European integration may jeopardize this outcome just in those countries that need most in terms of perspectives and stability: the Balkans.

Based on the analysis and conclusions reached in this book, supportive policies should have the following features.

1. Policies should be designed to strengthen networks more than focusing exclusively on individual actors and encourage the formation of social capabilities along with individual capabilities.
2. Policies should involve a plurality of decentralized and autonomous organizations since effective economic governance extends beyond the reach of individual organizations and should internalize spillover effects. There is also a need to encourage intermediate and mixed forms of governance, building upon local capabilities and institutional spillovers and including both the public, private, social, political, and nonprofit sectors.
3. Since institutions are in the making and the relation between the new formal and informal institutions is still unsettled, policies should aim at encouraging voice and negotiation and the formation of market-, democracy-, and pluralism-friendly procedural and recursive rationalities of behaviour. In an unsettled institutional context substantive rationality, which favours rule-bound behaviour, may have just formal or even perverse effects. Under these conditions, procedural and recursive rationality – favouring behaviour based on the accommodation to environmental constraints and strategic behaviour – should have priority in order to secure strategic vision, learning and adaptation.
4. Policies and the solutions pursued should be context-specific (for example consider the weakness of SMEs or poverty, or build upon the existence of universities and research centres) and pay attention to local path-dependencies to pursue transformation and development goals. In this way, policies would build upon spontaneous processes which have lower transaction

costs, better utilize the actors' assets (particularly knowledge), and lead to better sustainable solutions. However, policies should not become hostage to context-specificity and path-dependence that, in the unfavourable Balkan circumstances, would easily result in unwanted consequences. To this end and as far as spontaneous developments are insufficient, there is a great need for the state to provide a fundamental and strong role not only in institutional enforcement but also in arbitrating between decentralized authorities, pursuing collective strategic goals, upgrading human and social capital, supporting knowledge recontextualization, and, if needed, reallocating resources to these ends.

The final aim of policies should be to build the conditions for the development and wealth of local economies, polities, and societies by upgrading the administrative, economic, political, social and human base as the prerequisite for the success of transformation. This is not an easy undertaking since policies have important trade-offs and local policies coexist necessarily with more general policies and are under the influence of international events and policies. Therefore, they should pursue local goals by properly interacting with the general context. This is an important guarantee that policies based on mobilizing local resources do not degenerate into localism and an crucial factor in supporting local capabilities in anticipating and responding to changing internal and external circumstances.

5. Foreign-assistance programmes should take into account more the specificities of locality within countries, and should try to adapt the policy framework, which they often implicitly transfer to the beneficiary countries, to the variety of local circumstances. This would require paying more attention to the ways in which local economies function, and to the variation in local institutions within which economic incentives and agents' motivations are embedded.

Further research is needed to support the above conclusions in the case of the Balkans and elsewhere. This will hopefully make local development at the centre of attention.

## Notes

1. I thank various authors of this volume, an in particular Will Bartlett for helpful comments on a previous version of this introduction.
2. However, the intensity of transportation to individual goods is now greater than in earlier times due to a deeper infra-industrial labour division.
3. Please see note 3 on page 126 for an explanation of this term.

# 2
# EU Expansion and Regional Policy

*Paul Marer*

## Introduction

Since this chapter is about the regional policies of the EU, it is proper to introduce it with a brief discussion of the concept of regionalism and a definition and justification of regional policy.

A good point of departure is a statement of the obvious, namely, that there are significant differences among regions within Europe. Regions vary greatly in their economic capacity, institutional structures and the political, economic and social demands they articulate (Keating 1995). Some areas have a strong sense of identity, rooted in historical experience, language, culture or political tradition. Some have distinct civil societies. Some have autonomist or secessionist movements, aiming for independence or for reuniting ethnic groups that were separated by artificially drawn borders.

Be that as it may, the regional policy of the EU has long been inspired by the notion of 'cohesion'[1] (Allen 2000: 244). This rather vague term encompasses economic, social and political aspects of anti-disparity policies. Economically, the idea is to assist disadvantaged countries and regions to compete in the internal market. Politically, it is designed to demonstrate the value of Community membership in peripheral regions. That cohesion policies have served the EU's political purposes, at least in the poorer countries and regions, is clear. Survey data and citizen votes on EU membership show that the strongest support for membership by Spain, Portugal and Greece in the 1980s and by the CEE countries after 1990 had much to do with the expectation that these countries would be net beneficiaries from EU membership through the Community's regional policies (Keating 1995: 18–5). Similarly, the citizens of the poorer regions of the economically well-off countries, which also benefit from the Community's regional aid, tend to be the relatively stronger supporters, within their countries, of EU integration.

Furthermore, economic theory suggests that in the absence of appropriate accompanying policies, market forces unleashed by EU integration will not of themselves be sufficient to eliminate regional divergence, but rather the reverse (Armstrong 1995: 23). This is because the elimination of tariff and non-tariff barriers to trade, and of other obstacles to the free inter-regional and cross-border movement of factors of production, tends, on balance, to favour the 'core' of the EU. ('Core' refers here both to location close to the centre and to areas of relatively high level of development.) Therefore, the forces unleashed by the EU's ever-deeper economic integration (as well as by globalization) carry with them not only the hope for a more prosperous Europe, but also a threat to already disadvantaged areas. EU regional policy, just like those of its member countries, is also a response to this threat.[2]

The essence of EU regional policy is to reduce disparities in levels of development. However, this is not supposed to be viewed as handouts to underdeveloped areas. Rather, as it is stressed by the new EU Commissioner for Regional Policy, Danuta Hübner, it is about investing in regional competitiveness and jobs, thereby raising the endogenous long-term growth potential of the poorer regions, enabling them to attain a permanently higher level of development.[3] This process and the presumed outcome are seen as benefiting the entire EU.

The rest of this chapter chronicles the evolution of EU regional policies from 1957 through 2004; offers a brief discussion of the EU budget, as context for funding regional policies; discusses the criteria, the objectives and the allocation of EU Structural and Cohesion funds; reviews pre-accession assistance to the countries of CEE, with brief summaries of the PHARE, Instrument for Structural Policies for Pre-Accession (ISPA) and Special Accession Programme for Agriculture and Rural Development (SAPARD) programmes; summarizes aid and pre-accession assistance to the Western Balkans; describes regional policy coordination; projects regional aid through 2013; and concludes with a discussion of the efficiency and impact of regional aid policies generally and to the countries of CEE and the Balkans specifically.

## Evolution of regional policies, 1957–2004

The Treaty of Rome states: 'The Community shall aim at reducing disparities between the levels of development of the various regions' (Article 158). However, the only regional policy instrument included in the Treaty (at Italy's insistence) was the European Investment Bank (EIB).

Prior to 1975, the Community's regional policies were limited and fragmented. A more active policy, backed by funds, had its origin with the 1973 entry of the UK, a country that had a tradition of regional policy. And since the UK was bringing into the Community a number of problem regions in need of help, it was keen on having the European Community (EC) channel funds to them (Keating 1995: 19).

When regional policy became an issue, the Commission advocated approaches and measures that would have given it considerable power in formulating and implementing policy. For example, it proposed that a Commission-determined map should be used to specify areas that would be eligible for Community aid (EC 1973). However, the Council of Ministers approved a watered-down version of the proposal, restricting the extent of regional policy powers to be transferred from member states to the EC (EC 1975). In the meantime, member states continued with their own regional policies.

Although the new policy established the European Regional Development Fund (ERDF), it was the individual members who exerted the decisive influence over who was to receive aid and how the money was to be spent. The entire budget – quite small by recent standards – was allocated on the basis of country quotas, determined by the Council of Ministers through negotiations (not by the Commission on the basis of relative need and extent of the problems that regions faced), although the quotas did reflect need to a certain degree.

In each country, prospective recipients were those regions that were already identified by the member states for their own regional policy purposes. The states also controlled the flow of project applications, thus determining which localities, projects and firms could gain access to ERDF aid. Assistance was confined to project-based grants for infrastructure investments, with no attempt to package projects into synergistic programs to target regional problems (Armstrong 1995: 35–8).

Current EU regional policy owes many of its features to the significant set of reforms introduced in 1989 as part of the single market process. Its main features were (Armstrong 1995: 41–9):

- set up additional funds, established five specific objectives to be promoted by the various funds, and doubled the resources available, in real terms, for regional programs;[4]
- strengthened the degree to which various Community funds were to be used simultaneously and in a coordinated manner to tackle regional problems, moving from project-based to program-based assistance;
- introduced an iterative planning and grant-making process, which enhanced the role of the Commission and brought into the process representatives of regional and local authorities, solidifying a partnership of sorts between the central authorities of member states, regional/local authorities and the Commission; and
- abandoned the use of member states' own maps for identifying the regions eligible for assistance and charged the Commission to draw up its own map.

Some experts point out that subsequent policies, such as those embodied in the Agenda 2000 set of reforms and budget priorities adopted by the Council in 1999, have shifted much of the control of regional policy back to national governments because key decisions are being made not by the Commission but by bargaining among the member states (Allen 2000: 243–5).

Be that as it may, the modifications during and after 1989, and the dramatic increase in the funding for regional policy, owe much to the fact that during the 1980s and in more recent years several countries with development levels significantly below the EU average joined or were expected to join the EU.

## The EU Budget

To place the trends and programs in EU spending on regional development into perspective, this section offers a brief discussion of the EU budget processes.[5]

To ease the budgetary uncertainty caused by recurrent, cliff-hanging, annual budget negotiations, in 1999 the European Council (formerly, the Council of Ministers) tied the basic EU budget process into a seven-year cycle, which currently covers the period 2000 through 2006. The seven-year budget is called the 'Financial Perspective'. If major developments, such as the accession of new members, require it, the Council can modify the budget ('adjusted Financial Perspective'). This budget establishes a ceiling, expressed as per cent of each country's (and thus the EU's combined) Gross National Product (GNP) (subsequently changed to Gross National Income [GNI]). For 2000–2006, the agreed ceiling was 1.27 per cent. This means that no country can be asked to contribute more than 1.27 per cent of its GNI.

Actual contributions may of course be lower. Actual budgets have been below the ceiling in practically all years.[6] In recent years the budget has also declined as a percentage of GNP/GNI. For example, in the agreed 2004 EU 'austerity' budget, expenditures amounted to only 0.98 per cent in relation to the Community's GNI, even though the 2004 budget was the first for an EU of 25 member states. Since EU law specifies that the budget cannot run deficits, revenues and expenditures are the same, except for changes in the small reserve account.

Agreed Financial Perspective establishes annual expenditure limits for each category. Expenditures are dominated by two items, those required by the Common Agricultural Policy (CAP; 45 per cent of the 2004 budget) and Structural Operations (that is, regional aid; 35 per cent).

### Funding regional policies

EU regional policies are funded from four types of sources: (1) the so-called Structural Funds, which is a short-hand term for all the funds set up to fulfill particular regional policy objectives. Structural Funds (also called structural operations or structural instruments) is by far the largest source of regional aid; (2) pre-accession aid; and (3) miscellaneous other sources, which include external aid (for example, to the Balkans), portions of expenditures from other EU budget categories that tend to favour less developed regions (such as the rural development program financed by the CAP), and (4) resources for regional development provided by the European Investment Bank, an EU-affiliated institution.

Before discussing the purposes and amounts of these four types of resources for regional development, here is a brief overview of how the amounts in the EU budget that were to explicitly fund regional policies were modified for the period 2004–2006 as a result of the May 2004 accession of the ten countries.

For the period 2000–2006, 213 billion Euros were initially earmarked for all structural instruments for the 15 member states. In addition, the budget for the period included about 22 billion in pre-accession aid. As a consequence of the enlargement, 22 billion in additional structural funds were earmarked for the new member states for the period 2004–2006, within the Union's 'adjusted Financial Perspectives'. The total of about 257 billion Euros represents approximately 37 per cent of the EU budget projected through 2006.

The following approximation can be made of the total amounts available to the CEE countries from the main EU budget categories for regional aid (in billions of Euros):

| | |
|---|---|
| Structural funds earmarked for the new member states, 2004–2006: | 22 |
| Pre-accession aid (PHARE, ISPA & SAPARD programs), 2000–2006: | 22 |
| Total | 44 |

Structural funds are explicitly for regional aid. However, pre-accession aid may also be considered as largely regional aid, first, because all of it goes to countries that, upon accession, were the least developed areas of the EU by far, and, second, because a number of their program elements are explicitly for regional aid.

Through April 2004, pre-accession aid had been given or committed to ten CEE countries: the eight accession countries plus Romania and Bulgaria. The disbursement of committed aid for the eight countries will continue for more than a year after their accession and at least through 2008 for Romania and Bulgaria.

In 2004 a decision was made to create a new pre-accession aid program for the five Western Balkan countries of Albania, Bosnia-Herzegovina, Croatia, Macedonia and Serbia-Montenegro (including Kosovo), as detailed below. For this reason, the EU aid process and the aid experiences of the recipient countries of CEE is of interest not only in and of themselves but also as roadmaps for the Balkan countries.

Focusing on the Euro 44 billion total aid given or earmarked for the CEE countries, it should be noted that this total is slightly upward biased because the first item includes funds earmarked for Cyprus and Malta (totalling 0.2 billion Euros). On the other hand, the amount does not include (1) the small amount of regional aid provided to the CEE countries by miscellaneous other programs and sources, such as the European Investment Bank, and (2) a total of 3.4 billion Euros as 'Compensation' for the new members during 2004–2006 to keep them from becoming net payers to the EU, since their contributions to the EU budget start from the first day of their accession while the structural and other funds are being disbursed to them only gradually. To be sure, the general budget compensation is not earmarked for regional aid. Nevertheless, because it all goes to the new members, it may be considered regional aid, defined here as financial flows (except CAP) explicitly earmarked to countries with per capita GNIs below 75 per cent of the EU average. If so defined, the total rises to 47 billion Euros.

Most of the 44 billion Euros is being spent through multi-annual development programs, managed jointly by the Commission, the member states and regional authorities. EU subsidies supplement national aid.

The magnitude of the aid earmarked for the ten accession countries during 2000–2006 (44 billion Euros + 3.4 billion in budget compensation = 47.4 billion) gives us an estimate of the short-term direct cost of the enlargements of 2004 and 2007–2008 [7] for the EU 15. Let's assume, for simplicity's sake, that the full amount will be dispersed over a three-year period, 2004–2006. This means an average annual burden on the 15 of about 16 billion Euros, which is 42 Euros per person per year.[8] A more comprehensive assessment should also include the political, social and economic benefits of the enlargement for the older members. Also, the cost of enlargement should be juxtaposed with the cost of non-enlargement, such as the higher political and social tensions in the candidate countries that would result if membership and aid were denied to them. Although such costs cannot be estimated accurately, most experts judge that the hypothetical costs of non-enlargement would have been substantial.

A subsidy of 16 billion Euros per year for the combined population of 105 million for the ten countries means an average annual grant of about 150 Euros received per person per year. To be sure, a significant part of this money is paid to Western consultants on aid projects. Whether the populations of the CEE countries are receiving equivalent benefits is a complex question whose investigation is outside the scope of this chapter.

## Structural funds: criteria, objectives and allocations

The overarching criteria for EU regional assistance were established in the late 1980s by the reforms of then EU President Jacques Delores. They are:

- multi-annual provision of the expenditures (that is, the seven-year Financial Perspective);
- program- rather than project-based assistance (each country must submit a multi-annual national development plan, or NDP, that meets EU requirements);
- national co-financing of EU money; and

- the additionality of EU money with respect to national money (which means that the EU should co-finance only those projects that could not be implemented without its participation).

Although these criteria have not been always fully observed in practice (as is shown below, when discussing the Sapir Report), they do represent sound principles.

Policies to reduce regional disparities are supported mainly by four structural funds: the ERDF; the European Social Fund (ESF); the section of the EU's common agricultural fund devoted to rural development (EAGGF); and financial support for fishing communities as part of the common fisheries policy (FIFG).

These funds were slated to pay out about 213 billion Euros during 2000–2006. About 95 per cent of structural funding for the period 2000–2006 is concentrated on three objectives:

- Objective 1: Helping regions whose development is lagging behind to catch up.
- Objective 2: Supporting economic and social conversion in industrial, rural, urban or fisheries areas facing structural difficulties.
- Objective 3: Modernizing systems of training and promoting employment. Measures financed by Objective 3 cover the whole Union except for the Objective 1 regions, where measures for training and employment are included in the catch-up programs.

There are also four 'special initiatives' (that is smaller funds), accounting between them for about 5 per cent of the structural funds: cross-border and inter-regional cooperation (Interreg III); sustainable development of cities and declining urban areas (Urban II); rural development through local initiatives (Leader+); and combating inequalities and discrimination in access to the labour market (Equal) (Table 2.1).

*Table 2.1* Matrix of instruments and objectives of EU's structural funds for reducing regional disparities

| | *Objective 1* | *Outside Objective 1 regions* | *Objective 2* | *Objective 3* | *Interreg III* | *Urban II* | *Leader ±* | *Equal* |
|---|---|---|---|---|---|---|---|---|
| ERDF | X | | X | | X | X | | |
| ESF | X | | X | X | | | | X |
| EAGGF | X | X | | | | | X | |
| FIFG | X | X | | | | | | |

*Source*: http://www.europa.eu.int/comm/regional_policy/intro/working4_en.htm (also/working2_ and 3_).

In addition, there is the Cohesion Fund, set up in 1993 to co-finance transport and environmental infrastructure projects in member states with a per capita Gross Domestic Product (GDP) of less than 90 per cent of the Union average at the time. Between 1993 and 2003, Ireland, Greece, Spain and Portugal were qualified to receive grants from this fund. When the ten accession countries joined in 2004, additional amounts were added and one-third of the enlarged Cohesion Fund was allocated to the new members. Ireland, whose per capita income had moved above the EU average, has graduated: 2003 was the last year it could receive previously earmarked Cohesion Funds. Thus, at the end of 2004 there were 13 so-called 'cohesion countries' (the term refers to the countries eligible to tap the Cohesion Fund): the ten new members plus Greece, Spain and Portugal.[9]

Table 2.2 summarizes EU structural funds, including the Cohesion Fund, after the enlargement adjustment, for 2000–2006 by types of objectives and programs, separately for the EU−15, the EU+10 and the EU−25 combined.

Although there are numerous objectives and funds, Objective 1, (for which resources are mobilized from four structural funds), and the Cohesion Fund, which finances large-scale transport and environmental projects, together account for 95 per cent of the 2004–2006 regional aid earmarked for the ten accession countries from the so-called structural funds.

Table 2.3 shows the amounts in structural funds earmarked for 2004–2006 for each the ten accession countries, by main objectives.

The total for the ten accession countries in Table 2.3 (24.5 billion Euros) is larger than the 21.9 billion Euros shown in Table 2.2 because the latter is in 1999 prices while the former is in current prices.

The last column of Table 2.3 shows what per cent of each country's population are eligible to benefit from the structural funds. The percentages are based on the Commission's so-called Nomenclature of Territorial Units for Statistics (NUTS)-regions map.[10] We find that practically the entire population of the CEE countries is eligible to benefit from structural aid. Only in the case of the Czech Republic and Slovakia is the coverage 92 per cent. The shortfall is probably due to the way in which NUTS-regions were defined by and for these two countries.

## Pre-accession assistance to the countries of CEE

The EU had created three special financial programmes for 2000–2006 to help prospective members prepare for membership and to start narrowing their income gap with the rest of the Union: the PHARE, ISPA and SEPARD programmes. Each of these is described briefly. Some details on who can apply, how funding decisions are made and what types of projects are eligible and have been funded are given only under ISPA; for the other programmes, the procedures are similar.

*Table 2.2* Structural and Cohesion Funds budget for the EU-15, EU+10 and EU-25 combined, 2000–2006* (in billions of Euros)

| *Group* | *Objective 1* | *Objective 2* | *Objective 3* | *Interreg* | *Urban* | *Equal* | *Leader* | *Fisheries Fund* | *Cohesion Fund* | *Total* |
|---|---|---|---|---|---|---|---|---|---|---|
| EU−15 | 137.8 | 22.0 | 24.1 | 4.9 | 0.7 | 2.9 | 2.0 | 1.1 | 18.0 | 213.4 |
| EU+10 | 13.2 | 0.1 | 0.1 | 0.4 | 0.0 | 0.2 | 0.0 | 0.0 | 7.6 | 21.7 |
| EU−25 | 151.0 | 22.2 | 24.2 | 5.3 | 0.7 | 3.1 | 2.0 | 1.1 | 25.6 | 235.1 |

*Note*: *Spending under the structural funds varies considerably from year to year and from country to country. Payment to member states depend on several factors, such as how late in the budgetary year member states make requests for funding. In March 2004, the Commission earmarked from the given total a supplementary amount (performance reserve) of 8 billion Euros, or 4 per cent of total resources, for all successful programs (Objectives 1, 2, 3 and Fisheries).

*Source*: http://europa.eu.int/comm/regional_policy/atlas/factsheets/pdf/fact_eu_en.pdf.

*Table 2.3* Member states and structural funds and instruments, 2004–2006 (millions of Euros at current prices)

| *Country* | *Objective 1* | *Objective 2* | *Objective 3* | *Interreg* | *Equal* | *Cohesion Fund* | *Total* | *% of population in Objective 1 & 2 areas* |
|---|---|---|---|---|---|---|---|---|
| Cyprus | 0 | 28 | 22 | 4 | 2 | 54 | 113 | 31 |
| Czech Rep. | 1,454 | 71 | 59 | 69 | 32 | 936 | 2,621 | 92 |
| Estonia | 371 | 0 | 0 | 11 | 4 | 309 | 695 | 100 |
| Hungary | 1,996 | 0 | 0 | 69 | 30 | 1,113 | 3,207 | 100 |
| Latvia | 626 | 0 | 0 | 15 | 8 | 515 | 1,164 | 100 |
| Lithuania | 895 | 0 | 0 | 22 | 12 | 608 | 1,538 | 100 |
| Malta | 63 | 0 | 0 | 2 | 1 | 22 | 89 | 100 |
| Poland | 8,276 | 0 | 0 | 221 | 134 | 4,179 | 12,810 | 100 |
| Slovakia | 1,041 | 37 | 45 | 41 | 22 | 571 | 1,757 | 92 |
| Slovenia | 238 | 0 | 0 | 24 | 6 | 189 | 456 | 100 |
| Total | 14,960 | 136 | 126 | 479 | 252 | 8,495 | 24,451 | 98 |

*Note*: Due to different lengths of the programming periods for EU−15 and the 10 new member states (seven years and three years, respectively), it is not useful to compare the totals for these two groups of countries.
*Source*: See Table 2.2.

## PHARE

The PHARE programme was established in 1989, originally for Poland and Hungary. Subsequently eight other CEE countries were added: the six additional ones that eventually joined the EU in 2004, plus Bulgaria and Romania. The programme was designed to strengthen the administrative and institutional capacity of the prospective new members (30 per cent of the funding) and to finance investment projects to reduce their income gap (70 per cent).

A high priority of the PHARE programme is supporting economic and social cohesion in the candidate countries. Assistance takes the form of measures similar to those employed in member states through the ERDF and the ESF projects and programmes.

In an attempt to promote two complex objectives simultaneously, namely to improve competitiveness on the EU internal market and to reduce internal disparities, each country has been required to draw up a NDP that maps out its strategy, priorities and programmes for promoting economic and social cohesion on its national territory. This Plan constitutes the key steering document for programming PHARE projects. NDPs are updated as the candidate countries' own national and regional development strategies develop. The intention is that the NDPs should continue to evolve towards the development plans and programming standards used by the EU in its Structural Funds programmes.

## ISPA

The ISPA programme is similar to the PHARE programme. The main difference is ISPA's exclusive focus on environmental and transport infrastructure projects. Established in 1999, its rationale is also to enhance economic and social cohesion in the applicant CEE countries during 2000–2006.[11]

Application and grant procedures are as follows. The candidate countries propose, via their national ISPA coordinator, projects in the eligible sectors. The projects must be part of an ISPA sector investment plan already adopted by the candidate countries and by the Commission.

Applications are sent to the ISPA office of the Directorate-General of Regions. The application is examined by the staff and discussed with the applicant country when necessary. Once the Commission considers the project acceptable, it submits it for opinion to the Management Committee, composed of representatives of the member states. After having received a positive opinion from the Management Committee, the Commission adopts the project and submits a Financing Memorandum for signature to the applicant country.

ISPA concentrates on 'investment heavy' projects, that is, those that are particularly costly to implement. Priority has been given to assist projects that improve the quality and supply of drinking water and the collection and treatment of waste water, that modernize the collection and management of solid waste, and that reduce air pollution.

In the area of transport, ISPA focuses on building, upgrading and repairing the eligible countries' transport infrastructure and linking it to the expanding EU trans-European transport networks. ISPA assistance favours infrastructure projects that encourage sustainable forms of moving people and goods; in particular, projects of Community interest, such as those along the routes of multi-modal pan-European transport corridors. Keeping these criteria in mind, ISPA contributes to the development of railways, roads, ports and airports. ISPA also provides technical assistance, for example, to fund preparatory studies and to improve the administrative capacity of the bodies responsible for the management of ISPA projects.

For the period 2000–2006, a little over one billion Euros a year (in 1999 prices) were earmarked for the ISPA instrument. During its first four years of implementation (2000–2003), ISPA grants aided over 300 large-scale infrastructure investments in the 10 candidate countries of CEE. Assistance for them totaled 7 billion Euros; when matching funds provided by the national authorities and the private sector are taken into account, total investment is estimated to have been 11.6 billion Euros (at current prices).[12]

### SAPARD

The SAPARD, also set up in 1999, assists the same ten CEE countries (1) to deal with the problems of the structural adjustment in their agricultural sectors and rural areas and (2) to implement the *acquis communautaire* concerning the CAP and related legislation. The Directorate-General for Agriculture is in charge of programme implementation.

### Summary accession of the pre-accession programme

Table 2.4 summarizes the expenditures budgeted for each of the three programmes during the 2000–2006 Financial Perspective, total and for each of the seven years. The 22 billion Euros for the combined pre-accession aid for the CEE-10 for 2000–2006 agrees with the subtotal for pre-accession aid shown for the EU+10 countries in Table 2.2.

Since eight of the ten countries that were previously eligible for these three pre-accession programs became member states in May 2004 (in addition to

*Table 2.4* Pre-accession support budgeted for the ten CEE countries for 2000–2006 (millions of Euros in 1999 prices)

| *Programme* | *2000* | *2001* | *2002* | *2003* | *2004* | *2005* | *2006* | *Total* |
|---|---|---|---|---|---|---|---|---|
| PHARE | 1,560 | 1,560 | 1,560 | 1,560 | 1,560 | 1,560 | 1,560 | 10,920 |
| ISPA | 1,040 | 1,040 | 1,040 | 1,040 | 1,040 | 1,040 | 1,040 | 7,280 |
| SEPARD | 520 | 520 | 520 | 520 | 520 | 520 | 520 | 3,640 |
| Total | 3,120 | 3,120 | 3,120 | 3,120 | 3,120 | 3,120 | 3,120 | 21,840 |

*Source*: Based on B. Laffan and Mi. Shackleton (2000), Table 8.2, p. 231.

*Table 2.5* Financial allocation under pre-accession assistance for Bulgaria and Romania, 2004–2006 (millions of Euros at 2004 prices)

| *Country* | *Programme* | *2004* | *2005* | *2006* | *Total* |
|---|---|---|---|---|---|
| Bulgaria | PHARE | 203 | 220 | 237 | 660 |
| | ISPA | 135 | 147 | 158 | 440 |
| | SEPARD | 68 | 73 | 79 | 220 |
| | Total | 406 | 440 | 474 | 1,319 |
| Romania | PHARE | 474 | 513 | 552 | 1,539 |
| | ISPA | 316 | 342 | 368 | 1,026 |
| | SAPARD | 158 | 171 | 184 | 513 |
| | Total | 948 | 1,026 | 1,104 | 3,078 |
| Total | PHARE | 677 | 733 | 789 | 2,198 |
| | ISPA | 451 | 489 | 526 | 1,466 |
| | SAPARD | 226 | 244 | 263 | 733 |
| | Total | 1,353 | 1,466 | 1,578 | 4,397 |

*Source*: EU, 'Financial Statement Annex' to 'Roadmap for Bulgaria and Romania'.

Malta & Cyprus), 2003 was the final programming year for pre-accession assistance to these countries. To be sure, contracting is envisaged to continue through 2005 and payments till the end of 2006. Pre-accession aid was, however, substantially increased for the remaining candidate countries. Bulgaria and Romania together have been allocated some 4.4 billion Euros in pre-accession assistance for the period 2004–2006, as is shown in Table 2.5.[13]

## The EIB[14]

This is the financing institution of the EU. The Bank was established at the signing of the Treaty of Rome. Its current shareholders are the 25 member states of the EU. Each member's share in the Bank's paid-in capital is calculated based on the country's GDP-based economic weight in the EU at the time of accession. The combined weight of the 10 new member countries in the Bank's total (and newly enlarged) subscribed capital of 164 billion Euros is 5 per cent. Each new member will be paying in its share in eight instalments.

The EIB's mission is to provide long-term finance (usually 4–20 years, depending on the life of the assets being financed) for specific capital projects that further EU economic objectives, in particular, by financing projects located in the EU's weaker regions. The EIB operates like a development bank, borrowing on the capital markets (mainly through bond issues and other specialized capital market operations); it does not draw on the Community budget. Consequently, it makes no grants, only loans. Since it enjoys top credit rating, it is able to borrow at low rates. And since it is a not-for-profit organization, it passes on the resulting savings to its borrowers. EIB never finances more than 50 per cent of a project's total cost. The Bank acts as a catalyst, encouraging other banks and financial partners to participate in an investment.

*Table 2.6* EIB activity by groups of countries in 2003 (in billions of Euros)

| *Activity* | *Total* | *EU–15* | *CEE–10* | *Other* |
|---|---|---|---|---|
| Contracts signed | 42.3 | 34.2 | 4.6 | 3.5 |
| Loans approved | 46.6 | 37.3 | 5.7 | 3.6 |
| Loans disbursed | 35.7 | n.a. | n.a. | n.a. |

*Note*: n.a.: not available.
*Source*: European Investment Bank website.

Public- as well as private-sector bodies within EU states are eligible for Bank financing. There are no geographical or sectoral quotas. Similar organizations from non-member countries may also apply. In 2003, about 85 per cent of EIB lending went to projects located within the EU.

Table 2.6 summarizes the value of contracts signed, loans approved and loans disbursed during 2003, separately for the EU–15, the so-called 'Acceding and Accession Countries' (presumably covering mainly the CEE–10 countries, including Romania and Bulgaria), and EU's so-called 'Partner Countries'(in the Mediterranean Region and Africa).

It shows that in 2003 the CEE–10 countries accounted for somewhat more than 10 per cent of the Bank's total lending activities, and 12–13 per cent of the Bank's lending within the EU, which compares with their 5 per cent contribution to the Bank's capital.

## Aid and pre-accession assistance to the Western Balkans

Between 1991 and the end of 2001, the five Western Balkan countries had received in excess of 6 billion Euros through the EU's human and financial assistance (EC 2002c).[15] This aid had been provided not under the pre-accession budget item (and thus has not been included in the 44 billion Euros of total aid for the ten countries of CEE), but under the 'external aid' budget category.

Relations between the EU and the Western Balkans were dramatically altered in recent years, on the one hand, by the instability brought to the doorsteps of the EU during the 1990s by 'ethnic cleansing' and the wars in the Balkans and, on the other, by the pending accession of the ten CEE countries during the early part of this decade.

In 1999, the so-called Stability Pact – proposed by the EU – was agreed to by the international community to provide mutually reinforcing aid to the Western Balkans, subject to certain political conditions being met by the recipient countries.

In 2000, the EU announced its SAP for the Western Balkans. The SAP represents EU's contribution to the Stability Pact and its commitment to the eventual EU membership of some or all of these countries, subject of course to meeting membership preconditions. A key element of the SAP is a substantial financial assistance programme, called Community Assistance for Reconstruction, Development and Stabilization (CARDS). Another important element of the SAP is the offer to sign country-specific Stabilization and Association Agreements (SAAs) with those countries that are making sufficient reform progress and can thus move toward closer formal association with the EU. The SAAs are patterned after the so-called Europe Agreements that the EU had signed with each of the individual CEE countries during the 1990s. Such agreements specify a set of legally binding rights and obligations that must be met by both parties on the road to the signatory country's full integration into the EU. As of yearend 2004, the EU had signed SAAs with Macedonia and Croatia.

At the EU – Western Balkan Summit held in Thessalonica (Greece) on 21 June 2004, EU Commissioner for External Relations, Chris Patten, announced the upgrading of the SAP for all of Western Balkans by grafting on to the SAP a series of pre-accession programs, patterned on those that have proved their worth in the CEE countries in their preparation for accession. Specifically:[16]

- established the European Integration Partnership (EIP) program, which identifies short- and medium-term priorities for action in preparation for closer integration with the EU. This program, and its CARDS funding arm (which has earmarked assistance to the five countries totaling 5 billion Euros during 2000–2006) incorporates several features of the PHARE, ISPA and SEPARD programs;
- enhanced support for institution building, a key component of which is the so-called 'twinning programs': the secondment of civil servants from EU member states to work as advisers in the civil services of the Western Balkan countries;
- introduced yearly benchmarks for measuring each country's reform progress in specific areas, such as the legal system/enforcement and the fight against corruption and organized crime;
- invited the Western Balkan countries to associate themselves with EU common positions and declarations on Common Foreign and Security Policy issues;
- opened up these countries' participation in educational exchange programs Socrates and Leonardo.

These actions and new programmes demonstrate the EU's serious intention to hold out the prospects of eventual full membership for the Western Balkan countries. This important policy was made explicit by Chris Patten at the Thessalonica Summit of 2004:

> The map of the European Union will not be complete until the countries of the Western Balkans are included on it. [The new initiatives unveiled today] show that the EU will do all it can to help these countries prepare themselves, and that our wish to see them one day as fellow members is real.

EU's assistance policies and commitments for South-East Europe underscore the need for an improved understanding of EU's regional assistance policies and programmes generally and the positive and negative experiences of those programs, specifically in the countries of CEE. These issues are discussed in the remaining sections of this chapter.

## Regional policy coordination

This section identifies the actors involved in shaping EU regional policies; which ones have how much power in the policy game; how power has been shifting over time; and how disagreements get resolved.

Regional policy powers are exercised via three key sets of decisions (Armstrong 1995: 51):

- those that establish the size of the financial transfers between regions, that is, the budget, illustrated by the current debate on the EU budget for 2007–2013, summarized below, whose outcome will largely determine the funds available for regional assistance during the next seven years;
- those that determine the specific manner in which regional policy assistance is given, which was discussed briefly earlier in the chapter; and
- those that affect the coordination of regional policies among the member countries and the various EU agencies and programs, discussed briefly next, and with the regional policy efforts of member states, which is too complex a topic to cover in this chapter.

The main actors in the game are the central governments of the member countries, regional and local authorities, and the various EU bodies. Analysis of policy-making and coordination requires that each of these actors be further subdivided into distinct interest groups.

### Member governments

Countries need to be grouped into net contributors to and net beneficiaries from EU funding, even though any netting exercise is fraught with conceptual and practical difficulties. Memberships in the subgroups may also shift over time.[17] For example, Ireland, which used to be the largest net recipients of EU funding (and is still part of that group, owing to the length of the commitment–contract–disbursement chain), is now poised to become a net contributor. Understandably, its near-term policy concern is to delay the transformation as long as it can and to make the switch as painless as possible. At the same time, Ireland's position on longer-term regional policies is being aligned with those of the current net contributors.

### Regional and local authorities and the committee of the regions

Regional and local authorities are obviously important. But whether they are in a position to exercise influence, and to what extent, differ by country and region. Some states lack regional governments altogether; in others, regional/local governments exist but are not effective because they have little or no independent revenues or because they lack internal cohesion or the capacity to mobilize politically. In such cases it is difficult to articulate regional/local interests; making them effective is more difficult still (Keating 1995: 12).

In fact, in both situations (in states with no *de jure* or *de facto* effective regional institutions) national governments have intruded on local matters where there has been EU regional policy to be formulated or implemented. Some argue, therefore, that EU regional policy has proved to be a force for centralization within states. Others contend that EU regional policy has promoted administrative decentralization and the emergence of local civic organizations, among other reasons, because both central governments and the EU need them as partners (Keating 1995).

Regional and local authorities simultaneously cooperate and compete. They cooperate and try to form partnerships with the Commission (and vice versa) to pressure member governments to provide the regions both more resources and more autonomy in the use of those resources. At the same time they compete with each other for resources, both within each country and across the member countries in preparing winning proposals and in lobbying the Commission, the Council and Parliament for their approval.

The Maastricht Treaty provided for the establishment of an EU-wide Committee of the Regions (CoR), one of only two advisory bodies formally attached to the EU (the other is the Economic and Social Council). Its members and an equal number of alternates are appointed for four-year terms by the Council of the EU, acting by a qualified majority on proposals from the respective member states. The delegates, who must be elected representatives of, or politically accountable to, a regional or local assembly, may be reappointed.[18] The CoR has a two-fold mission: to represent the citizens' direct interests in the process of shaping Community policies and to keep its citizens informed of relevant EU activities. However, the CoR is internally divided and its membership 'debilitatingly diverse', with powerful regional leaders from Germany and Belgium sitting next to representatives from English town parishes (Bomberg and Stubb 2003: 63).

Initially, the CoR was made up of 222 members and an equal number of alternates. In anticipation of further enlargement of the Union, the Treaty of Nice (2000) decreed that the CoR could have up to 350 members. The 2004 enlargement added 95 members, currently making it into a 317-person political assembly.

With respect to competition among the regional bodies, independently of the work of the CoR, many regional governments and other types of regional interests have attempted to forge direct individual links with decision-makers in Brussels. The European Council of Ministers, representing member states, is responsive to such lobbying only to the extent that member governments are responsive. Most lobbying has, therefore, concentrated on the Commission.

Several regions have established offices in Brussels (around 1990 there were 54; today there are many more). According to one observer (Keating 1995: 13–14):

> The concrete benefits of regions lobbying with the Commission are questionable. While the Commission is always happy to talk to regions, thus extending its own information sources, it is rarely able to respond to specific demands, given the rules about funding and programs. For this reason, the quality of information assembled by the regions and their technical competence are more important than the fact of having a representative office in Brussels. The directorates-general responsible for regional and structural policies had to some extent become allies of the regions in promoting a more *communautaire* perspective and maintaining pressure on the Council.

### EU bodies

Turning to the third major player in regional policy, the EU itself, the division of powers and the relations between the Council, the Commission and Parliament are pretty well known, as are the conflicts as well as the checks and balances between them. For as long as the EU has been in existence, there has been a tug-of-war for power and influence between the Commission and member governments. Representatives of member governments make up the European Council of Ministers (within which there is hard bargaining on the issues), while elective representatives comprise the Parliament (whose power has been gradually increasing), and whose members represent partly the interests of their countries' (typically as formulated by their central governments) and partly the positions of the political parties they represent.

With respect to policy implementation, let us recall our previous brief description of how ISPA policies are implemented. The reference here is to the continuous, legislatively required back-and-forth steps between the Commission and the Council. It stands as an example of how other regional (and unrelated) policies involving resource transfers are implemented. Whether calling it unnecessary bureaucracy, unavoidable conflict between the Commission and the Council, or desirable checks and balances, it is a complex process that is essentially here to stay.

The Commission itself does not always speak with a single voice on regional policies. For example, there is a conflict between competition policy, monitored by the Competition Directorate, and regional policy, in the hands of the Regional Directorate. Competition policy frowns on subsidies because they distort competition. Paradoxically, one justification of grants to poorer regions is that the very market forces unleashed by increased competition generated by the Single Market Act reinforce some of the disadvantages of backward regions, so regional aid is needed to mitigate them.

Various compromises have been reached at different times between the directorates. During the 1970s the Competition Directorate used to fix ceilings for total permissible subsidies for each region. Later on rules have become more flexible. The Competition Directorate approves regional aid more readily mainly in those cases where the aid promotes the economic development of areas where the standard of living is abnormally low or where there is serious underemployment. To obtain approval, the aid must be exceptional in nature, limited in time, and ensure that the resulting distortions to competition do not outweigh the advantages of the aid in terms of economic development.[19]

Another potential trade-off area is the environment. Ever stricter environmental regulations (in the hands of another directorate) have been imposing particularly strong burdens on the less developed regions because they tend to undercut the poorer regions' cost advantage. Again, regional policy can be a mitigating factor through grants for improving the environment, as was discussed under the ISPA program.

## Regional aid prospects through 2013

During the decade of the 1990s and the first half of the current decade, the EU has been rather generous in providing financial assistance to the CEE countries. However, there are clear indications that the era of generosity is turning into a long period of austerity. The main responsible factor behind this is the sustained weak economic growth performances of EU's three heavyweight Continental economies, those of Germany, Italy and France.

Slow growth has been exacerbating their governments' difficulties in dealing simultaneously with three major fiscal pressures: the ageing of their populations (pressure on the pension systems); non-sustainability, in the face of increasingly severe global competition, of the generous benefits of their social welfare states; and the sudden rise in the number of EU members, candidate members (Romania, Bulgaria, the Western Balkan countries and Turkey), and other hopefuls (such as Ukraine), all hoping for substantially larger net resource flows from the EU in the future than they have been receiving up to now.

In February 2004 (and again in July 2004) the Commission presented to the Council (and thus to member governments) its proposal for the 2007–2013 Financial Perspective. Keenly aware of the net contributing members' fiscal situation and prospects, the Commission proposed a budget ceiling of 1.14 per cent of EU GNI within an own resources ceiling of 1.24 per cent of GNI (the current ceiling is 1.27 per cent), of which 0.41 per cent would be dedicated to cohesion policy (versus 0.37 per cent during the current budget period).

At about the same time the governments of the six net contributors to the EU budget – Germany, France, the UK, Austria, the Netherlands and Sweden – sent a joint letter to the Commission, proposing a 1 per cent of GNI budget ceiling for 2007–2013. Given their status as net contributors and their voting weight in the Council, they have a strong bargaining position. As a consequence, it is likely that the final outcome will be closer to 1 per cent than to the 1.24 per cent or even the 1.14 per cent proposed by the Commission. And since it has been agreed earlier that expenditures on CAP will not decline significantly in absolute amounts, this means an austerity budget for all cohesion programs, since there are no other big items in the budget that can be cut.

## Efficiency and impact of regional policies

Focusing first on impact, it should be pointed out that even under the best of circumstances, 0.4 per cent of GNI (maximum of 40 per cent of an EU budget of around 1 per cent of GNI) cannot be expected to make a big dent on regional inequalities in the short- or medium term.

Moreover, in assessing the impact of regional policies on reducing differences in development levels among the EU members, it must be recognized that the impact of distinct national policies and institutions on growth rates are and will remain, as a rule, greater than the impact of EU regional assistance programmes. No reliable ways have been found so far for separating the impacts of these two complex sets of variables. Take, for example, Ireland versus Greece. Both countries had obtained, over many years, substantial and roughly comparable levels of EU assistance relative to the size of their economies. Ireland has performed remarkably well – not only reducing but eliminating per capita income differences *vis-à-vis* the richer members – while Greece's progress has been less impressive. Since responsibility for success has many claimants, Ireland has been given as an example of the positive contribution of EU regional assistance.

The official position of the Commission is that regional aid clearly has positive impacts in the recipient as well as the donor countries. This position has been well articulated by the incoming Commissioner for the Regions, Hübner, in her many speeches on the topic (see Danuta Hübner's website). She notes that regional spending programs contribute to rising employment and income levels in the recipient countries as well as in other members (in the latter, because most EU-funded projects are carried out in part by contractors from other member countries). She then notes, further, that:

- a large part of EU's cohesion funds are directed to environmental and transport projects whose benefits spill over national boundaries, which makes a strong case for EU-level action;
- EU's seven-year financial perspective stretches beyond national electoral cycles, thus contributing to the financial stability of the recipient countries;
- EU's cohesion policy is a vehicle for the exchange of best practices in regional development policy;[20]
- in financing big infrastructure projects, their long-term impacts are particularly important because long after the initial round of spending has been completed, the consequences of the improved stock of human capital and

physical infrastructure will continue to show up in the form of higher productivity and enhanced profitability for local businesses, benefits that do not show up in 'any net payer versus net contributor' calculation.

The influential Sapir Report of 2004 – prepared by a high-level group of independent experts commissioned in 2002 by Romano Prodi, President of the European Commission, to review the entire system of EU economic policies – has this to say on the impact of EU regional policies (Sapir *et al.* 2004: 76):

> In practice, there is simply not enough relevant regional GDP data for statistical procedures to distinguish the effects of cohesion policies in the absence of data on other regional characteristics, such as initial income, human capital, local industrial structures, quality of local administration, the peripheral nature of the region, and of random influences. The net result is that it is not possible to establish conclusively what the relative performance of these regions would have been in the absence of EU aid.

The Sapir Report did examine, nevertheless, the statistical evidence available and offers an excellent discussion of the conclusions that can and cannot be drawn (Sapir *et al.* 2004: 69–83).[21]

Turning to issues of the efficiency of EU regional aid, the Sapir Report calls attention to two sets of problems. One concerns how aid flows are allocated by the EU; the other, the ability of the local agencies to effectively absorb the earmarked funds.

With respect to the efficiency of fund allocation, the Report points out that while the three main principles underlying current EU cohesion policy (multi-annual programming of expenditure, national co-financing, and additionality of EU money with respect to national money) are sound, the principal weakness of the policy is insufficient focus. One problem is that intra-EU negotiations on which particular countries and regions are to receive how much are driven mainly by judgments about the net budgetary balances of member states. This problem arises because the Council needs unanimity for its decisions, which gives each and every government a significant bargaining power (Sapir *et al.* 2004: 177):

> Each government worries more about being able to flag a negotiation success (that is obtaining a significant share of EU money to be spent on its own territory) than about being sure that the money is spent on worthwhile projects, let alone those fostering convergence in the EU as a whole.

Another problem of insufficient focus is that policy instruments are often given several objectives at the same time (Table 2.1 illustrates this). The Report recommends that it would be better to assign a single objective to each policy instrument (Sapir *et al.* 2004: 6). The Report also points out that the EU typically does not prioritize those investments that would have the largest impact. In other words, lots of objectives and projects are getting some support instead of each of the fewer and more focused objectives and projects obtaining adequate funding (Sapir *et al.* 2004: 176–7).

A related problem is that monitoring focuses insufficiently on output as compared with input. The Report recommends that the disbursement of EU convergence funds should be tied more to the attainment of *ex ante* declared 'output' results (for example, of having an additional Y per cent of schools linked to the internet, or having an additional Z per cent of public employees able to speak a foreign language), rather than on 'input', such as having spent X millions on an objective (Sapir *et al.* 2004: 179).

Turning to the ability of local agencies to make good use of the funds earmarked for them, the Sapir Report points out the importance of the quality of local institutions, such as public administration, in managing EU as well as national development assistance. The Report points out that those areas with low quality local institutions find it difficult to spend Community funds allocated to them. The most frequently used indicator of performance for managing EU funds is the so-called 'disbursement rate', which is the difference between the amount of money allocated to a given country or region and the actual amount paid out to it.

Experience with the EU's pre-accession aid to the countries of CEE shows that the actual disbursement ratios were rather low (50–70 per cent of commitments) and that substantial delays in using the funds were also frequent (Sapir *et al.* 2004: 129–30).

The limited administrative capacity of the new members manifests itself in two distinct areas. First, there is a chronic deficit of well-prepared projects that would be both part of a national development program and meet the stringent substantive and procedural requirements imposed by EU rules on the use of its funds. Second, the capacity of local administrations to evaluate projects and to interact between local agents and EU authorities is limited. Some expertise on using EU funds has already been developed, but it is mostly concentrated in central government administrations; by contrast, local offices are largely understaffed, their personnel lack skills (language or knowledge of procedures) needed to process effectively and expeditiously all documentation pertaining to projects. In their words, inadequate capacity to effectively absorb EU regional assistance is singled out as the main problem for the CEE countries, a problem that is even more serious in the Western Balkans and in such other transforming economies as Ukraine.

Capacity to absorb foreign EU regional assistance has three aspects (Horvat 2004):[22]

- *Macroeconomic absorption capacity*. This refers to whether or not the country in question has reached the 4 per cent of GNI maximum limit the EU has established in 2002 for structural and cohesion funds that can be allocated to any member country in a given year. Since so far none of the CEE countries have been earmarked EU funds that approach this limit, macroeconomic absorption capacity has not been a constraint and is unlikely to become one, owing to the increasingly severe long-term financial problems faced by the EU budget.

- *Financial absorption capacity*. This refers to the ability of EU members to co-finance EU-supported programmes and projects since co-financing is a requirement of structural assistance. Sources of co-finance include central and local government budgets and any other domestic or international contribution that the government is able to tap. While the author is not aware of any formal studies on financial absorption capacity, it is, presumably, not a binding constraint for any country.
- *Administrative absorption capacity* (AAC). This is defined as the ability and skill of central, regional and local authorities (a) to prepare, on a timely basis, national plans, programs and projects that meet EU standards; (b) to arrange the required coordination among the principal partners; and (c) to cope with the vast amount of administrative and reporting work required by the Commission to properly finance, monitor and evaluate the implementation of the programs and projects.

AAC is the critical variable for the CEE and other transition economies. Although the AACs of the transforming economies cannot be measured accurately, first and foremost because new member states are only at their first programming period (2004–2006), approximations can be made, based on these countries' experiences with pre-accession funds, as well as on their ability to prepare, on a timely basis, acceptable national plans, programmes and projects for purpose of obtaining structural and cohesion funding.

Based on a comprehensive review of the literature, including Commission documents, and his own survey of some of the factors that define ACC, Slovenian economist A. Horvat compared and ranked the AACs of five CEE countries – the Czech Republic, Estonia, Hungary, Slovakia, and Slovenia – as of April 2003.[23]

Horvat found that Hungary and Estonia are 'sufficiently able' to administer structural funds, with certain weaknesses, to be sure. The Czech Republic and Slovenia were ranked somewhat lower, with 'serious weaknesses' that need to be addressed. Slovakia's administration was found to be 'not yet sufficiently prepared for structural funds management'.[24]

A 2002 report by the EU Commission on the countries of South-East Europe also emphasizes the weakness of their administrative capacities, pointing out that their public administrators are generally neither well trained nor equipped, that there is insufficient understanding of the role of government in democratic, market-oriented economies, and that even where new laws were introduced, implementation has remained weak. 'Strengthening human resources throughout the public sector [is] crucial "for the countries" development, including for their ability to effectively absorb EU and other foreign assistance' (EC 2002b).

The real contribution of Horvat's study – especially for the countries that are preparing or aspiring for EU membership – is the author's identification and systematization of the factors that define ACC.

## Conclusions

This chapter has two main conclusions. First, that it is more than likely that EU regional aid of various kinds will continue to be available for the transforming economies of Central, Eastern and Southern Europe during the next decade. However, as a group, these countries should not count on significant increases in the amounts of transfers. Even so, regional aid will continue to be substantial. Secondly, that policymakers in all these countries, but especially in the less developed ones, should concentrate their efforts on improving the administrative absorption capacity of EU (and other) aid programmes.

## Notes

1. Cohesion as an objective was written into the Single European Act (SEA) in 1985 to signify the importance of promoting the development of poorer countries and regions of the EU.
2. To be sure, countervailing forces are also at work. Growth at the centre triggers land-price rises and wage increases, which make peripheral locations more attractive for investors. So too does the increasing congestion and poorer quality of the environment in metropolitan areas.
3. Speech at the Centre for European Reform in Brussels, 9 December 2004, as reported on website http://www.europa.eu/ies/SZMLONS/SPEECH-04-527_en[1].doc.
4. While only three of the five objectives (that is, to develop structurally backward regions, to assist the conversion of regions in industrial decline, and to promote the development of rural areas) were overtly regional in nature, the other two objectives – to combat long-term unemployment and to modify the structure of agriculture – implicitly biased support toward the poorer regions.
5. The information in this section is based, unless otherwise specified, on the website of Terry Wynn, member of the European Parliament and the Chairman of its Budgets Committee during 1999–2004: http://www.terrywynn.com/eubudget/images/table7.gif.
6. Between 1986 and 2004, EU expenditures as per cent of GNP/GNI have moved as follows: 0.99, 0.96, 1.03, 0.94, 0.94, 1.03, 1.09, 1.18, 1.04, 1.04, 1.14, 1.12, 1.09, 1.07, 1.09, 1.08, 1.05, 1.04, .98. (Source: Terry Wynn's website, cited above.)
7. In April 2005 the European Parliament voted in favor of Romania and Bulgaria joining the EU in 2007 or 2008, depending on the speed with which they will implement the reforms demanded by the EU.
8. In 2003 the population of the EU–15 was around 380 million.
9. The Cohesion Fund co-finances major projects rather than programs and thus makes it possible to avoid having the cost of these works disrupt budgetary efforts

in the countries to satisfy the Maastricht Treaty's budget rules for economic and monetary union.

10. NUTS = Nomenclature of Territorial Units for Statistics, established in the late 1970s by Eurostat, provides a single, uniform breakdown of territorial units in the EU. One of its purposes is to frame Community regional policies, notably economic assistance.
11. Source: EU website http://europa.eu.int/comm/enlargement/pas/ispa.htm. For the countries that became members in May 2004, projects previously financed under ISPA are now under the Directorate General for Regional Policy and are handled as part of the Cohesion Fund policy.
12. Source: EU website http://europa.eu.int/comm/regional_policy/funds/ispa/ispa_en.htm
13. During this period Turkey is scheduled to receive 1.05 billion Euros in pre-accession aid.
14. The information in this section comes from the Bank's website, http://www.eib.org/about/
15. The Annex to the Report provides details.
16. EU website: Commission, External Relations, 'The EU's Relations with South-Eastern Europe' (7 January 2005).
17. For insightful discussion, see (http://www.terrywynn.com/eubudget/images/table7.gif).
18. http://www.COR.EU.INT/EN The UK website, http://www.lgiG.gov.uk/ukint-e1.htm, lists the number of delegates for each country.
19. Source: EU website, SCADPlus, 'National Regional Aid'.
20. In 2003, the EU established a new program, Industrial Change Network (ICN), to compile a database of best practices of public bodies across Europe, with the aim to improve the efficiency of regional development policies. (See www.interreg3c/Net/sixCMS for details.)
21. For example, prior to the creation of the Euro, exchange rate fluctuations pollute all income data and purchasing power adjustments are inevitably imprecise.
22. This research paper is based on the author's review of the literature on aid absorption.
23. Horvat's study is based on his 2004 PhD dissertation at the Vienna University of Economics and Business Administration. Currently, Horvat is a staff member of Slovenia's National Agency for Regional Development. He can be contacted at andrej.horvat@gov.si
24. It is possible that in the two years that have elapsed between Horvat's survey and the preparation of this chapter, considerable improvements had occurred in the AACs of these countries.

# 3
# National and Local Governments: Institutional Rebuilding and Politics in the Balkans

*Simona Piattoni*

## Introduction

Just barely has, in May 2004, the EU completed the most significant round of enlargement to date, by admitting ten new countries and roughly 75 million people, that the issue of further enlargements to the Balkans is already on the table of the new Commission and the European public opinion. Sheer economic convenience – the creation of an even larger common market – cannot explain the drive towards the inclusion of the Balkan countries in the European Union, as it is exceedingly difficult to calculate the short- and long-term costs and benefits for current member-states and for prospective members. It is rather the historical mission of the European Community (EC)/Union, of securing peace through prosperity and prosperity through peace on the European continent, that stands out as the main rationale for enlargement to the Balkan area. In turn, this finality poses European institutions with probably unprecedented challenges (see Chapter by Gozi).

This chapter will focus on the European policies for securing economic and social cohesion to highlight the complexity of the challenges which the Balkan countries (and the other member-states together with them) are bound to face in these first decades of the 21st century. Some of these problems have emerged in the past during the first 15 years (1988–2004) of life of the reformed (European Regional Development Policy) ERDP – a collective term to denote structural action through Structural Funds, the Cohesion Fund and other financial instruments of the EU. Additional problems will emerge in the remaining years of the current (1999–2006) programming cycle and during the upcoming (2007–2013) programming cycle, which will see the full inclusion of the current enlargement countries into ERDP. The problems will be multi-faceted as they will have economic, institutional, legal, cognitive and political dimensions. The aim of this chapter is to extrapolate from past experience to anticipate some of these challenges.

The first section will briefly describe the evolution of ERDP since its inception in order to highlight the transformation of some of its goals from purely economic to more institutional objectives. The second section will dwell on the impending reform of the Structural Funds (due to be completed by 2006), which will have to solve the difficult problem of how to secure sufficient funds for the social and economic catching-up of the new ten member-states while still guaranteeing a certain amount of resources to the lagging or suffering regions of the older 15 member-states. The third section will then focus on the challenges that the Balkan countries can be expected to face in meeting the institutional, procedural and substantive requirements of ERDP at the moment of their accession. The responses to these problems may be of different types: the fourth section will draw on the comparative literature on the 'Europeanization of structural policy' to typify some such responses and forecast some of the possible difficulties. The fifth section will conclude by speculating on the never-ending process of adaptation which older and newer members must face, due to the continuing changing nature of the objectives and procedures of European structural policy.

## The evolution of structural policy 1975–2006

The European Regional Development Policy, or structural policy, at the Community level was inaugurated in 1975, but was later deeply reformed in 1988 (and again, less thoroughly, in 1993 and 1999) to take into account the increasing complexity and challenges stemming from successive enlargement waves. It will be reformed again in 2006, to accommodate the problems of the latest enlargement round. Indeed a veritable parallel development of enlargement waves and Structural Funds reforms can be observed. Structural policy is one of the most important policies of the Union for two reasons. First, it constitutes one of the largest items in the EU budget, amounting to roughly one third of it, and redistributes resources which approximate 0.45 per cent of the GNP of the Union. Second, by involving sub-national entities in the decision-making processes concerning the ideation, implementation and monitoring of the development plans funded by the Structural funds, it calls into question the internal structure of several member states (Ansell *et al.* 1997).

Several reforms have punctuated the history of the Structural Funds. These have often been the result of package deals struck at Council meetings – the Regulations regarding the Structural Funds are part and parcel of the budgetary negotiations, hence are matters reserved to the Council – and have often brought about unexpected consequences which then prompted further changes (Marks 1992). Unanimity is required for all those Council decisions concerning the 'widening and the deepening of the Union', which often involve the internal redistribution of the Union's own resources. The politics of 'package deals' manages to push forward complex agendas because each member-state has enough at stake to withhold veto (Marks 1992). It is not by chance that progress in the Structural Funds has normally been preceded or followed by Community enlargements: more generous disbursements of Structural Funds have frequently been the side-payment or the prize for agreeing on major steps towards 'a wider (and deeper) union' (Table 3.1).

*Table 3.1* The parallel unfolding of enlargements and reforms of the Structural Funds, 1973–1999

| *Enlargement* | *SF reforms* |
|---|---|
| 1973: Accession of Denmark, Ireland and the UK | 1975: Inauguration of the ERDF |
| 1981: Accession of Greece | 1985: Agreement on Integrated Mediterranean Programmes (IMPs, 1987–1992) |
| 1986: Accession of Portugal and Spain | 1988: Reform of the Structural Funds (ERDF, ESF, EAGGF, EIB) |
| 1995: Accession of Austria, Finland and Sweden | 1993: Second reform of the Structural Funds; creation of the Cohesion Fund (Objective 6 added in 1995, FIFG added in 1996) |
| 1998: Negotiations with Eastern and Central European countries for accession | 1999: Third reform of the Structural Funds |
| 2002: Enlargement to Eastern and Central European countries decided at Nice | 2002: Negotiations on fourth reform of the Structural Funds |

*Source*: Brunazzo and Piattoni (2004a:153).

The accession of Denmark, Ireland and the UK the last two countries in particular, magnified the problem of internal regional economic disparities which, until then, had plagued Italy alone. Moreover, it was clear that upon accession, the UK would be a net contributor to the Community budget, which is mainly financed through a levy on VAT intake. The British government thus felt compelled (by its public opinion) to try and find compensation for this inconvenient situation (Bache, 1998). The decision was thus made to design specific policy instruments to address the problems of industrial decline, which affected some British regions.[1]

This first enlargement, then, led to the creation of the ERDF dedicated to the creation of industrial infrastructure, the promotion of industrial investment, and the absorption of industrial unemployment. Until the mid-1980s, European regional development policy consisted of five main policy instruments including the just mentioned ERDF. The other four were: the ESF dedicated to the improvement of labour mobility, particularly the facilitation of youth entrance into the job market and the retraining of long-term unemployed; the European Community for Coal and Steel (ECCS), which had sustained (since the 1950s) divestment of excess steel productive capacities and had facilitated the retraining of steel workers; the loans of the EIB, which collected money on the market and lent it at favour rates to firms involved in regional development plans; and the EAGGF, born in 1962 and targeted at the support of the less-favoured agricultural areas. This Fund was in turn divided into two sections: the Guarantee section, dedicated to the subsidy of farmers' income, and the Guidance section targeted at the improvement of agricultural efficiency. Despite good intentions, during the first 15 years of existence, this policy acted more as a reimbursement to member-states for their budget contributions than as a veritable redistributional policy aimed at helping the troubled regions of the Community.

The second enlargement wave, which brought into the Community Greece in 1981 and Portugal and Spain in 1986, caused a thorough reform of the Structural Funds. The first impulse for reform came from Greece's threat to veto the accession of Portugal and Spain into the Community if sufficient compensatory measures had not been devised. Greece feared that the market for Mediterranean products would be flooded by Portuguese and Spanish production thus undercutting the demand for Greek production. Hence the idea of devising a special programme – the Integrated Mediterranean Programmes (IMPs) – which were meant to encourage the reconversion from traditional Mediterranean produces towards new produces for which competition was lower. To reach this goal, an integrated approach combining investment in fixed capital, infrastructure for the industrial transformation of agricultural products, and the re-training of the labour force in Mediterranean regions was needed. Hence, the idea of devising a programme which would integrate all existing Funds towards one transformative goal.

In 1986, when Portugal and Spain joined, this integrated approach had started to show its superiority: hence the idea to apply it to the rest of ERDP to address the development problems of the incoming countries whose per capita GNP was, at the time of accession, lower than 90 per cent of the Community average. Such a situation was clearly untenable, particularly at a time when further steps towards economic integration, eventually leading up to the Single European Act, were being taken. The IMPs effectively 'communitarianized' the ERDP by fundamentally entrusting to the Commission the ideation, implementation, supervision and evaluation of regional development plans. In carrying out these tasks the Commission was assisted by the planning authorities of each member state and, for the first time, also by the planning authorities of the regional governments.

The need to secure the agreement of the four poorest member-states – Greece, Ireland, Portugal and Spain – to the completion of the Single Market was behind the decision to drastically reform the Structural Funds in 1988. The 1988 reform can be without doubt considered as a 'package deal' between the richer member-states, which were vitally interested in the completion of the Single Market, and the poorer member-states, which were concerned about being left behind. The reform, that is, served both the immediate purpose of securing unanimity for this crucial step forward in integration and the long-term goal of helping the lagging countries take advantage of the economic growth that was expected to ensue from it. The Funds' endowment were therefore significantly increased and the organizational innovations already experimented with the IMPs were introduced full-force.

Regional policy and enlargement became intertwined also during the 1999 reform, which posed, for the first time in urgent terms, the problem of the incompatibility between regional policy and agricultural policy.[2] The 1999 reform round anticipated some of the concerns that govern the current 2006 reform negotiation round: the lagging regions of the EU-15 member states will probably lose most structural support once the new member states join the Union. Hence the 2000–2006 programming cycle will probably be the last cycle which will help redress the internal disparities of the current member states. In view of the management problems that the incoming members states would most likely encounter, efficiency and effectiveness criteria were further strengthened already in the 1999 regulation (Suttcliffe 2000; Hooghe 2002; Sorrente 2002).

With the 2004 enlargement inter-country disparities became significantly bigger than intra-country disparities. This will imply a massive redirection of Structural Funds away from the current member states to the new member states. The criteria according to which the Funds will be distributed will have to be thoroughly discussed, past policy instruments will have to be reassessed, and new instruments will have to be devised. Regulation reform negotiations will be quintessentially a political process.

As we have seen, reforms thought for the problems of one set of countries get inscribed into the *acquis communautaire*, which then constitutes the bottom-line on which further reforms are conceived and implemented. The incremental nature of the European Union does not allow for sudden changes or drastic U-turns. For example, the latest enlargement countries have had to create a regional tier because the regional level had been one of the main issues, as well as the corner-stone for their solution, of structural policy in a Europe of 12 member-states. Likewise, the issues and solutions devised for a Europe of 25 members will have an impact onto the Balkan countries ten years or so from now. This is the reason why it is a good idea to take a look at the current debate on the 2006 structural policy reform, which in all likelihood will have a durable impact also on the Balkan countries at the time of their accession.

## The 2006 structural funds reform

The Structural Funds regulation reform process is very complex and contains both formal and informal elements. At this moment, the process of reform concerning the 2007–2013 programming cycle is in its informal stage, in which the Commission drafts the proposal in close consultation with the member states that decide to follow the negotiations. This informal phase was launched in 2001 with the adoption of the Commission's *Second Cohesion Report on Economic and Social Cohesion* (EC 2001a), followed by the adoption of the First progress report (EC 2002a) and the Second progress report (EC 2003) and, lately, of the *Third Cohesion Report on Economic and Social Cohesion*

(EC 2004). Some member states and European institutions have adopted specific opinions and resolutions. Looking at the opinions and official documents approved by the different institutions one can have an idea of what are the most important issues around which the debate is now structured. Following the *Second Progress Report* (EC 2003), the main topics of the debate on the future cohesion policy are three: the definition of priorities, the reform of the implementation process, and the financial aspects of the future policy.

The *definition of priorities* will directly impinge upon which regions of the current 15 member states will continue to receive Structural Funds in 2007–2013. If the criteria for the definition of lagging regions will remain unchanged (that is 75 per cent of EU average GDP), 17 currently funded regions (among which six German regions, for a total of 11 million inhabitants) will cease to receive the funds, while 29 (mostly southern) regions will still receive aid (Viesti and Prota, 2001). Clearly, the maintenance of the current criteria would operate not only a redistribution of funds from older to newer member states, but also a redistribution of funds among the older member states (Table 3.2). The question, therefore, is not only whether western European citizens are willing to help their central and eastern European neighbours, but more specifically whether northern citizens are willing to sustain this redistributive effort towards their eastern and southern neighbours.

Moreover, among the richer northern member states, some carry a heavier burden than others: Germany contributes to the EU budget a lot more than, for example, France which gets back through the CAP much of what it contributes. The definition of structural criteria will therefore involve also a most thorny discussion about the future of the Common Agricultural Policy – an issue already raised in 1999 with the 'Agenda 2000' document but which has not yet found an acceptable solution. A solution will have to be found by 2013 when also the latest enlargement countries will be fully entitled to agricultural support. The contours of such a solution might imply either the definition of 'special criteria' or the development of new lines of intervention and support, particularly in the field of transportation infrastructure. Extrapolating from past experience, which has proved that it is easier to add new policy instruments than to redefine the overall architecture of the existing policy, we can anticipate the creation of new Funds and objectives rather than the redefinition of past criteria.

The second large set of issues concerns the *reform of the implementation process*. This entails both a constitutional dimension – the role of the regional tier within each member state – and an administrative dimension – the differential levels of administrative performance within each member state and the need for simple but watertight procedures. Starting from the latter, the larger the share of budgetary resources devoted to structural policy, the tighter and more difficult to evade the rules governing its implementation. Unfortunately, some of the very rules designed to avoid waste and wrongdoing work against the effective utilization of the funds. One of the requests

*Table 3.2* Summary statistics for regions falling below the 75% threshold (based on GDP/head in PPS, 2000)

| | *In the EU−15* | *In the EU−25* | | *In the EU−27* | |
|---|---|---|---|---|---|
| *Index used:* | *EU−15 = 100 E−22603* | *EU−15 = 100 E−22603* | *EU−25 = 100 E−19661* | *EU−15 = 100 E−22603* | *EU−27 = 100 E−18530* |
| No. of regions falling below the 75% threshold | 48 | 85 | 67 | 99 | 68 |
| *of which in EU−15* | *48* | *48* | *30* | *48* | *18* |
| Population in those regions (million) | 68 | 137 | 116 | 168 | 122 |
| *of which in EU−15* | *68* | *68* | *47* | *68* | *24* |
| Population as a proportion of EU−15-25-27 | 18 | 30 | 26 | 35 | 25 |
| *EU regions as a proportion of EU−15 total (%)* | *18* | *18* | *12* | *18* | *6* |
| Average GDP/head (PPS) of regions falling below the threshold | 65 | 53 | 54 | 47 | 46 |
| *of which in EU−15* | *65* | *65* | *69* | *65* | *68* |

*Source*: Viesti and Prota (2001).

repeatedly put forth by the member states has been the reform of the 'Fund by Fund' system of accounting – which fragments what should in theory be integrated – and the excessive involvement of the Commission in the management of the Funds.

A partial solution to this problem has been already found within the current regulation, which leaves implementation and monitoring to national and regional authorities and limits the role of the Commission to that of supervisor. The 'reserve clause',[3] moreover, acts as a stimulus towards an efficient use of the money. Sometimes, however, financial inefficiency conceals inter-institutional tensions between central and regional authorities. The instrument of 'tripartite contracts' introduced by the White Paper on Governance should serve to iron out such difficulties. The explicit pressure of the Commission towards the creation of a regional level, where it does not exist, or of its empowerment, where it already exists, only exacerbates this problem. This is the kind of issue which elicits the concerns of various EU institutions and member-states.

Debates about definition of criteria and reform of policy implementation find their most concise summary in the issue of the *financial endowment of the Funds* for the foreseeable future. While the total amount of resources available in 2007 should be about 44 billion Euros, only roughly a third of it should accrue to enlargement countries. A comparable amount, roughly 46 billion Euros, should be devoted to CAP (Viesti and Prota, 2001). Ailing regions of the current member states, which do not receive any CAP money, would thus be penalized *vis-à-vis* all other comparably needy regions.

The position of the different member states can be easily anticipated through a simple convenience calculus (Viesti and Prota, 2001). Unsurprisingly, Spain, which released a memorandum in April 2001, is particularly concerned about the discontinuation of Cohesion support due to the statistical effect brought about by the new member states. Its main concern is the total endowment of the Structural Funds. Ireland, in its turn, quickly redrew its own map by turning from a single NUTS 2 region to a two NUTS 2-region country – the poorer parts of the country all falling within one region. In this way, Ireland will be able to retain Objective 1 status in most of its relatively underdeveloped regions and 'phasing out' (from Objective 1) status in the rest. Germany proposed two solutions. The first is designed to 'contain the damage' of the statistical effect, keep the current approach to Structural Funds, and request a thorough reform of the CAP. The second foresees a more generous distribution of the Funds, but puts responsibility for regional policy back to central authorities (which would obviously allow German authorities to use those resources as they please, that is, to sustain also some regions which, on a EU−15 scale, would be cut off from structural aid). The Netherlands takes a similar position. France and Denmark are favourable to maintaining the status quo, which advantages them through the inverse redistributive effect of the CAP. The UK has an interest in keeping Objective 2 in place. Italy, in two

Memorandums released in June 2001 and December 2002, opposed the idea of re-nationalizing structural policy. Banking on its experience with local development in the North-East and Centre (and, increasingly, in the South), the Italian government stated that effective development action has often more to do with the mobilization for productive uses of endogenous resources than with the transfer of massive (financial) resources from outside. It consequently proposed to build more robust indicators of underdevelopment, capable of detecting the pool of unutilized endogenous resources and identifying the truly critical areas which regional statistics might conceal, and to create central-local partnership on the model of those experimented in Italy.

The Commission's positions are contained in several official documents and have been presented in different forums and inter-institutional meetings. The main issues are outlined in the *Second Report* (EC 2003) which 'develops a set of conclusions and recommendations with a view to opening a debate on the future of cohesion policy after 2006 in an enlarged European Union'. The same issues have later been reiterated and better specified in the *First* and *Second Progress Report* (EC 2002a, 2003) and in the *Third Report* (EC 2004). The European Commission emphasizes that the forthcoming enlargement to central and eastern European countries will result in an important increase in social, economic and territorial disparities and, as a consequence, the Commission will continue to 'support those actions that are most likely to contribute to the reduction of the economic, social and territorial disparities in the Union' in the new regions but also in the disadvantaged ones previously assisted by cohesion policy (p. XXV).

Looking ahead, the Commission recommends integrating cohesion policy with other EU policies. In particular, coordination has to be sought between cohesion and competition policy: 'Competition and cohesion policies are complementary, since the ceiling imposed on regional State Aids benefits the less prosperous countries most of all. This thrust of policy needs to be pushed further to establish more equitable conditions for competition, while taking account of the role played by services of general interest in territorial cohesion' (p. XXXVII).

Recognizing that enlargement will substantially reduce EU average GDP levels and that disparities in EU-25 will be wider than in EU-15, the Commission proposes four options for determining eligibility and temporary support. The first is the maintenance of the present threshold of 75 per cent (of EU average GDP), irrespective of the number of countries joining the Union. This option would deny aid to a large number of regions in the current EU−15. The second option starts from the same principle but adds the proviso that all current Objective 1 regions which, due to the statistical effect, would result to lie above this threshold should receive temporary ('phasing-out') support. The third option envisages setting a higher average GDP threshold (for example 90 per cent), which would include a larger set of current needy regions than the 75 per cent threshold but would not protect those regions which, as a consequence of the statistical effect, would suddenly result to be richer. The fourth option consists in setting two thresholds of eligibility, one for the regions in EU−15 and one for the candidate countries. A special kind of support might be provided for particular regions, such as border regions and outmost regions. In particular, intervention in the last kind of regions is supported by article 299(2) of the Treaty that allows the EU to maintain and reinforce actions to promote their integration into the Community.

Writing about the distribution of competencies and powers, the Commission favours the strengthening of regional and local authorities in opposition to the state. Moreover, the Commission recommends that, 'if in the future indirect zoning is the method retained for targeting resources, it would be essential that it is accompanied by guarantees regarding the involvement of regional and local authorities', where by indirect zoning the Commission means that eligible areas are decided by national governments on the basis of a set of parameters established by the Commission, following the approach adopted by some Community Initiatives. Whichever the final outcome of this long and complex negotiation process, we may expect with some degree of confidence that the new (and old!) member states will be subjected to the following challenges.

Currently, negotiations have entered their more formal, but also more delicate phase. The Commission proposal is out and soon the Council will have to decide on the financial perspectives of the Union. The current debate sees the northern member-states pitted against a forming front of southern member-states on the issue of the future endowment of the Structural Funds. The northern members want to reduce the Union's own resources to 1.00 per cent of the Union's GNI, while the southern member-states want keep the current 1.24 per cent (these are ceilings which the Council may decide not to reach year by year). The difference in budget would first and foremost be translated into corresponding cuts in structural and cohesion policy, with significant redistributive consequences both for older and newer member-states. But, given the proposed parameters which still give primacy to the 75 per cent threshold, it is particularly the older but poorer member-states which would suffer from such constrained financial perspectives.

## The goals of Europeanization

The overarching goal of the Community was *economic* until at least the SEA of 1986: the creation of a large common market in which European economic actors could compete freely and reap the benefits of a much larger market than the national markets. Larger economies of scale, it was assumed, would allow for the exploitation of comparative and competitive advantages and secure sustained rates of growth once post-war reconstruction had been completed and after the two oil crises had been weathered. This simple and appealing recipe clashed against a much more complicated reality (made of non-tariff barriers, insufficient factor mobility, different social security and other welfare state provisions and, not least, different currencies) which created large internal imbalances while not necessarily securing sustained growth (Mele 2002). Further rounds of enlargement increasingly highlighted the presence of regional imbalances not only across member-states but also (and much more) within member-states. In order to chip away at one bastion of competition discrimination – national currency management – the Treaty of Maastricht established the Economic and Monetary Union, which in turn necessitated a structural policy with dynamically redistributive incentives rather than static compensatory effects.

ERDP was initially conceived (in typical EU fashion, one might add) as both responding to an *economic* logic – by correcting the effect of 'pure' economic forces, which made the core productive and commercial locations stronger and the peripheral locations weaker – and as pursuing the political ideal of an ever 'closer and more harmonious Union'. The idea of ERDP, however is not so much to compensate for situations of under-development or decline, but to help regions with economic problems develop or restructure. In this sense ERDP should be different from the beginning from CAP which has had a strong (although decreasing) compensatory rationale.

Instrumental and idealistic motivations got intertwined in the case of ERDP as they have done in the case of so many other EU policies. The economic record of ERDP, however, has been somewhat mixed. On the one hand, particularly after the creation of the Cohesion Fund – which is centrally managed, is directed exclusively at redressing infrastructural and environmental imbalances and has proved to have a much stronger impact on the receiver countries than the Structural Funds or the Community Initiatives – authentic and remarkable economic progress has been observed in Spain, Portugal and, particularly, Ireland (Mele 2002). On the other hand, the progress of some regions which have received European structural aid since the inception of ERDP – such as some southern Italian regions – and even of regions which have received both Structural Funds and Cohesion Fund money for quite some time – such as some Greek regions – have not displayed comparably spectacular development results. While the reasons for such a mixed record may be different – ranging from the presence/absence of social capital to the different incidence of EU per capita help on the level of per capita GDP – the unevenness of developmental results across the EU is cause for economic reassessment of ERDP.

So, even though only mixed economic results have been achieved, European structural action has been maintained and even strengthened. What are, then, the other possible goals served by this policy? I underlined above the *political* goals served by this policy: by acting as side-payment for crucial decisions about the 'deepening and widening of the European Union', structural policy has greatly helped the advancement of the European integration process. Just as the first ERDP (1975) was a side-payment to compensate the

UK for excessive budgetary contributions so have the IMPs been the token exacted by Greece in exchange for its agreement to accession of Spain and Portugal and so has the Cohesion Fund been the currency with which mainly Germany paid for the costs of EMU in the weaker economies of the Union such as Spain, Portugal, Greece and Ireland (but, interestingly, not eastern Germany).

The side-payment nature of structural policy and the enactment of reforms at each enlargement round point to the third important goal of ERDP: *the construction of efficient and effective institutions*. Precisely because structural policy has become increasingly salient over time in economic and political terms, member-states, particularly large net contributors to the EU budget, have more and more demanded 'value for money'. This has meant securing that the money thus transferred would be well spent. In practice, this overarching goal has taken the shape of ever tighter programming and spending procedures and has entailed the ever closer oversight of the European Commission. In the beginning, in order to compensate for the member-states' tendency to cash in the funds without necessarily employing them for developmental purposes, emphasis was put on *additionality* of EU funds *vis-à-vis* national, local or private effort in favour of ailing regions. The *concentration* of funds towards few, well selected axes of development and the elaboration of developmental *programmes* were also inspired by the need to direct funds towards few, manageable tasks rather than sprinkling the Funds over myriads of small-scale projects whose cumulative impact was often negligible. Finally, *subsidiarity* and *partnership* were introduced to make sure that those institutional and non-institutional actors who are closest to the problems and which command the knowledge and resources which guarantee that programmes are well-conceived and well-implemented would be involved at all policy stages in order to secure its success.

The original economic (and political) goals were thus enriched by institutional considerations concerning the level at which decisions were made and implemented and concerning the efficiency and effectiveness of structural action. This in turn, implied increasing emphasis on ex-ante and ex-post *evaluation*, in order to make sure that developmental goals were matched by appropriate actions and that the degree of success or failure of the policy could be adequately assessed. In this drive towards increased efficiency and control, detailed and rigid guidelines were devised which ended up stifling structural action and creating institutional winners and losers of structural policy. To give just few examples, while the Spanish regions have been empowered by the Structural Funds and have found themselves at the centre of many crucial policy-making circles, German Länder were initially relatively disempowered and found themselves suddenly marginalized in those very circles which they had traditionally dominated (Anderson 1991; Jeffery 1997, 2000; Börzel 2002). The central and regional governments of several member-states found the situation unappealing and clamoured for policy fine-tuning. The 1993 'counter-reform' somewhat simplified the procedures and relaxed the direct involvement of the Commission while tightening the remaining procedures and strengthening the Commission's indirect supervision. It also restored the centrality of the national authorities and granted special rights to 'special' regions.

Despite these rigidities, the 'Europeanization' of structural policy had several positive effects. First of all, it truly addressed problems of Community-wide imbalances thus seeking to redress the effects of the Common Market and helped the realization of the EMU. Secondly, it created a tool with 'direct' redistributive effects (that is, from the richer to the poorer areas) trying to compensate for the 'inverse' redistributive effect (from the poorer to the richer areas) built into the Common Agricultural Policy. Thirdly, it gave a sense to the regions of Europe (the new receivers of the Structural Funds) – and, through them to the citizens of Europe – that the Community took seriously its mission of creating ever more prosperous and comparable living conditions across Europe, thus infusing some practical sense into the notion of 'European citizenship'. Fourth, it gave European regions and citizens a new sense of 'ownership' of the policy, thus mobilizing fundamental grass-roots energies without which – so the New Development Economics teaches us (Krugman 1991) – no real development can actually occur. Last but not least, it made it possible for the Commission to oversee the programming and delivery of the policy, thus giving it a real chance to account for the money which was being spent and for the result which were being achieved. The upshot of all this was nothing less than the re-launching of the European integration project, which had stagnated for lack of vision and for the cross-vetos of the member-states for some 15 years.

This drive towards homogenization of ERDP had also some negative side-effects, the most glaring being the excessive rigidity and cumbersomeness of the procedures and the impossibility to adapt them to the widely different administrative and policy styles of the member-states. While the 2003 reform diluted some of the rigidity built into the 1999 regulations, the drive towards efficiency and efficacy continued. The challenge soon became that of finding a balance between the need to impose a common template to the problems of lack of economic and social cohesion and that of adjusting for national and local peculiarities. In an attempt to strike the right balance between the drive towards efficiency and the attempt to reduce social economic disparities among European regions, more and more programmes (particularly Community Initiatives) were created. With successive rounds of enlargements, development problems were becoming increasingly differentiated ranging from relative under-development to industrial decline, from problems connected with peripheral location to problems of scarcity of population, from problems connected with agriculture to problems related to fishing.

In light of this literature, we can now anticipate some of the challenges that the Balkan countries will probably encounter. Building on the description of the economic programmes created for the CEE and the SAP countries contained in Marer (Chapter 2, this volume), I will mostly dwell on the implementation difficulties which are likely to emerge.

## The challenges of Europeanization

Europeanization can be defined as 'The processes of (a) construction, (b) diffusion and (c) institutionalization of formal and informal rules, procedures policy paradigms, styles and 'ways of doing things', and shared beliefs and norms which are first defined and consolidated in the making of EU public policy and politics and then incorporated in the logic of domestic discourse, identities, political structures, and public policies'(Radaelli 2003: 30). In the case of structural action, the challenges of Europeanization seem to be of a dual order: economic and institutional. While Marer (Chapter 2) amply tackles the former, I will here dwell on the latter.

Institutional complexity is the main challenge that the Balkan countries can expect to meet in their EU-sustained development action. Obviously, 'lessons' cannot be drawn in any immediate meaning of the word from the experience of any current member-state, including perhaps even the recent SEECs (Paraskevopoulos and Leonardi 2004). While the challenge of (re)constructing a market economy and a liberal democracy after many years of planned socialism or autarky besets both the South-East European (SEE) and Balkan countries, the magnitude of economic and institutional problems varies enormously among them. Moreover, the problems of the Balkan countries are of a (macro) regional nature, in the sense that they affect as much each individual country as their mutual relations. A crucial pre-condition for sustained growth is not only the creation of functioning economic, political and legal institutions within each country, but also the creation of institutions which regulate inter-regional relations. To give just one example, trade agreements will have little impact – or, paradoxically, may have a perverse effect – if they do not facilitate also inter-regional trade. In its turn, inter-regional trade will not take place if trans-border commerce is not subjected to fairly even conditions regardless of the country of origin of the products. Obviously, uniform trans-border commerce regulations cannot apply until the region is fully pacified and the relations among ethnic groups fully normalized (Chapter 4 by Berloffa and Segnana in this volume).

New policy tools will have to be used to help these countries in their structural catching-up in addition to the more conventional and better experimented country-by-country and (micro)region-by-(micro)region instruments. Albania, Bulgaria, Bosnia i Herzegovina (BiH), Croatia, the Former Yugoslav Republic of Macedonia (FYROM), Romania and Serbia and Montenegro (SCG) have been extended the same programs which had been originally devised for Poland and Hungary (PHARE, ISPA, SAPARD) and later extended to the other accession countries the Check Republic, Estonia, Latvia, Lithuania, Slovenia, and Slovakia. In addition to these programmes and to the immediate relief programmes such as ECHO, SAP countries have recently started to receive regional aid in the form of the Community Assistance for CARDs programme, which foresees the deployment of 4,650 million Euros between 2000 and 2006 for investment, institution-building and stabilization measures. Since the Council Regulation EC 2006/2000 (5 December 2000), CARDs streamlines assistance to the countries of the Western Balkans. It has both a national and a regional dimension: this latter will use 10 per cent of the available funds, equalling for the 2002–2004 period 197 million Euros.

This latter is of particular interest to us here as its main objectives are: '(1) reconstruction, democratic stabilization, reconciliation and the return of refugees; (2) institutional and legislative development, including harmonization with EU norms and approaches to underpin the rule of law, human rights, civil society and the media, and the operation of a free market economy; (3) sustainable and social development, including structural reform; (4) promotion of closer relations and regional cooperation among SAP countries and between them, the EU and the candidate countries of central Europe' (http://europa.eu.int/comm/europeaid/projects/cards/index_en.htm). The Regional Strategy is embodied in a Multi-annual Indicative Plan (MIP) which gets detailed in Annual Action Plans. The idea behind CARDs was born at the Feira (Portugal) European Council in June 2000 – which foresaw, for the SAP countries, the 'credible prospect of EU membership, once the relevant conditions are met' – and was later sealed at the Zagreb Summit. One cannot overemphasize the importance of fair inter-ethnic and minority treatment as a fundamental premise for the improvement of the institutional and legal preconditions for economic development. Where fundamental human rights are violated and where social and economic interactions are thwarted by inter-ethnic strife or minority oppression and retaliation, no rule of law may exist and, as a consequence, no economic activity can flourish. Where borders are more porous to smugglers, criminals and various kinds of illegal trafficking while legal commerce is hindered by complex and differentiated tariff regimes, there can be no inter-regional trade. Where political and legal authorities are prone to all types of corruption, there can be no basic trust. Under these circumstances, any prospect for economic development is necessarily rather dim (EC 2000).

The *first* institutional challenge that the future enlargement (SAP) countries may encounter regards the presence or absence of *institutional veto-players*. The comparative literature shows (Green Cowles *et al.* 2001) that the reception of new policies or the modification of existing policies may be hindered by actors who have a stake in the status quo. Particularly if a country already has a national programme aimed at redressing interregional imbalances, EU Structural Funds may be implemented with greatest difficulties as the tacit knowledge embedded in a certain 'way of doing things' may be difficult to change. Moreover, if state resources institutionalize a class of civil servants, whose status comes from implementing the national policies, then these may resist the innovations entailed by EU regulations. Therefore, change is slowest precisely where there already exists a policy legacy and standard operating procedures. Whether or not the SEECs will encounter the same problems depends on whether they harbour such policy traditions. Indeed, from a cursory and limited survey of their structural policies, this may prove to be a minor problem.

Even where the institutional problem does not exist – or should be overcome with relative ease – there may be a problem of creating the right incentive structure so that money is appropriated, perhaps with procedurally perfect techniques, but for the 'wrong' sort of aims. The most common mistake according to the literature is to first secure the money and then think of a good way of spending it. Development plans are often 'pipedreams' which cannot be really implemented, or are made up of a myriad of individually insignificant projects which do not amount to any real development plan. By the time regional (and national) actors devise a credible development plan, time has elapsed and the EU asks to see the results. Lacking these, the funds are withheld, redistributed to more deserving (because better at spending) regions, and even the smaller projects flounder.

The *second* challenge is also linked to the institutional level but is best described as a *learning process*. It is very complex to master the procedures necessary to draft credible (integrated) development plans and the corresponding Operational Programmes, appropriate the matching funds (even though in this case they will constitute a small part of the overall investment), implement the spending decisions, monitor expenditures, and evaluate the congruence between stated objectives and achieved results. It took some twenty years for some EU regions – among them, some Italian regions (Leonardi 1998; Piattoni 2003; Brunazzo and Piattoni 2004a/b) – to master these complex processes: it is only reasonable to expect that it may take as much for the SEEC regions to do the same. Yet, learning may be faster the higher the policy stakes. A clear assessment of the urgency of the situation and an accurate evaluation of the magnitude of the problem may speed up the learning process in the Balkans. Also, the lack of pre-existing national programs of regional development may paradoxically facilitate the learning process as the actors who may lose from the adoption of this policy will be few while the winners may be many. Finally, the presence of think-tanks and other institutions for policy design have proved to act as facilitating factors in overcoming cognitive problems and easing the learning process (Radaelli 1999). This latter factor would point to the crucial role that the new political, managerial and intellectual elites may play in the implementation of European policies and the diffusion of European procedures (see Chapter 7 by Grancelli and Chiesi in this volume).

The *third* likely institutional challenge has to do with the lack of *an intermediate level of government*. The SEE, because of their small size and because of their socialist past, often lack an intermediate (NUTS 2) tier of government (see Woelk in this volume). When they harbour significant inner divisions, these are often linked to inter-ethnic problems. Moreover, being mostly underdeveloped, planned economies they also lack a vibrant organized civil society. One of the characterizing features of European structural action is the involvement of sub-national governmental tiers – be they purely administrative or be they also legislative – in the ideation and implementation of structural policies as well as the involvement of 'social partners' (trade unions, employers associations, Chambers of Commerce, Universities, environmental and equal opportunities groups, and so on). While the actual involvement of social partners is a matter left to the central government (in adherence to the subsidiarity principle), the involvement of sub-national governmental tiers is mandatory. With the exception of the Cohesion Fund and the European Social Fund – which are directed at the whole nation – all other structural measures (ERDF, EAAGF, and the Community Initiatives) explicitly require the involvement of NUTS 2 units. Most of the SEE countries lack any regional/county/district articulation before the municipal level and most of them will resist this institutional innovation. However, if they comply, they will most certainly meet the following problem. The third challenge then may also be one of *lack of political vision*. Development is not a mere technical question, but involves priority-setting, consensus-building, burden-sharing. Without politically legitimate authorities which make development into their principal goal there cannot be any efficient management of the funds. It may be better to have central authorities which are clearly committed to development than regional authorities which do not have the vision and the legitimacy to carry out development plans. The opportunity for corruption – of many types – is large.

The *fourth* challenge, then, has to do with the creation at the national and local level of the *technical expertise* which is necessary to handle competently EU programmes. True enough, already Poland and Hungary had been specially assisted in their effort to create or revive a sub-national level of government and interesting experiments aimed at easing the acquisition of the technical and managerial knowledge had been attempted (the so called 'twinning experiments'). Such efforts will most certainly continue in the SEECs, but in this case the steepness of the learning curve should not be underestimated. Particular attention will have to be devoted to the accumulation of that human capital which has proved so crucial in the success cases (for example Ireland). Once more, existing institutional actors may resist this kind of adaptation and act as veto-players. On the one hand, inter-ethnic strife may risk to surface again should decentralization proceed too fast and too deep. On the other hand, a certain measure of decentralization may help handle consensually relations among ethnic 'pillars' which would otherwise be at each others' throat. Much will depend, as the literature tells us, from the vision of the respective elites and their willingness to accommodate inter-ethnic differences. This fourth challenge is also linked to the difficulty of managing the EU-level of decision-making. National and regional authorities must be able to interact with Brussels in all the relevant arenas – a task which may be particularly daunting for smaller countries. Smaller countries may be relegated to the role of policy-takers, rather than policy-makers, and may have to dance to the tune of the bigger countries. Their small size may however allow them to express greater coordination than some of the larger countries and to sit in more crucial decision-making arenas than most European regions. The capacity for coordination at the national and European level among national and regional actors is one of the main factors of success or failure in structural policy, as the Italian experience shows.

The *fifth challenge* has to do with the creation of minimal levels of trust. According to the new orthodoxy in developmental economics, minimal levels of trust and a modicum of social capital are essential ingredients in any developmental recipe. Where people distrust each other and are unwilling to cooperate, little economic progress is possible. In countries which have experimented central planning – which made cooperation unnecessary and, rather, bred opportunist behaviours – and in which ethnic conflicts are endemic, trust may be a particularly scarce commodity. Part of the developmental effort will have to be devoted to 'reconciliation', the recognition of human rights, and to the accommodation of ethnic minority and political refugees. This is a whole new challenge, and probably most daunting, on which little knowledge can be gleaned from past experience.

For all of the above reasons, progress can be expected to be slow and difficult. While the statistical effect of starting from very low levels of development will foster the illusion that progress can be quick, past experience teaches that in reality real catching up is extremely slow. It is not exaggerated to expect that development will take decades and that, perhaps, full social and economic cohesion will never be achieved, just like it seems to be escaping even the original six member-states. The Italian experience teaches that all of these challenges, save perhaps only the last one (although Italy, too, is not immune from a certain amount of inter-regional prejudices), may slow down the catching up process and the attainment of social and economic cohesion.

## Conclusions

This chapter has focused on the main institutional challenges which lie ahead of the Balkan countries assuming that the Stabilization and Accession process will continue to unfold. While the management of the current development programmes directed at the Balkan countries (PHARE, ISPA, SAPARD, CARDs) are co-managed by the European Commission and the national governments, and in this respect reproduce the structure of the Cohesion and Social Funds, the SAP countries will have to equip themselves with intermediate (NUTS 2) levels of government in order to receive the Structural and EAGGF Funds. The 'Europeanization of regional development policy' in these countries will pose a set of institutional challenges linked to: (1) the possible resistance of institutional actors who favour the status quo and resist institutional adaptation, (2) the difficulties inherent in acquiring new policy tools, new standard operating procedures, new 'ways of doing things', (3) the difficulties linked to the creation of an intermediate level of government and to the interaction with a weak civil society, (4) the need to achieve coordination and cooperation among different institutional levels, and (5) the creation of that minimum level of trust and social capital without which no economic development can take place.

Likewise, the Europeanization of Regional Development Policy poses equally tall challenges also to the current (old and new) member-states and to the European institutions. The temptation to retrench from the task ahead and to tighten up 'fortress Europe' may be strong, but ultimately resistible. The nineties have proved beyond doubt that the European Union cannot ignore what happens on its eastern border and that the only way to secure peace and prosperity is by annexing the Balkan countries to its liberal and democratic sphere. The costs of Stabilization and Accession process may be high, but those of failure even higher.

## Notes

1. While Ireland's underdevelopment problems were mainly agricultural and could therefore be addressed through the Common Agricultural Policy and the Guidance section of the European Agricultural Guarantee and Guidance Fund (EAGGF-Guidance), Britain's problems, like Italy's, required financial instruments specifically targeted at industrial problems.
2. See 'Agenda 2000' (EC 2000). The CAP redistributes resources from the poorer to the richer regions. It is therefore at odds with Regional Policy, which redistributes resources from the richer to the poorer regions. Especially in view of enlargement, the CAP needs to be reformed.
3. The 'reserve clause', at the beginning of the programming period, sets aside 4 per cent of the total EU contribution to be released only if given spending targets are met within one year of the period mid-term.

# 4

# Inequality, Poverty and Growth: the Balkan Case

*Gabriella Berloffa and Maria Luigia Segnana*

## Introduction

The economic experience of the Balkan countries is striking with respect to several aspects. In the last decade the region has been the poorest European area with a large percentage of the population living below the poverty line. At the same time, in the last couple of years, the economies of these countries have grown at higher rates than the EU economy and inflation has remained low. However, unemployment is high, the informal sector is large, and institutions are poor. The launch of the SAP by the EU with the five Western Balkans (SEE5) has created a new momentum for trade integration/liberalization in and of SEE but each country finds itself at different stages of integration and faces different problems and challenges. The process has important implications for trade integration and institutional upgrading; and trade policies and institutional upgrading have been recognized as key priorities for private sector development and economic growth in the Balkan region.

The aim of this chapter is threefold:

1. to draw a picture of the present situation of the Balkans with respect to growth performances, income distribution and trade policies currently followed;
2. to highlight some features that are specific to the region; and
3. to examine their implications for the sustainability of growth in the long run.

The incidence of poverty and the need to recover from a decade of impressive losses in GDP, make it urgent for the Balkans to design and implement effective growth-enhancing policies. Trade is one of the main candidates. However, as shown by a huge literature, the specific characteristics of trade patterns are crucial in determining the sign and the magnitude of the trade–growth relationship. Moreover, since the Balkans face the difficult task of ensuring the sustainability of growth in a situation where inequality is rising and poverty rates are extremely high, particular attention has to be paid to the distributional consequences of trade. Indeed, if trade and growth worsen the income distribution, the speed at which poverty may be reduced in the region will be much slower, and the prospects of future growth will be questioned because increasing inequalities generate problems for the accumulation of physical and human capital and undermine the already fragile socio-political stability of the region.

The marked spatial, regional, and ethnic dimensions of poverty and inequality in the area suggest that, if economic growth bypasses the areas where the poor are concentrated, it will further increase inequality and exacerbate spatial and social gaps in standards of living. Therefore, the local development of the poorest regions becomes a strategic goal if one wants to design effective policies for a process of economic growth that not only allows poor people to share in the benefits but that also impedes poverty from becoming a constraint on future growth. In this framework, the consequences of the Stabilization and Association processes with the EU and within the area on local development need to be carefully examined.

This chapter is organized as follows. In the following section we present some stylized facts which characterize the Balkans with respect to growth, trade integration, and income distribution. Next, we illustrate the link between trade and growth, and its consequences on income inequalities. We show that in and of themselves trade and trade-related policies are not necessarily growth-supporting policies, and that they imply redistributive effects, both in income and geographical distribution of economic activities. These effects are critical in the Balkans because, even independently of trade, growth is generating increasing inequalities. We then discuss the consequences of inequalities for growth and poverty reduction. We show that the distributional changes that accompany the growth process are a crucial determinant of the poverty–growth elasticity, and that a high level of inequality may lead to lower growth. Finally, we argue that trade liberalization and other growth-enhancing policies will not yield the desired benefits unless there are parallel efforts for institutional upgrading.

## Stylized facts in the Balkans

The case of the Balkans is striking with respect to some 'stylized facts':

- with respect to growth: their experience is rather different from the CEECs;
- with respect to trade: their experience is rather different from the CEECs and recent data do not show either uniform or widespread common experience; and
- with respect to poverty/inequalities: inequalities are increasing as well as poverty with important spatial, ethnic and regional components.

### Empirical evidence on growth and trade integration

The growth experience of the Balkans through the 1990s has been quite different from that of other countries in CEECs and in the Baltics (CSB). While, on average, the whole region started to recover and by 1998 the GDP level was back to the 1990, in SEE and particularly in the Balkans recovery started a couple of years later and it was stopped by various events in the second half of the 1990s. Within the Balkans, only Albania in 2002 had a GDP higher than in 1990; for all other countries the level of GDP was lower than in 1990. For Serbia and Montenegro (S&M) the level of GDP in 2002 was half of that in 1990.

On the trade side, the SAP in 1999 has created a new momentum for trade integration/liberalization in and of five countries of SEE5, the so-called Western Balkans further enhanced by the SAA, already signed with FYR Macedonia and Croatia. These processes are key to economic recovery and regional stability, as combination between credible government commitment to reforms and better conditions in access to large EU markets. They envisage the establishment of FTAs between the EU and each of SEE5 as well as between the countries themselves, based on contractual undertakings. A step forward was the Memorandum of Understanding (MOU) reached in June 2001 which envisaged the conclusion of *bilateral*[1] free trade agreements over the next two years where the SEE5 countries were joined by Bulgaria and Romania; Moldova has joined later. The process of trade liberalization in SEE has by now almost been completed with some 23 (out of 28) agreements signed, though a number of them still need to be ratified.

The main features of trade patterns over the last period can be identified with respect to the EU and SEE7. The trade performance[2] of the Western Balkans in the last decade has lagged behind and has been worse than that of other economies in transition in CEECs. Over the period 1992–2000 they show growing exports on average by only 0.3 per cent per annum and much faster growing imports (6.8 per cent per annum). At the same time, the openness of the SEE5 as measured by the ratio of total trade in goods and services to GDP, varies considerably from a high 1.0 to around 0.4 in Albania and Serbia–Montenegro, with countries less open than other countries of similar size in CEECs and trend neither strong nor uniform (Michalopoulos 2003). Data reported by Uvalić (2004) show destination and origin of trade flows with the EU and the SEE7 and they enable us to draw the following conclusions:

- With respect to the EU: it emerges as the major trade partner for most SEE countries and throughout most of the period. Anyway, this cannot be generalized: SEE countries' export performance has been unstable, while on the import side the situation has been more uniform; in 2002, for three of the SEE4 countries (the four countries originating from former Yugoslavia), only less than 50 per cent of their exports (imports) were directed (came) to (from) the EU.
- With respect to the SEE: the weight of regional trade is extremely variable and identifies two sub-groupings: it is very important for the four countries

originating from former Yugoslavia (SEE4) and much less important for the other three countries (Albania, Romania and Bulgaria) with a very low share of trade flows, going to the other SEE countries, lower than 5 per cent and never surpassing 10 per cent. The reliance of the SEE4 on intra-SEE trade applies primarily to exports and much less to imports so that trade imbalances are less striking in intra SEE than with the EU.

The composition of trade flows, however, has not changed significantly. SEE5 countries' exports are concentrated in heavy manufactures, with SITC 5-7 accounting for over 50 per cent of exports in all countries except Albania where manufacturing exports are concentrated in textiles and shoes. Agricultural exports play little role. The composition of intra SEE5 patterns of trade show that:

- manufactures account for a relatively low share of intra-SEE5;
- merchandise mutual trade diverge significantly from those that these countries have with the EU where manufactured goods account for a dramatically larger share than in their mutual share; and
- some countries (for instance Albania versus Croatia and versus Macedonia) seem to be locked in a traditional division of labour as suppliers of production inputs (ores, agricultural raw materials, minerals and non ferrous materials) in return for manufactures.

All mutual trade remains mainly of the *inter-industry-type* with limited exchanges occurring within the same sector.[3] This shows that differences in factor endowments rather than economies of scale associated with supplying a larger market and fixed costs of production continue driving this trade; this also points to the low level of interaction among firms operating in the same networks of production and distribution as suppliers of parts and components. As specialization associated with intra-industry trade poses fewer adjustment problems[4] than inter-industry trade, the low(high) share of intra(inter)-industry trade suggest serious implications for regional trade liberalization effort. It may produce significant inequalities in regional development and income distribution, affecting whole sectors and skill-gap. In this case, adjustments triggered by liberalization do affect whole sectors as well as factors income.

Trade policies (Michalopoulos 2003) have not encouraged export expansion and many of the fundamental export support institutions were either absent or totally ineffective. Policies towards merchandise imports have been liberalized in most countries and territories, in particular Albania, Bosnia and Herzegovina (BiH), Croatia and Kosovo. The trade regime has also been liberalized in Serbia and Montenegro, though there are a few residual restraints which would have to be eliminated as part of the accession to the WTO. The situation was worse in FYR Macedonia where there was a much longer list of products under licensing from the Ministry of the Economy for protective purposes which is being terminated before WTO accession.

What is important to underline for the purposes of this chapter is the following:

- Looking at the trade performance, trade cannot be at the moment a good candidate to explain the growth performance of the Balkan countries.
- The main features of intra-SEE5 trade indicate a limited potential for growth as the dominant inter-industry flows may produce significant inequalities in regional development and income distribution.
- Recent Stabilisation and Association processes of the Balkan countries with EU *exchange* EU prospects for accession and preferential access with institutional upgrading and engagement in mutual regional cooperation. The combination of credible government commitment to institutional reforms and better conditions in access to large EU markets might stimulate economic growth but it also leaves many issues open to negotiations and different solutions at two different levels: the local institutions for trade and the institutional set-ups.

## Poverty and inequality in the Balkan case

As outlined by the presentation of *World Development Indicators 2004*, in Eastern Europe and Central Asia, the number of people living on less than US$2 a day[5] rose from 8 million (2 per cent) in 1981 to over 100 million (24 per cent) in 1999, dropping back to slightly more than 90 million (20 per cent) in 2001 (presentation of the WDI 2004). As can be seen from Table 4.1, the proportion of people living with less than US$4 a day is striking. Even if the incidence of poverty is particularly deep in CIS countries, countries in South-Eastern Europe are not much better off, with the exception of Bulgaria and Croatia.

Good quality data on poverty for the Balkans are available only for very recent years. The national poverty lines from the WB poverty assessments are between US$2 and US$4 a day. The proportion of people in absolute poverty in these countries rises from 8.4 per cent in Croatia to 28.9 per cent in Romania (Table 4.2).

Whereas many poor people in transition countries are generally well-educated, in the Balkans poorly educated individuals make up the majority of the poor and have the highest poverty risk (Table 4.3). Beside low levels of educational attainment, household size and inactivity are the main demographic factors driving poverty in almost all the Balkans (Table 4.4).

What is important to underline for the purposes of this chapter is that, with the exception of Croatia, in all the Balkans poverty has marked spatial, regional and ethnic dimensions:

- As regards the spatial dimension, rural areas are consistently poorer than urban ones. In Albania, Macedonia and Romania, about two-thirds of poor

*Table 4.1* Absolute poverty rates of transition economies in Europe and Central Asia (selected years 1995–1999)

| Country | Survey year | Headcount index US$2.15/ day | Headcount index US$4.30/ day | Ratio of survey Mean consumption to private consumption | 1998 GNP in US$ per capita Atlas method | 1998 GNP in US$ per capita 1996 ppp |
|---|---|---|---|---|---|---|
| Tajikistan | 1999 | 68.3 | 95.8 | 1.02 | 370 | 1,040 |
| Moldova | 1999 | 55.4 | 84.6 | 0.67 | 380 | 1,995 |
| Kyrgyz Republic | 1998 | 49.1 | 84.1 | 0.83 | 380 | 2,247 |
| Armenia | 1999 | 43.5 | 86.2 | 0.62 | 460 | 2,074 |
| Azerbaijan | 1999 | 23.5 | 64.2 | 1.39 | 480 | 2,168 |
| Georgia | 1999 | 18.9 | 54.2 | 0.88 | 970 | 3,429 |
| Russian Federation | 1998 | 18.8 | 50.3 | 0.85 | 2,260 | 6,186 |
| Albania | 1996 | 11.5 | 58.6 | 0.68 | 810 | 2,864 |
| Turkmenistan | 1998 | 7 | 34.4 | 0.89 | 502 | 2,875 |
| Romania | 1998 | 6.8 | 44.5 | 0.43 | 1,360 | 5,571 |
| Macedonia FYR | 1996 | 6.7 | 43.9 | 0.69 | 1,290 | 4,224 |
| Latvia | 1998 | 6.6 | 34.8 | 0.68 | 2,420 | 5,777 |
| Kazakhstan | 1996 | 5.7 | 30.9 | 0.45 | 1,340 | 4,317 |
| Bulgaria | 1995 | 3.1 | 18.2 | 0.67 | 1,220 | 4,683 |
| Lithuania | 1999 | 3.1 | 22.5 | 0.69 | 2,540 | 6,283 |
| Ukraine | 1999 | 3 | 29.4 | 0.95 | 980 | 3,130 |
| Slovak Republic | 1997 | 2.6 | 8.6 | 0.75 | 3,700 | 9,624 |
| Estonia | 1998 | 2.1 | 19.3 | 0.8 | 3,360 | 7,563 |
| Hungary | 1997 | 1.3 | 15.4 | 0.47 | 4,510 | 9,832 |
| Poland | 1998 | 1.2 | 18.4 | 0.67 | 3,910 | 7,543 |
| Belarus | 1999 | 1 | 10.4 | 0.99 | 2,180 | 6,318 |
| Croatia | 1998 | 0.2 | 4 | 1.18 | 4,620 | 6,698 |
| Czech Republic | 1996 | 0 | 0.8 | 0.81 | 5,150 | 12,197 |
| Slovenia | 1997/98 | 0 | 0.7 | 0.94 | 9,780 | 14,399 |

*Note*: Recent household survey data are not available for Bosnia and Herzegovina and Uzbekistan. Private consumption data are not available for Tajikistan Turkmenistan Kazakhstan Georgia or Moldova. GDP per capita in current prices is used instead, GDP per capita (first half 1999) are used for Ukraine. The poverty headcount numbers are based on the international poverty lines of US$2.15 and US$4.30 per person per day.
a) The survey did not cover the capital city Tirana.
*Source*: World Bank (2000b).

households live in rural areas. Pockets of poverty in urban areas, especially in urban slums, are present in all countries, but especially in Macedonia and BiH where poverty is widely distributed among smaller 'mixed' (or semi-urban) communities across the country (where many people who left rural areas during the war found refuge).

– Regional differences in the incidence of poverty are also a marked phenomenon in the Balkans. In Albania, 44.5 per cent of those living in the

*Table 4.2* Poverty rates in the Balkans (headcount indices)

| | *Year* | *National poverty line* | *US$4* | *US$2* |
|---|---|---|---|---|
| Albania | 2002 | 25.4 | 59.3 | 10.8 |
| Croatia | 1998 | 8.4 | 4 | n.a. |
| Macedonia | 2000 | 20.7 | n.a. | 7.5 |
| Romania | 1998 | 28.9 | 44.5 | 6.8 |
| S&M | 2002 | 10 | n.a. | n.a. |
| BiH | 2001 | 19.5 | n.a. | n.a. |

*Note*: n.a.: not applicable.
*Source*: World Bank (2003a,b,c,d).

*Table 4.3* Composition of poor people according to their educational attainment (%)

| | *Albania* | *S&M* | *BiH* | *Croatia** |
|---|---|---|---|---|
| Primary & less | 84.0 | 66.6 | 68 | 71 |
| Secondary | 10.0 | 30.8 | 8 | 18 |
| Vocational | 5.3 | | 22 | 9 |
| Higher | 0.7 | 2.6 | 1 | 2 |

*Notes*: *These percentages refer to the composition of households according to the educational attainment of the head.
*Source*: World Bank (2000a,b,c,d).

*Table 4.4* Composition of poor households according to the employment status of the head (%)

| | *Croatia* | *BiH* |
|---|---|---|
| Employed | 34 | 33 |
| Unemployed | 9 | 13 |
| Retired and other inactive | 57 | 55 |

*Source*: World Bank (2003a,b,c,d).

Mountain region is poor, compared to 25.4 per cent overall. In Romania, the North-East hosts the largest number of poor (25 per cent of total poor), and faces the highest poverty risk (43 per cent compared to 32–33 per cent in the South and 22–23 per cent in Central and West). A country as compact as Montenegro has 1:2 differences in poverty rates between the poorest and the richest region; the Montenegrin North is the home of 54 per cent of the country's poor. Regional differences in poverty rates in Serbia are even greater, exceeding 1:3 between better off Belgrade and the poorest rural areas of South Eastern Serbia.

- Poverty has in 2002 a quite clear ethnic characterization: The ISSP survey in Montenegro found that the poverty rate among Roma exceeds 50 per cent (using the same baseline definition), which is five times the average incidence (World Bank, 2003b, Vol. 1). In Romania, three out of five Roma live in severe poverty, and only one out of five is not poor.
- In many cases these various dimensions overlap so that, for example, in Macedonia the geographical concentration of poverty is partly in areas where ethnic tensions are the highest. In BiH poverty is strongly geographically concentrated in particular communities, which suffer from a combination of economic dislocation and social cleavages that dramatically reduce social capital of these communities. Often these communities have a high concentration of refugees.

This spatial and regional differences in poverty rates clearly affect the overall income distribution. Indeed the increase in poverty rates over the 1980s has been accompanied by an increase in overall income inequality. Although data on inequality for all the Balkans' countries are available only for very recent years, we can look as an example to the experience of Romania, Bulgaria and Croatia. From the end of the 1980s to the end of the 1990s, the Gini index increased from 0.23 (measured on income) to 0.30 (measured on consumption) in Romania; from 0.23 to 0.41 in Bulgaria, and remained roughly stable in Croatia (but for this country data problems are more relevant than for the other two).[6]

The incidence of poverty and the need to recover from a decade of impressive losses in GDP, make it urgent for the Balkans to design and implement effective growth-enhancing policies. Trade is one of the main candidates. However, as described above, the specific characteristics of trade patterns are crucial in determining its growth-enhancing potential. Therefore, attention has to be paid to the nature of trade that a specific policy would induce because, according to it, trade may push the economy's resources towards activities that generate long run growth, or divert them from such activities. We will discuss this point in the next paragraphs.

## Trade, growth and the adjustment costs to trade integration

Trade liberalization programmes have brought important economic and social changes in countries where they have been implemented. The literature focuses upon trade-growth linkages and their consequences on inequality/poverty (Winters *et al.* 2004). The first focus is crucial because trade has been seen as a determinant of economic growth gaining the status of a 'stylized fact' in the growth literature.[7] But trade policies inevitably involve redistribution so that the second focus comes into play. Trade integration can be a direct or indirect determinant of within-country inequality, acting through changes in commodity prices affecting functional income distribution and resource allocation across sectors, or through international relocation of production processes (outsourcing). In both cases trade might be a source of inequality. These results are critical because, even independently of trade, growth is already generating increasing inequalities in the Balkans. Thus, specific attention has to be paid to distributional consequences of trade and growth.

## The growth impact of trade: any consensus estimate?

The usual size of the welfare gains from trade liberalization generates disappointing static estimates, seldom larger than 1 per cent of GDP. Why is trade liberalization often a priority policy for closing the 1 per cent difference in per capita incomes between developed and less developed economies? The solution is the often invoked dynamic relationships, with the widely accepted conclusion that international trade and economic growth are positively and significantly related.

The large body of empirical literature on the subject has emphasized the statistical significance of the trade-growth relationship more than its economic significance. The trade-growth nexus is quantitatively important because the 'consensus' estimate shows an average coefficient of 0.22 across a very large number of cross-section and time-series sources of growth regressions models that tested the relationships between trade and growth (Lewer and van der Berg 2003). Many researchers have found evidence that this coefficient is different between groups of countries, suggesting that trade generates more growth in developed economies than in developing ones. Some problems and questions arise when conducting balanced evaluation of this empirical result and we focus on two.

First, opinions differ on the empirical evidence for at least three reasons:

1. *Trade indicators*. The empirical literature is still affected by serious limitations, and it is unable to generate satisfactory indexes of trade policy orientation. Indicators of trade policy have been inappropriately used, and they have been selected in order to systematically bias the results so that they show a statistically and quantitatively significant link between trade liberalization and growth (Rodriguez and Rodrik 2000).
2. *Multicollinearity, simultaneity, omitted variables bias and measurement errors and so on,* or the well-known problems that can lead to inconsistent results in many of the empirical studies of trade and growth, studies often motivated by the newer econometric methods and better data sets that promised to correct the statistical problems of earlier studies. Problems are often identified in the correlations between trade and growth, trade and institutions or countries' institutional quality (Rodrik *et al.* 2002).
3. *There is a gap between the results at the firms level and at the macro level.* The proponents of trade liberalization have argued that at the firm level, it will force firms to produce closer to the production possibility frontier, and that the frontier will move out more rapidly. Empirical results provide little

evidence that firms derive technological or other benefits from exporting *per se*; the more common pattern being that efficient producers tend to self-select in export markets. In other words, the causality runs from productivity to exports, not vice versa. These results hold across countries at different levels of development (Roberts and Tybout 1996) and indicate a potential gap between firms' absorption of exporting experience and countries absorption of trade benefits: in other words, between the positive impact of trade at macro level (Harrison, 1996) and the debatable impact of learning by exporting at micro level (Tybout 2001; Bernard and Jensen 2004). While no evidence is available at the firm level for the Balkan countries, there is some evidence supporting the learning by exporting model, where the causality goes from exports to productivity, for some transition economies: Russia, Ukraine and Belarus (Bleaney *et al. 2000*).

Secondly, the question is whether or not there is any positive and economically significant link between trade and growth. Or in other words, whether or not the many econometric improvements have substantially aided comprehension of why the statistically significant relationship is robust across many samples, data sets and regression models, corrected for omitted variables and simultaneity, and so on. The 'missing discrimination' problem is still unresolved: Rodriguez and Rodrik's criticism that trade merely serves as a proxy for other important policy variables cannot be easily rejected. The discrimination among institutions, geography and trade in explaining striking cross-country income variations around the world (Rodrik *et al.* 2002), concludes that the institutional explanation outweighs the other stories. Furthermore, the specific channels through which trade influences growth are still undervalued. For instance, the channel identified by Frankel and Romer (1999), but also the six channels identified by Wacziarg (2001) (with simultaneity of growth and trade), indicate that the most important channel through which trade influences growth is investment, which accounts for 63 per cent of trade's total growth effect, with technology (22.5 per cent) and stabilizing macroeconomic policy (18 per cent) accounting for the remainder. Channels can be ranked and investment is a key link, with the consequence that poor investment policies may undermine trade benefits.

At the end of the story, trade-growth nexus cannot be only an empirical matter. The theoretical framework offers different explanations of the growth effects of trade: they vary according to whether the forces of comparative advantage push the economy's resources in the direction of activities that generate long run growth (through externalities in R&D, expanding product variety, upgrading product quality and so on) or whether they divert them from such activities. For instance, a subset of countries may indeed experience trade-diminished growth in the endogeneous framework, depending on their initial factor endowments and levels of technological development.

Thus, there is no definite general theoretical link between trade protection and growth once real world phenomena such as learning, technological change and market imperfections are taken into consideration.

### The inequality impact of trade

Trade liberalization programmes most likely entail net benefits for the society as a whole, but could affect both the relative country's position and the within-country relative households positions. In the Balkan case there is evidence that reading inequalities or adjustment costs to economic integration only through the 'lens' of trade liberalization may be misleading because an important role has been and is played by internal[8] and area-specific factors. But adopting these lenses, adjustment costs to trade reforms encompass a wide variety of potentially disadvantageous outcomes showing distributional and geographical effects.

Adjustment costs of trade affect wage inequality[9] via the factor income share, or via outsourcing. In both cases trade may be a source of within-country inequality for one or all trading partners (for instance North and South).

The literature on the interaction between trade and technological change and the increasing global production sharing (outsourcing) and matching across the world (Feenstra and Hanson 1996a,b; Feenstra 1998) generate different predictions from standard Stolper-Samuelson (SS) results: i) increasing skill-gap in both countries; ii) methods of production shifting towards skilled labour within sectors; iii) significant impact of trade even without changes in relative price. Specifically, when trade is conduit for skill-upgrading between North and South, it ends up with trade as a source of inequality within both countries an thus a source of deterioration in global inequality. A similar phenomenon has probably affected middle-income countries rather than lower-income ones (Berman and Machin 2000). This case can be significant in the Balkan case as it is consistent with the weight of the outsourcing processes from the EU and within the area.[10] This would generate a widening skill-gap even within sectors because outsourcing[11] may be perceived as a kind of endogenous technical change biased in favour of skilled workers.

Not only outsourcing but even the conventional Stolper–Samuelson effect is consistent with trade-induced inequalities: they are generated by a consistent reallocation of resources across sectors rather than within sectors and the associated distributional impacts on functional income distribution. The high share of inter-industry flows identified by the stylized fact on trade show that reallocation across sectors of economic activities induced by trade integration may play a significant role.

In both cases (the conventional SS and the outsourcing) trade may be a source of wage inequalities, acting within and between sectors, and thus at the basis of the fears on trade-induced adjustment costs.

But diffuse fears may have been justified even at another level: to some extent by the findings of the new trade theory and geography models focussed on the spatial distribution of economic activity induced by trade integration, in other words by the spatial inequalities of economic activities. While the new trade theory suggests that the overall benefits are likely to be significantly larger than those predicted by traditional approaches, economic geography models allow for the possibility that gains – especially during the early stages of integration – will be distributed in favour of a more developed partner, the EU for instance or the most developed areas in the Balkans. Economic geography models suggest that firms operating under the conditions of imperfect competition and economies of scale, that is, in increasing returns-to-scale industries, inevitability implies a relocation of industrial activity to highly developed areas with better forward or costs linkages.

In presence of distributional and geographical consequences, trade policy reforms will not yield the desired benefits unless there are parallel efforts to address the redistribution of the gains from trade and the interaction between trade openness and domestic redistributive policies: the form of support inside the welfare state may matter as much as the size. It is an open problem the kind of social compensatory arrangements, the opportunity/safety nets and the interaction between a social responsible open trade regime with the policy context. But distributive and redistributive dimensions of trade integration are to be taken into account if one wants to ensure the political viability of the process.

## The poverty and inequality impact of growth

The examination of the distributional consequences of trade policies is particularly relevant in the Balkan case, because there is evidence that, even independently of trade, the pattern of economic growth experienced by these countries in the most recent years is already generating increasing inequality. Indeed, although data on inequality for the Balkan's countries are available only for very recent years, there is a flavour that inequality is rising in the region. In Romania, for example, we observed a decrease in inequality during the 1996–2000 recession and an increase in the subsequent recovery. This means that economic growth in Romania seems to lead to an increase in inequality. The same is true for Macedonia, for which modest but volatile growth since 1996 has been countered by rising inequality of incomes over the same period.

This evidence is in contrast with some results about the relationship between growth and inequality for the transitional region as a whole. Using a panel of inequality estimates for 24 transitional countries for the period 1989–1998,[12] Ivaschenko (2003) finds support for a normal U-shaped relationship between income inequality and per capita GDP: below some threshold level of development economic growth is associated with falling income inequality, whereas above the threshold it leads to an increase in inequality.[13] Although the level of per-capita GDP in the Balkans is far below this threshold,[14] we do not observe that economic growth leads to decreasing inequality. The reason for this discrepancy may be either that Ivaschenko's study suffers from severe measurement problems in the data because it involves changes in income distribution before and after transition (Garner and Terrell 1998; Keane and Prasad 2000),[15] or the particular nature of the forces influencing income distribution and growth in the first years of transition. In any case, Ivaschenko's result does not appear robust enough to be used as a general model to predict whether the process of economic growth will be associated with increasing inequality or will eventually lead to a decline in the latter.

The evidence on the inequality consequences of growth in the Balkans is coupled by the effect of growth on poverty reduction. The lack of data makes it very difficult to have a clear picture of the poverty–growth elasticity in the whole region. However some interesting examples can be mentioned. Romania is the only country that showed a decline in poverty, but poverty levels in 2002 are still much higher than in the mid 1990s (poverty increased from about 20 per cent in 1996 to 35 per cent in 2000 and then declined to 28.9 per cent in 2002). Moreover, the elasticity of poverty to growth *decreased* from −3.2 in 1996 to −1.8 in 2002. During the recession of 1995–2000 poor people were hurt relatively less than rich people, whereas between 2000 and 2002 the poor did not appear to share the benefits of economic recovery (especially the rural poor). See growth-incidence curves below (Figure 4.1)

In Croatia the elasticity of poverty with respect to growth is estimated at −2.1. However, the type of economic growth that Croatia had, failed to generate enough economic opportunities, and has benefited primarily those who have kept their jobs. In the other countries, there is some evidence that poverty rates have increased (at least until the end of the 1990s) or remained stable. In Albania, despite strong economic performance, poverty has remained high: for the US$2 poverty line, poverty rates decreased from 11.5 per cent in 1996 to 10.8 per cent in 2002, whereas for the US$4 poverty line it increased from 58.6 per cent to 59.3 per cent (however, the survey in 1996 did not cover the capita city Tirana). In Macedonia, poverty rates increased from 18.1 per cent in 1996 to 20.7 per cent in 1998, and remained roughly unchanged afterwards (as measured against constant real national standards). In Serbia and Montenegro, from 1990 to 1999 poverty increased by more than 100 per cent.[16]

Summarizing, in these paragraphs we have shown that the effects of trade liberalization on economic growth are not univocally positive, neither at the theoretical, nor at the empirical level. On one side, there is some evidence that exporting increases productivity for some transition economies, even if there are no specific studies for the Balkans. On the other side, emerging trade patterns in the area are likely to increase inequality within these countries by widening skill-gaps and spatial differences. Moreover, even independently of trade, growth is already generating a worsening of the income distribution in the Balkans. These results are critical because, as will be shown in the next

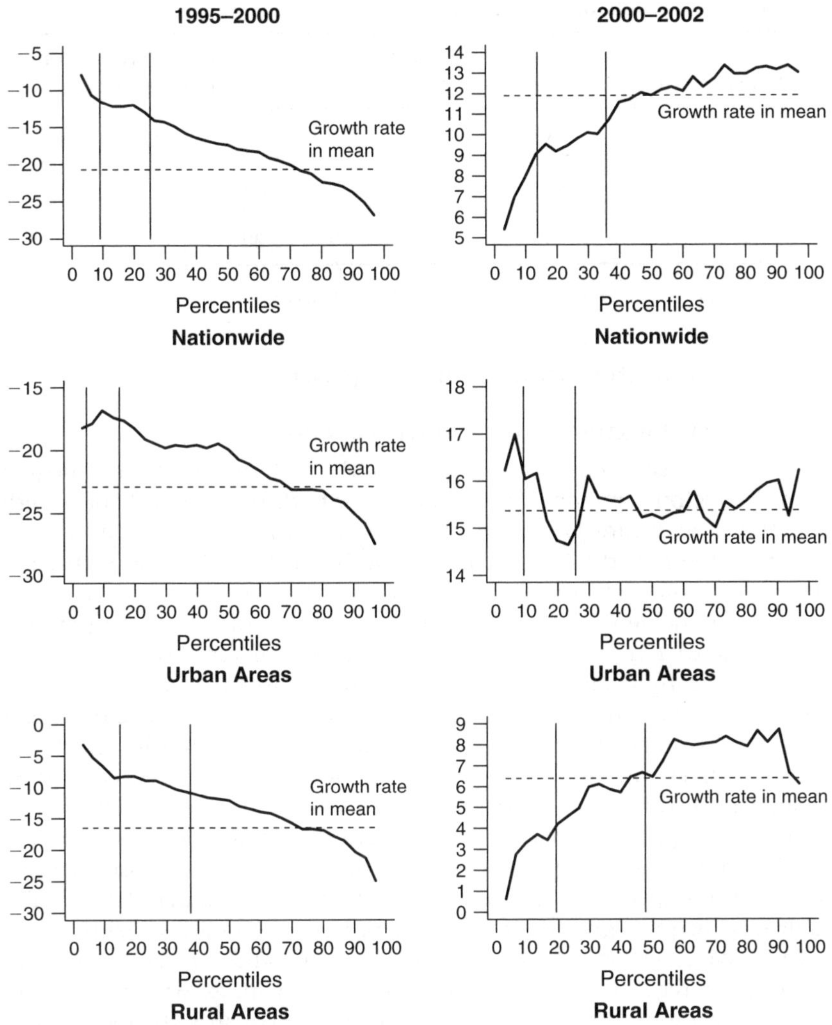


*Source*: World Bank (2003a), vol. 1.

*Note*: The 2 vertical lines indicate the % of people in extreme poverty (left-hand line) and total poverty (right-hand line).

*Figure 4.1* Growth–incidence curves: cumulative growth in consumption per adult equivalent

paragraph, increasing inequalities can generate problems for the accumulation of physical and human capital and undermine the already fragile sociopolitical stability of the region, with significant negative consequences for the future prospects of growth.

*Table 4.5* Poverty projections for BiH under different scenarios (%)

| *Annual growth* | *Poverty in 10 years with constant inequality* | *Poverty in 10 years with increasing inequality* |
|---|---|---|
| −3 | 74 | 88 |
| −1 | 26 | 29 |
| 0 | 20 | 22 |
| 1 | 15 | 18 |
| 3 | 6 | 20 |

*Source*: World Bank (2003c), vol. 1. Simulations based on LSMS.

## Inequality and the sustainability of growth

### The prospects for growth and poverty reduction

The slow response of poverty to growth and the pattern of increasing inequality in the region represent a real concern for both the prospects of poverty reduction and future growth in the region. With respect to the former, almost all the Poverty Assessments in the Balkans call for a growth based strategy to reduce poverty. This call is clearly based on the evidence that *on average* the incidence of absolute poverty tends to fall with growth.[17] However, as we have seen in section 3.3, in the Balkans the poor do not seem to benefit greatly from the process of economic growth. Even if we look at the experience of other less developed countries, there is a huge dispersion around the average relationship and, within the lowest quintile, growth has the least effect on the income of the poorest (Foster and Székely 2001; Karshenas 2001; Ravallion 2001; Bourguignon 2002; Lustig *et al.* 2002).

The distributional changes that accompany the growth process are a crucial determinant of the poverty–growth elasticity: when growth increases inequality, the speed at which poverty can be reduced is much slower.[18] This result has been recognized also in some of the poverty assessments for the Balkans. We have poverty projections for Serbia and BiH under different assumptions regarding the evolution of the Gini index which show that when growth is accompanied by an increase in inequality the reduction in poverty is significantly lower than when it is distribution neutral or, better, when the distributional changes favour the poor (see Tables 4.5 and 4.6).

Bourguignon (2002) shows that the distributional effects of growth depend crucially on the underlying evolution of the *supply of skilled labour*: if the latter lags behind growth, then the rate of return to skill is bound to increase, resulting in more inequality. In addition, the demand for skilled labour is affected by the *structure* of growth which may result from *policy choices*. For instance, 'the reason why demand for skilled labour grew so much in Taiwan may have to do with the openness of the economy and the strong changes it caused in the structure of production toward sectors more intensive in both

*Table 4.6* Poverty projections for Serbia, 2002–2006

| | *2002*[d] | *2003* | *2004* | *2005* | *2006* |
|---|---|---|---|---|---|
| GDP growth rate | 4.0 | 4.0 | 4.0 | 4.0 | 4.0 |
| Growth rate of private consumption | 6.3 | 3.0 | 2.0 | 2.3 | 2.3 |
| Pro poor growth[a] | 10.6 | 8.9 | 8.0 | 6.9 | 6.3 |
| Equally shared growth[b] | 10.6 | 9.4 | 8.7 | 8.1 | 7.5 |
| Pro-rich growth[c] | 10.6 | 10.0 | 9.7 | 9.2 | 8.9 |

*Notes*: [a]Improving distribution (Gini index falls by 1% per year, consumption of the poor grows by 17% against 10% on average); [b]distributionally neutral growth (consumption of an average poor grow as fast as the average, 10% over the 2003–2006); [c]worsening income distribution (Gini index increases by 1% per year, consumption of the poor increases by only 2% over the entire period versus 10%); [d]actual.
*Source*: World Bank (2003b), vol. 1. Staff estimates based on SLS data and Government Serbia (PRSP 2003).

physical and human capital'.[19] In any case, according to Lustig *et al.* (2002) 'a sole focus on maximizing per capita income growth may be less than successful in reducing poverty if the growth bypasses geographic areas or sectors in which the poor are concentrated'. Since in the Balkans poverty has marked spatial and regional dimensions, growth policies yielding a worsening of the income distribution or an exacerbation of the spatial differences will have a strong impact on the speed at which poverty can be reduced. In this situation, local development becomes a strategic goal for effective poverty reduction policies.[20]

The distributional consequences of a given growth pattern are crucial not only for equity or 'humanitarian' concern, but also because inequality and poverty may be harmful for the prospects of economic growth in the long run. Indeed, a large number of studies point towards a possible negative effect of inequality on growth especially in the long run. This view is supported by empirical studies on the relationship between inequality and growth usually carried out on a panel of countries (including both developing and developed countries). A number of issues can be raised concerning these results. For example, it is not clear whether this relationship is different for countries at different stages of development, nor it is clear how inequality is related to other known growth determinants.[21] However, the negative effect of inequality on growth is highlighted also in a large number of theoretical studies, which have identified various channels through which high initial inequality may lead to lower growth. These channels mainly work by relating inequality in various ways to a lower accumulation of physical or human capital, which in turn leads to lower growth.[22] These effects are likely to emerge only after sufficiently long time periods, especially if human capital rather than physical capital accumulation plays the main role.

Inequality may have a direct negative effect on growth even in the short run when it generates *sociopolitical instability*. Indeed, a highly unequal and polarized distribution of resources creates strong incentives for organized individuals to pursue their interests outside normal market activities or the usual channels of political representation, engaging in rent-seeking behaviour or other manifestations such as violent protests, assassinations and coups. In turn, sociopolitical instability discourages investment by creating uncertainty over the political and legal environment, and by disrupting market activities and labour relations.

This effect may be particularly important for the Balkans. We have shown in the first section the devastating effect on economic growth of the conflicts in S&M and BiH over the 1990s. Furthermore, Keane and Prasad (2000) find that the relationship between social transfers and growth in transition economies has in fact been strongly positive. In particular, they argue that in the case of Poland, transfers may have been a critical component for ensuring social stability and setting the stage for rapid reforms during the early years of transition. Therefore, for these countries, a short-run argument about the importance of socio-political stability for growth can be added to the long-run arguments that highlight a negative effect of high inequality on growth.

It is worth noting that if growth bypasses geographic areas or sectors in which the poor are concentrated it will increase inequality and exacerbate spatial and social gaps in standards of living. This on the one hand becomes a constraint on physical and human capital accumulation; on the other hand it could undermine the already fragile socio-political stability of the area. Therefore, local development becomes a strategic goal not only for the reduction of poverty and inequality but also for the long run sustainability of growth.

### Institutions and institutional set-ups

In the Balkans, trade related institutions show serious specific weaknesses, many of them are linked to the conflicts in the region and to the way the conflicts have been resolved.[23] These institutional weaknesses can be seen in light of the three dimensions of the trade related institutional set-ups. The regional, the European and the global one involving the accession to the WTO.[24] The first two dimensions point out to the importance of designing the pace of SEE and SEE5 mutual trade liberalization and are strictly connected with the third one.

European partnerships for Western Balkans (March 2004) is supposed to create a policy-induced integration along the first two dimensions: trade integration with the EU and intra-regional trade liberalization among the countries.

The strengthening of the overall economic relationships with the EU and within the area are often negotiated bilaterally, setting up a network of bilateral free trade area. In this case there will a tendency for the EU to tailor each one in response to the protective pressures felt by the individual governments in the region. But given the commitment to enter into preferential arrangements with the EU, liberalization of trade among the countries in the region would appear desirables in order to avoid the familiar 'hub and spokes' (Baldwin *et al.* 2003) pattern of trade. Integration-induced advantages would go to richest countries, areas and firms, simply because of their better market accesses: the results would be the hub getting the bulk of the benefits, especially regarding investment and affecting significant the spatial distribution of production activity.

Even within the area, an uncoordinated series of bilateral FTAs, involving different product coverage, depth of preference, rules of origins is likely to introduce significant trade diversion without generating significant benefits in terms of the economies of scale, technology transfers or international bargaining power. As a consequence, the preferential arrangements would not lead to 'dynamic gains', which Balassa early identified as critical to a preferential trade agreement's success, a very significant danger because of the small size of the Balkan countries. In other words if preferential treatment is not extended to intra-regional SEE5 trade, the area risks to be victimized again by the hub and spokes syndrome, that offers higher benefits to rich and large areas while impoverishing small and poor. They may further exacerbate 'agglomeration economies' effects, that is investment tend to be attracted to regions with already high intensity of investments thus contributing to deepening of regional differences in the level of economic development.

As a result, the establishment of a set bilateral free trade arrangements, rather than a single free trade area, especially in the context of weak and sometimes corrupt customs services is not likely to enhance trade prospects but, on the contrary, it may lead to significant efficiency losses. Maintaining the bilateral approach may be not in the countries' long-term interests.

But regional integration into an FTA has to be accompanied with multilateral liberalization. And this is where the third dimension has a role to play. Liberalization in intra-regional trade has to significantly reduce Most Favourite Nation (MFN)-based tariff rates and open to EU imports at a similar pace as to those from other preferential partners within the region. The empirical evidence provides strong support to the finding that integration among developing countries may lead to divergence in economic performance in presence of very diversified external trade policies. This result depends on the level of preferential tariff margins simply because the higher they are, the more pronounced relocation of economic activity to a more developed partner is.

These observations point out to the importance of designing the pace of SEE5 mutual trade liberalization in ways that would both reduce the incentive to shift industrial activity from poorer to richer regions and to trade diversion due to SEE5 small economies size. Openness, through lowering MFN tariff rates, can help scaling down the level of protection given to firms including those from more developed SEE5 countries as well as the potential for trade diversion. But this has to be accompanied by substantial institutional upgrading because institutional weakness or inadequacy can act as a hidden tax on trade flows.[25] Anecdotical evidence on insecurity abounds, not only in the Balkan case, with different types of insecurity (from predation, theft, corruption, extortion and from imperfect enforcement) all implying a price mark-up analogous to a hidden tax on trade, a source of hidden costs. These results significantly constrain international trade where legal system poorly enforce commercial contracts and where economic policy lacks transparency and impartiality. What emerges in this case is not only the room for specific institutional upgrading but also the need to focus on the interplay between elite's vested interests and the global and local political/institutional dynamics within a country. This interplay between private and public sector governance has been often under-emphasized in program design often focused on misgovernance within public sector only (Kaufmann 2003). Not only insecurity matters but how much it matters and to whom it matters is a crucial field of applied research in the Balkan countries in order to avoid the deepening of regional differences.

## Conclusion

This chapter examines the striking economic experience of the Balkans over the last decade. Despite being the poorest European area with impressive poverty rates, they are experiencing very high rates of economic growth. At the same time, the priorities for private sector development and economic growth are placed on trade policies and institutional upgrading. While efforts to complete reforms, ensuring a proper functioning of democratic institutions and a full respect of human and minority rights, uphold the rule of law, fight organized crime and corruption, as well as those to improve the business climate and the competitiveness of industries are urgent, they have to be accompanied with an assessment of the consequences of trade reforms for both growth and inequality and on the conditions under which growth is sustainable in the long run.

In this chapter we have shown that the effects of trade liberalization on economic growth are not univocally positive, neither at the theoretical, nor at the empirical level. Emerging trade patterns in the area are likely to increase inequality within these countries by widening skill-gaps and spatial differences. Moreover, even independently of trade, growth is already generating a worsening of the income distribution in the Balkans.

These results are critical for both the prospects of reducing poverty and of ensuring a sustainable growth path. If trade and growth worsen the income distribution, the speed at which poverty may be reduced in the region will be much slower. Furthermore, increasing inequalities generate problems for the accumulation of physical and human capital and undermine the already fragile socio-political stability of the region, questioning the future prospects of growth. The marked spatial, regional, and ethnic dimensions of poverty and inequality suggest that, if economic growth bypasses the areas where the poor are concentrated, it will further increase inequality and exacerbate spatial and social gaps in standards of living. Thus, local development becomes a strategic goal not only for the reduction of poverty and inequality but also for the long run sustainability of growth.

Trade policy reforms will not yield the desired benefits unless there are parallel efforts to institutional upgrading, addressing the redistribution of the gains from trade and the interaction between trade openness and domestic and local redistributive policies. The form of support inside the welfare state may matter as much as its local size. It is an open problem the kind of social compensatory arrangements, the opportunity/safety nets and the interaction between a social responsible open trade regime with the policy context. But distributive and redistributive local dimensions of trade integration are to be taken into account if one wants to ensure the political viability of the process.

## Notes

1. The countries in the region have so far eschewed efforts to set up a single FTA, opting for setting up a network of bilateral FTAs. The main reasons appear to be political.
2. It should be noted that a lot of trade data are unreliable and in some cases distorted. Unsatisfactory trade statistics are clearly identified by Uvalić (2004) as well as different conclusions that arise because of the different definition of SEE.
3. This observation is drawn from the values of Grubel-Lloyd indices reported in Kaminski and de la Rocha in World Bank (2003e) indicating very low levels of intra-industry trade among SEE5 countries and huge imbalances.
4. The theory holds that intra-industry is a win-win situation for all, as consumers enjoy an expanded range of products and nobody suffers a loss of income. See Facchini and Segnana (2003).
5. While in many parts of the world the US$1-a-day line is used to measure absolute deprivation, the US$2-a-day line is more appropriate for the region because its climate necessitates additional expenditures on heat, winter clothing, and food.
6. A pattern of increasing inequality characterized all transition economies during the late 1980s and 1990s, although the extent of the increase varied greatly from country to country. In Hungary, for example, the increase was surprisingly modest (the Gini coefficient for per capita income rose only from 0.21 in 1987 to 0.25 ten years later). in the Czech Republic, Poland, and Latvia, inequality rose more substantially, but the distribution remained fairly egalitarian. In the Commonwealth of Independent States (CIS) the increase in inequality far exceeded anything ever seen before: in Russia, Armenia, Moldova, Tajikistan, and Turkmenistan, income Ginis almost doubled.
7. See stylized fact no. 6 'Growth on output and growth in the volume of international trade are closely related' in Jones (2002: 15).
8. See Cornia (2003) for the role of internal and external liberalization in explaining distributive impacts of trade reforms.
9. This exclusive focus may be misleading, because the costs of adjustment to trade integration do not consider exclusively wage inequality but also employment response to trade liberalization.

10. See the role of Albania in the outsourcing processes within the area.
11. Similar results are generated in the case of technology catch-up. See Trefler and Zhu (2004).
12. Poland, Slovenia, Czech Republic, Hungary, Romania, Estonia, Belarus, Kazakhstan, Bulgaria, Lithuania, Russia, Kyrgyzstan, Latvia, Ukraine.
13. Since in the transition economies the economic collapse and subsequent recovery were clearly not caused by inequality, it is possible to use this case to assess the effect of economic growth on the distribution of income without worrying too much about the effect of income inequality on growth.
14. The threshold is estimated between US$6405 and US$8337 PPP-adjusted GDP per capita, US$1992.
15. According to Milanovic (1999) most calculations may slightly overestimate the true change in inequality but not by much and not in all cases.
16. For Croatia there was no representative household budget survey between 1991 and 1998; in BiH the first representative household survey was conducted at the end of 2001.
17. For developing countries, Ravallion (2001) reports estimates of the poverty–growth elasticity that vary from −2.5 to −1.96. Moreover, the elasticity of the *average* income of the lowest quintile of the population is not significantly different from −1 (Dollar and Kray, 2001).
18. Kakwami, Khandker and Son (2003) show that the total poverty elasticity, which determines the extent of country's poverty reduction, depends on the growth elasticity of poverty, the inequality elasticity of poverty, and the inequality elasticity of growth.
19. Two other variables that appear particularly important in explaining different growth-inequality relationships are the *distribution* of schooling within the population of working age and the *convexity of earning profiles* with respect to education (Bourguignon 2002).
20. By comparing rates of poverty reduction across states of India, Ravallion and Datt (2002) showed that the response of poverty to nonfarm output growth varied significantly among states, reflecting *systematic differences in initial conditions.*
21. For example, policies aimed at reducing inequality may have different impacts on growth according to the level of education or trade openness; and vice-versa, policies that affect the latter may have very different impacts on growth according to the initial level of inequality.
22. They refer mainly to credit constraints, fertility and macroeconomic fluctuations. For a detailed description of these channels see Berloffa and Segnana (2004).
23. Examples abound: the problems associated with customs administration, the collection of excise taxes and tariffs, the representation of trade interests, the presence of adequate export finance and insurance, the separate customs administrations in BiH and in S&M.
24. For instance with the related implementation of Sanitary and Phytosanitary, Technical Barriers to Trade and Trade Related Intellectual Property Rights.
25. See Anderson and Marcouiller (1999). According to the survey of Anderson and van Wincoop (2004) trade costs vary widely across countries (larger in developing countries by a factor of two) and across product lines by factors of as much as ten or more.

# 5

# Reforms of Local Government in SEE: Closer to Europe?

*Jens Woelk*

## Introduction

The process of constitutional transition and transformation of the state in the Western Balkans is still far from being concluded.[1] In addition to the complex processes of democratization, the political and economic reconstruction of the countries in former Yugoslavia[2] has to face the problem of administrative and territorial reform of a formerly socialist political and legal system.

This chapter will analyse the current process of territorial and administrative reorganization at local level in former Yugoslavia as an important aspect of reconstruction and precondition for gradual integration into the political, legal and economic space of the European Union. Starting with a short exploration of the traditions of local self-government in former Yugoslavia, the ECLSG is introduced as the main international document of reference: its provisions are used as parameters for comparison and a critical evaluation of the reform-process. The ethnic question, which conditions autonomy as well as institutional structures in a number of countries, will be discussed, too. At the end, some reflections on the effects of 'conditionality' will add to the considerations of local autonomy as an important element in the process of transformation.

## Traditions of local self-government in former Yugoslavia

The principle of local self-government was enshrined in the Federal Constitution, adopted on 27 April 1992, but not defined, a task left to the Constitutions of the Republics: 'the right of local self-government shall be guaranteed, in accordance with the constitution of each member republic' (art. 6.4). This specified the right laid down in the paragraph before, according to which 'a member republic shall autonomously organize its government under its own constitution' (art. 6.3).

Yugoslavia had a long and deep-rooted institutional tradition of local self-government (LSG) with the municipality as its basic and central unit.

According to the former constitutional assumption (and the utopian theory of a communal system following the Marxist conception of the commune), state power was exercised for its own benefit, thus transforming the municipality into a 'mini State'. The basic local unit or commune was in first place an institutional form of an ideally conceived community of people rather than being considered a step in the vertical division of authority (Höcker-Weyand 1980: 124ff; Ramljak 1989: 58). This concept was implemented after the conflict with Stalin in 1948, since institutional equivalents for some dimensions of the Soviet model had become necessary: thus, workers' self-management in the economy and the 'communal system' in the administrative – political sphere were introduced gradually and developed (see Smerdel 1989: 16ff.; Vujacic 2001; Žagar 2004). Municipalities, as the basic socio-economic communities, were radically transformed from branch offices of central state power to political and territorial units with a relatively high degree of administrative autonomy; this process was accompanied and strengthened by the vast decentralization of powers (in implementation) to the municipalities and – to a lesser extent – to the districts as the second level.

In accordance with the general assumption of the municipality being competent for implementing all administrative affairs, the formal–legal difference between the spheres of own, autonomous powers and transferred State-powers ceased to exist: all affairs were implemented as the municipalities' own affairs; the right to self-organization, financial independence and an own budget was granted. Since municipalities had generally increased in size and taken over most of the tasks of the districts, the latter had increasingly become a burden and were consequently abolished in the 1960s; on the other hand, local communities and local offices were introduced at a sub-municipal level in order to guarantee certain services close to the citizens.

The institutional structures reflected those at central level: all municipalities had an assembly as a representative body (composed of two chambers first, the chamber of producers and the chamber of citizens, and three chambers since 1974: the chamber of local communities, the chamber of associated labour and the socio-political chamber), councils as executive bodies of the assembly as well as administrative bodies. Direct participation of workers and citizens was realized in particular through the delegate system with the election to the respective chambers in the assembly by the members of elected delegations and the delegates obliged to take into account their guidelines as well as to inform them (see for further details Ramljak 1989: 63ff.).

The administrative bodies were politically controlled by the municipality's assembly and by the executive council; their work was also subject to the control of legality by central authorities with means ranging from providing assistance to the right of substitution. However, from extreme centralization which characterized the system at the beginning, it evolved to an almost complete lack of any control over municipalities: this was partly due to a distinction of supervision according to the nature of competences (original, transferred or of general interest), partly a result of the continuous strengthening of the position of Republics and Autonomous Provinces.

Of course, the realization of the communal system in practice was not perfectly corresponding to the ideological principles and not even to the constitutional and legal framework as well as different in the single Republics, even before the dramatic changes of the 1990s. In addition, there were some inherent contradictions: the parallel structures in social affairs due to the co-presence (and competition) of territorial units with the institutions of the self-managing communities of interest established by the 1974 Constitution; the principle of the monotype municipality in the face of great social and economic diversity as well as economic disparities; the limits of direct government through workers and citizens due to the increased size of municipalities; the principle of equality of citizens as opposed to the principle of the dictatorship of the proletariat and the production principle (special delegates of workers in the chamber of associated labour); the factual dominance of the League of Communists, institutionally strengthened by the introduction of the socio-political chamber in the municipality's assembly; the reduction of central supervision according to the fiction of the self-governing municipality although the huge majority of tasks were related to the transferred sphere of activity. Especially the latter phenomenon led to an almost complete (*de facto*) autonomy of the municipality.

## The ECLSG

The Council of Europe conventions and treaties relevant in the sphere of local self-government comprise the ECLSG, the European Framework Convention on Transfrontier Co-operation, Framework Convention for the Protection of National Minorities and the European Charter for Regional or Minority Languages.

The ECLSG, in force since 1 November 1988,[3] is the first multilateral legal instrument to define and safeguard the principles of local autonomy and one of the criteria for the accession of new members to the Council of Europe (CoE). This explains the high number of ratifications, currently 38 out of 46 Member States. In South-East Europe the Charter has been ratified by BiH, Bulgaria, Croatia, Moldova, Romania, and FYROM. Not being a full member State of the Council of Europe, the Federal Republic of Yugoslavia could not accede to the ECLSG; its successor, the State Union of Serbia and Montenegro is a Member since 3 April 2003, but did not yet sign or ratify the Charter, as exclusive competences regarding local government are vested with the Republics, that is Serbia and Montenegro, respectively.

The substantive provisions on the principles of local self-government are contained in the first part of the ECLSG (articles 2–11). However, the objective of protecting a minimum of basic principles of local self-government is balanced with the acknowledgement that these necessarily affect the structure and organization of the state itself. As expression of a compromise between these two positions, the ECLSG follows a 'menu approach': 20 out of 30 paragraphs of part I (principles) have to be chosen and implemented, but these are legally binding in the domestic legal system only in so far as the Member States bind themselves (art. 12). In order to guarantee a certain minimum, an essential core of 10 out of 14 provisions has to be chosen in each case. These commitments can subsequently be added to by the parties.

Unlike other instruments under the CoE, the ECLSG does not provide for an institutionalized system of control of its application, beyond a requirement for parties to supply all relevant information (article 14). However, the presence of the Congress of Local and Regional Authorities in Europe (CLRAE) with direct access to the Committee of Ministers ensured political control of compliance by the parties with the requirements of the Charter. In 1994 the CLRAE established a monitoring system with a special committee assisted by a working group of 11 independent experts. In its activities, three different categories can be distinguished: (a) general reports on the implementation of single articles of the ECLSG in different countries; (b) individual reports on specific countries; and (c) monitoring on request.

A common feature, regarding the choice of binding provisions as well as the monitoring system, is the conviction that acceptance has to be created for a positive environment in which local self-government can develop: instead of the imposition of standards or judgments on individual cases, dialogue has been chosen as the instrument for finding sustainable solutions. Thus, the ECLSG certainly represents the most important vehicle for the circulation of legal models of democratic local administration, whether its principles have been imitated (with a view of getting closer to the requirements of European integration) or whether they have been used as self chosen reference (corresponding to a deliberate political choice of values and ideals).[4] For this reason, the ECLSG provides a useful tool for the analysis of local government reforms aiming at adhering to its principles as well as for comparison given the wide margins of discretion in choosing and realizing the single provisions.

## Organization of local self-government in SEE today

Accordingly, the wide definition of 'local authorities' in the ECLSG comprises both the local and the intermediate level (article 13). In fact, local government may be constituted on multiple levels of local authorities or as single tier systems consisting of a single level of local authorities with corporate status. Local self-government units represent the common interests of the citizens of the local community as well as those of the whole entity. Their basis is economic and social integrity as well as a close network of local population (Kandeva 2001, p. 29). In all countries of the area, the local self-government units (despite differences in name, such as municipalities, communes, villages) have a uniform design and equal powers and functions. However, a special status is usually given to the capital and, in some cases, also to the bigger cities. Despite the symbolic value of this distinction, it does not necessarily correspond to different (that is more) powers.

In Republika Srpska (BiH), the territory is divided into 64 municipalities and two cities governed by special laws (Serb Sarajevo and Banja Luka). In the Federation there are 84 municipalities and also two cities (Sarajevo and Mostar). The 'city' is defined as a unit of local government and self-governance forming 'a single urban, cultural, economic and administrative territorial entity linked with daily needs of citizens' between municipalities (art. VI.A.1. Constitution of the Federation as amended in 2004).

In Serbia there are 140 municipalities besides the capital city Belgrade and three 'cities' (Novi Sad, Nis and Kragujevac). The Montenegrin territory is divided into 21 municipalities; the administrative center is Podgorica and the – historical – capital Cetinje (art. 7 Constitution). In FYROM, there are currently 123 Municipalities with Skopje, as the capital, enjoying a constitutionally protected distinct status (art. 115 Constitution of FYROM); the number of municipalities will decrease remarkably according to the Law on Territorial Division adopted in August 2004. No regional structure exists in Montenegro and FYROM. Apart from Kosovo with its unresolved final status, only Voivodina has a special status as an autonomous Province, while the rest of Serbia does not have an intermediate territorial level; further decentralization is an issue to be resolved within constitutional reform, both federal and Serbian.

Croatia's territorial structure is made up of 426 municipalities, 121 cities and 20 counties have been established by law, including the city of Zagreb, which has the status of both, a town and a county. According to the new Croatian Local and Regional Self-Government Law (2001), 'city' status is given to all county seats, to municipalities with more than 30.000 inhabitants as well as to those with special significance in historical, economic or geographical terms. (see Table 5.1)

## Constitutional and legislative foundations of local self-government

A legal – or better – constitutional basis constitutes an important guarantee for the principle of local self-government. According to articles 3 and 4 ECLSG, it should be enshrined in written law in order to become a 'right' to local self-government. In all countries local self-government enjoys constitutional status and is organized according Western models based on political democracy and autonomy of the local level. Details regarding functions, procedures, relations with the State (authorities) and citizens as well as issues like supervision and control are regulated in a set of specific laws (general administrative laws; general laws on local government; specific laws on single issues, that is local taxes and finances, local elections, municipal property). A first necessary distinction, however, is to be made between federal and unitary states: in the

*Table 5.1* Territorial organization and municipalities in the Western Balkans

| | *BiH (FBH – RS)* | *Croatia* | *FYROM* | *Montenegro* | *Serbia* |
|---|---|---|---|---|---|
| Area ($km^2$) | BiH: 51,129<br>FBH: 26,110<br>RS: 24,811 | 56,542 | 24,856 | 13,812 | 88,361 |
| Population | BiH: 3,922,205<br>FBH: 2,318,972<br>RS: 1,490,993 | 4,496,869 | 2,022,547 | 650,575 | 7,498,001<br>(without Kosovo) |
| Intermediate entities | FBH – 10 cantons<br>RS – none | 20 counties | None | None | 29 merely administrative districts (plus autonomous Province of Voivodina) |
| Number of municipalities | RS: 64 municipalities (2 cities)<br>FBH: 84 municipalities (2 cities) | 425 municipalities<br>122 cities (total: 547 LG units) | 123 municipalities<br>(2005: 84) | 27 municipalities | 140 municipalities<br>3 cities |
| Special Status of the Capital | | Zagreb | Skopje | Cetinje<br>(Podgorica) | Belgrade |

Croatia and Bosnia and Herzegovina are the only countries with true intermediate territorial bodies. However, due to its asymmetric and federal nature, the case of BiH is a special one: due to their nature as constituent bodies in the respective federal systems, neither the two entities nor the ten Cantons which only exist in the Federation and which are responsible for all issues of local government can be regarded as an intermediate level in formal terms, even though the cantons, at least in functional terms, might be compared to such intermediate authorities.
*Notes*: RS: Republika Srpska (BiH); FBH: Federation of Bosnia and Herzegovina (BiH).

former, the federal level often does not have the power to regulate local affairs as this competence is reserved to the member states or entities.

BiHs State Constitution was designed to derogate most powers to the entity level and below. Accordingly, the Constitution makes no mention of local self-government as the authority in matters of local and regional self-government is vested in the two entities (the Federation of Bosnia and Herzegovina and the Republika Srpska which have substantial powers to pass legislation and impose taxes), which therefore regulate these matters through their Constitutions and respective legislation. Currently, there are 11 systems of local government in Bosnia and Herzegovina, ten of which show considerable variation in the distribution of powers, taxes, allocation of resources, and so on.

The Constitution of the Federation of BiH contains only few and basic provisions on local government (section VI, arts 1–6). In 2004, proposals for the substantial amendment of these articles have been made,[5] strengthening local self-governance by determining basic principles to be observed by the ten cantons of which the Federation consists and which have jurisdiction to legislate in the sphere of local self-government. All cantonal Constitutions contain detailed provisions in special chapters on 'municipal authorities'. At the level of ordinary legislation, a Federation 'Law on the Basis of Local Self-Government', adopted in September 1995 after the first ratification of the ECLSG by BiH during the War, defines local self-government and establishes a number of essential rules; subsequently, all cantons passed their own laws on local self-government, filling this framework.

The RS has no intermediate tier of government between its central institutions and the municipalities; here the entity level performs tasks that belong to the cantons in the Federation. The Constitution of 1992 grants municipalities 'self-rule' in all matters delegated to them by the RS entity (arts 5, 100–103). The RS has a rather centralized administrative structure and an entity-level Ministry of Local Government regulates and conducts dialogue with its 64 municipalities. A new Law on Local Self-Government was passed in 1999; it has been amended substantially in November 2004.

Serbia and Montenegro present a similarly differentiated picture: as the Constitutional Charter of the State Union (4 February 2003) does not contain any competences regarding local government, all principles as well as detailed regulations are reserved to the two Republics.[6]

The Constitution of Serbia of 1990 provides for the municipality as a form of territorial self-government while reserving most decisions to a respective law (art. 7): thus it contains only few basic provisions regarding the basic functions and tasks of LSG-units (art. 113), their entitlement to revenues (art. 114), their statutes to be adopted by the Municipal Assembly as their basic legal act, the forms of participation by citizens (elections and referendum, art. 116), as well as the possibility of introducing the merger of two or more municipalities into a 'city' (art. 117) and a special status for the capital Belgrade (articles 7 and 118). Districts in Serbia are administrative territorial units which function as territorial branches of the central government administration: they have neither autonomy nor elected bodies. The new Law on Local Government, adopted in February 2002, has been positively assessed by the Council of Europe. It envisages more competencies and resources for local administrations, limits on undue interference by Republican authorities, greater involvement of citizens, and specific provisions on protection of minorities. In June 2002 a new Ministry for Public Administration and Local Government has been established and a new Law on Local Elections been adopted.

Montenegro's Constitution of 1992, refers to the principle of local self-government in the following way: 'The territory of Montenegro shall be a single and inalienable territory. Montenegro shall be organized in territorial units – municipalities' (art. 8). 'The right to a local self-government shall be guaranteed. Local self-government shall be exercised in the municipality and in the capital' (art. 66). Article 99 concerns the delegation of powers to the local self-government while articles 113 to 118 provide for the competencies of municipalities. However, only in July 2003 a set of laws has been adopted, notably the Law on Local Government, the Law on Financing of Local Government and the Law on Election of Mayors. The new legislation provides for genuine municipal competencies and some own resources (through municipal taxes and other charges).

A 'right' of citizens to local and regional government is guaranteed by the Croatian Constitution of 1990 (Chapter VI). Despite the 'unitary and indivisible' character of the Republic (art. 1), since 2000 a two tier structure of local and regional self-government has been established (through constitutional changes, articles 133 ff.): the counties' (*Zupanije*) main function is to coordinate the activities of the municipalities and to organize the delivery of public services at a regional level. A new Croatian Law on Local and Regional Self-Government and a Law on the Election of members of representative bodies of local and regional self-government units entered into force on 1 July 2001. The new Law clearly states that the main territorial subdivisions (municipalities, towns and counties) are legal entities (article 9) and defines local government responsibilities.

Articles 114–17 of FYROM's Constitution of 1991,[7] guarantee the 'right of citizens to local self-government'. According to the principle that there are 'no territorial solutions to ethnic issues' (art. 1.2. Ohrid Framework Agreement), no intermediate, regional level has been established. The whole system of local government consists of only one level (the municipality) and is based on the self-government principle. 'Local self-government is regulated by a law adopted by a two-thirds majority of the total number of Representatives' (art. 114): as other territorial solutions have been ruled out, this requirement of a qualified majority for an ordinary law regarding the organization of the local level and its competencies shall provide an additional guarantee to all ethnic groups. The status of the 'City of Skopje as a particular unit of local self-government' is regulated by a special law (art. 117). A new Law on Local Self-Government in FYROM was adopted on 24 January 2002. Its enactment and implementation as well as the adoption of further laws related to the decentralization process (esp. the one on Territorial Division) are among the key points in the Framework Agreement.

Besides the mentioned differences between unitary and federal states, an important difference in the constitutional provisions results from the period in which the Constitutions have been adopted: although in all Constitutions LSG is conceived as a 'right', in some of them, notably those adopted at the beginning of the 1990s, it is framed as the 'right of citizens to local self-government'. This might be seen (and be in future interpreted) as a modern reference to democratic involvement from the bottom-up, but is historically linked to the citizens' right to manage local affairs under the concept of self-management in former Yugoslavia, a concept of political rather than of legal nature.

The existence of ethnically pluralistic societies together with recently gained independent statehood, often after traumatic experiences, explain the emphasis on expressions like 'single and inalienable' or 'indivisible and inviolable' territory in a number of Constitutions (for example art. 3 FYROM Constitution and art. 1 Constitution of Croatia) which have to be balanced with the autonomy of local government. Thus, it is important, that most Constitutions already contain detailed blueprints for the structure and the organization of local government as well as principles regarding the distribution of competencies which constitute a framework for the legislator, but might also be used by Courts as criteria in resolving controversies.

All laws on local self-government are the results of relatively recent reforms and reflect the principles adhered to with the ratification of the ECLSG. The case of Serbia and Montenegro is of particular interest: although their respective Constitutions providing the constitutional guarantee for local autonomy have remained unchanged and although both States have not ratified the Charter yet, both new laws on LSG have already been drafted using the ECLSG as the main reference.

## Scope of local self-government and its relations with the central government

The unambiguous definition of functions, financial means and self-government property is a basic condition to be fulfilled to allow local self-governments to function independently. The ECLSG refers to the 'right and the ability' (art. 3 para. 1), that is the legal right to regulate and manage certain public affairs, which must be accompanied by the means of doing so effectively (in particular adequate financial resources). A declaration of these principles can be found in all examined Constitutions. But local autonomy operates 'within the limits of the law' (art. 3 para. 1): a more specific and detailed definition of its scope in ordinary laws is therefore necessary. Although it is not possible to define precisely, once and for all, what affairs local authorities should be entitled to, regulate and manage, it follows from the 'right' to LSG that powers of local authorities have to be pre-determined and laid down by law, thus allowing for legal certainty and protection of the single municipalities. Furthermore, this is required by the principle of separation of powers: being part of the executive, also the local administration has to operate on the basis of the legality-principle.

## Areas/competencies of LSG and methods of allocation

As it is neither possible nor appropriate to enumerate local powers exhaustively, the ECLSG contains only general principles on responsibilities and nature of local powers (art. 4). Following from their conception as political entities acting in their own right to promote the general welfare of their inhabitants, local authorities should have the right to exercise their initiative in all matters having local implications (art. 4 para. 2). This is supported by the general principle according to which the exercise of public services and responsibilities should be decentralized (para. 3), unless the size or nature of a task is such that it requires to be treated within a larger territorial area or there are overriding considerations of efficiency or economy, it should generally be entrusted to the most local level of government.

In the legislation under review, general clauses and enumeration can be distinguished as the two main methods of determining the scope of local government powers. The general clause establishes the rule that the municipality is entrusted with all functions which are not expressly excluded or transferred to other authorities by law. This bottom-up approach, which fully corresponds to the one laid down in the ECLSG, can not be found anywhere in its true form. By contrast, and following the (top-down) assumption that all rights and authorities are originally vested in the (central) State, which can delegate them when appropriate, the legislation of some countries still relies on the explicit allocation of powers to local self-government, according to the principle of enumeration and in contrast with the ECLSG. Art. 17 LSG Law of FYROM contains a long and detailed list of 'concrete activities' to be 'independently' performed by the units of local self-government. The enumeration of local powers used to be the method in federal Yugoslavia. Its legacy is particularly strong in the RS Law on LSG: 15 articles describe the original responsibilities of municipalities (arts 12–27). Although the new Serbian Law on LSG (2002) introduced a residual clause in favour of local governments – which 'engage in other activities of direct interest to the local population' –, this is to be found at the very end of a long and detailed list of original responsibilities of municipalities (art. 18, no. 35)!

According to Croatia's Constitution, cities and municipalities 'carry out affairs of local importance that directly realize the needs of the citizens', and that have not been assigned by constitution or law to other bodies; this is followed by two lists of areas constituting the sphere of self-government of municipalities and cities on one hand, and of counties on the other (art. 134). Together with the principle of subsidiarity in the following paragraph, this comes quite close to the spirit of a general clause. The following areas are listed as obligatory fields of local self-government activities: housing and the arrangement of settlements; zoning and town planning; utilities for the municipal economy; concern for children; welfare; primary health care; pre- and elementary schooling; culture, physical education and sports; consumer protection; protection and improvement of the natural environment; fire-fighting and civilian protection. The sphere of regional self-governments covers 'operations of regional importance', particularly in the domains of education; health care; zoning and town planning; economic development; transports and transportation infrastructure; planning and development of the network of educational, health care, social and cultural institutions. Other major services (for example, education) are typically provided, financed and controlled by sector ministries. In the countries with a two tier LSG-structure, such as Croatia, this is combined with the 'dual subordination' of local governments at the second level (counties). In each county there is an office of the state administration as decentralized authority of the central government. Although powers should normally be full and exclusive, overlapping responsibilities between municipalities/cities and counties are a frequent problem as many affairs have local, regional and/or national implications. A first step to resolve this problem is the clear and unambiguous determination of the scope of the powers and (financial) responsibilities of elected local authorities and territorial representatives of the State.

According to all laws, local authorities can also exercise delegated powers of supra-local authorities: the Serbian Law on LSG consequently distinguishes the 'original scope of responsibilities' from 'delegated responsibilities' (art. 3). However, a practically important question is whether they are able to take account of local circumstances when implementing delegated functions (as laid down in art. 4 para. 5 ECLSG) and whether these delegated powers are accompanied by sufficient guarantees and financial means. In most cantonal Constitutions in BiH, for instance, the delegation of powers from the cantonal to the municipal level requires a law to be adopted with a two-third majority, but only in three Cantons also a legal obligation exists for identifying the related financial resources. The FYROM Law on LSG provides for the delegation of activities from organs of State administration to LG units 'for a more rational exercise of the rights and duties of its citizens and for the satisfaction of certain needs of direct interests of the citizens' (art. 19 par. 1) while establishing the duty for the Republic to provide for the required funds (par. 3). A similar provision can be found in art. 28 para. 2 RS Law on LSG.

The delimitation of responsibilities between local self-government and other layers of government is not very clear and poses problems in nearly all countries. Although consultation of local authorities regarding matters outside their scope, but by which they are particularly affected, is usually expressly laid down as mandatory,[8] a lack of communication results in poor coordination between different levels of government. Often middle-tier authorities still work as territorial agents of the central government. The recent reforms in Croatia show that they might also become territorial units which bridge state and local policies guaranteeing the execution of central government policy on local territories and providing coordination of the activities of local self-government authorities. In addition, the middle-tier authorities will have an important task in the preparation of EU integration as the level for implementing EU regional policy. The potential of decentralization for balancing power between central and local governments is not yet fully recognized and far from being exploited.

As results from the comparison basic utility and communal services in the Western Balkans are mostly decentralized to the local level. However, there are considerable differences in the development of concrete facilities which mostly depend on the – different – degree of autonomy of local government decision-making powers (Kandeva 2001: 34f.): it is usually the State to determine the general standards in the field of public service delivery, together with financial indicators. Municipalities are mostly limited to formulate the policy and devise methods for service provision as well as to select those services they provide themselves.[9] Due to strict allocation of funds for specific purposes, municipalities are very often extremely limited choosing their own preferences or priorities in public service delivery. These limits are even stricter, where enumeration is the general method for the distribution of functions.

### Efficiency: size and involvement of the private sector

The issue of size of the single LSG units is generally subject to a compromise between democracy and efficiency: citizen participation is more difficult to organize effectively where the size of territory and/or population increases, while this usually favors sustainability and quality of service delivery creating economies of scale (Steering Committee on Local and Regional Democracy 2001; Swianiewicz 2002). Smaller and smallest LSG-units lack the financial means to provide adequate services, have difficulties to attract qualified staff and might thus become more easily dependent on the central government, while the duplication of administrations causes additional costs without efficiency gains: 5.000 inhabitants are indicated as an approximate threshold below which significant efficiency losses are experienced (Verheijen 2001: 38). However, territorial fragmentation of local government is not seen as such a widespread problem as it used to be in CEE countries (Swianiewicz 2002), as the average size of municipalities is generally bigger. As a consequence, the establishment of forms of self-government below the municipal level is foreseen in all examined countries: in Serbia as 'local communities' by municipalities as their sub-units; in Croatia as 'territorial committees' and in FYROM as 'neighbourhood (village and suburbs) communities'. These legal entities with own rights express common local interests through directly elected councils.[10]

In all countries, the creation of new local governments and the abolition or territorial changes of existing ones is subject to a regulation by law and often has to correspond to criteria such as local needs, common economic interests and historical tradition (for example art. 9 RS Law on LSG 2004). Although a matter reserved to the final decision of Parliament, usually both, the concerned local authorities as well as the local population, have to be consulted (the latter through a referendum), as in art. 15 FYROM Law on LSG and art. 12 Serbian Law on LSG. This requirement of consultation (and consent) is fully in line with art. 5 ECLSG and shall protect the local community. An important alternative to centralization or to the fusion/merger of smallest and smaller municipalities into bigger ones is cooperation: in all countries, the right to associate is guaranteed. Local authorities are allowed to engage in functional cooperation, can establish consortia for certain purposes, and establish cross-border relations (in accordance with art. 10 ECLSG, for example art. 12 Serbian Law on LSG).

Most public services at local level are still delivered by public corporations established by the municipalities or the government. On the whole, the process of transfer of public services, formerly provided by state monopolies, such as education, health care, water and electricity supply, from central to local government continues. Even provisions on 'horizontal subsidiarity', that is involvement of the private sector in the fulfillment or management of public tasks and functions (not specifically foreseen in the ECLSG), can be found in the new legislation of FYROM ('may acquire revenues by conducting business and other profit-making activity', art. 64 Law on LSG) and Serbia (art. 6 Law on LSG: 'may establish enterprises, institutions and other organizations engaged in public services'), where also contracts with private local or foreign enterprises as well as concessions or licensing can be applied. These alternative forms are seen as an innovative means for raising effectiveness, reducing costs and improving accountability in the performance of certain activities and services by the local administration. However the citizens' choice is still not considered in the normative regulation of public service delivery with their demands and preferences as criteria and priorities (Kandeva 2001: 35). In addition, forms of partnership between local governments and NGOs have the potential to create a wider political and social base of political decisions as well as to improve their efficiency and successful implementation.

### Relationship with state administration, supervision and judicial remedies

All countries have opted for the continental system of supervision of local authorities' activities based on the distinction between own (specific, typical competencies and functions) and delegated responsibility: the administrative supervision of the former is limited to legality-control aimed at 'ensuring compliance with the law', whereas regarding the latter (execution of delegated functions) also a control of expediency is possible (in accordance with art. 8 ECLSG). All laws meet the demand for supervision according pre-established rules and procedures with detailed provisions, including those which regulate cases of direct intervention, such as substitution or nomination of a government's commissioner. The respective provisions at least implicitly – by foreseeing a gradual approach of these interventions – respect the principle of proportionality (art. 8 ECLSG para. 3), even though it is not expressly stated. In BiH, the provisions in the cantonal laws had to be amended in 2000 in order to be brought in line with this principle, but there remain doubts regarding art. 13 of the FBiH Law on LSG, which does not expressly mention proportionality.

In some cases, the authorities exercising control over the activities of local self-government authorities are part of the middle-tier administration: in Croatia the function of a county governor, as a representative of state authority and as a supervisor of the legality of local self-government activities, has been separated from the function of county mayor (as President of the county executive board). In other countries, such as FYROM, supervision is exercised directly by the Central government (art. 68 ff. Law on LSG). The same is true for Republika Srpska in BiH, where such supervision is conducted through the entity government, and, similarly for the Federation of Bosnia and Herzegovina, where the specific competent cantonal ministries are determined, with some variations, in the respective cantonal legislation on local government; some cantons have authorized their parliaments to dissolve local councils under certain conditions and to appoint commissioners for the management of the municipalities. Art. 44 of the LSG law of Hercegbosna Canton authorizes the governor of the canton to examine normative acts adopted by the municipal councils with the right to reject them in case of alleged illegality or unconstitutionality – practically a veto power, although the final decision is made by the Constitutional Court (Jokay 2001: 106).

The relationship between the central and local levels can be considered an indicator of the extent of democratization and modernization of a country's government. In most of the countries compared, this relationship still appears 'somewhat strained' (Kandeva 2001: 30). In part, this is certainly due to their recent adoption and the lack of practical experience with decentralization and new spheres of autonomous functions, but it might, at least partly, also be explained as a reaction to the described experience with the progressive loosening of the control over municipalities' activities in former Yugoslavia. In addition there are usually fears by the governing parties not to create too wide and uncontrolled spaces for opposition parties at local or regional level.

Given this situation, the judicial remedies for defending LSG rights against regional or national intervention (as provided for in art. 11 ECLSG) are most important. Such remedies for the protection of local powers are foreseen in all countries; the general rules regarding the control of constitutionality and legality also refer to the legal protection of LSG. Accordingly, in Croatia, Montenegro, FYROM and Serbia, the defence of local powers can even give access to the Constitutional Court (art. 128 of Croatia's Constitution, art. 113

para 5 of the Montenegrin Constitution, art. 85 of the FYROM Law on LSG and in art. 122 Serbian Law on LSG).

## Administrative structures and financial resources

Regarding the administrative structures of local authorities, all examined laws contain general principles in order to guarantee a uniformity of local government. In Croatia, the Constitution and the new legislation allow for greater freedom of internal organization, but in some cases detailed regulation raises the question of how much room is left to the single LSG-unit in adapting its administrative structures to local needs (as requested by art. 6 ECLSG). Most laws leave some liberty regarding the organization and selection of staff (being the remuneration and status legally defined), as well as for the compensation for elected officials or representatives. A distinction between ordinary staff and leading positions is common: the latter are usually elected and appointed for a certain period. An interesting example for a specific institution is the 'Chief Architect of the Town' to be designated in FYROM's larger and urban LG units (with a town as the seat of the unit, articles 24, 52 and 53 LAW on LSG): appointed by the Mayor for a four years term of office he or she is involved in all issues concerning urbanism and architecture. Similarly, a main architect and a municipality manager can be engaged by Serbia's Mayors on contract base (arts 54 ff. Law on LSG). In some countries, special supervisory boards have to be established by the municipal council for 'supervising the material and financial operations' of the LSG unit; these boards have to inform and report back to the council (articles 50 ff RS Law on LSG) and, in some cases, also to the Ministry of Finance (arts 67, 72 FYROM Law on LSG).

Inadequate financing is a common problem for most local governments all over Europe. As sufficient financial resources are crucial for the exercise of legal rights, the ECLSG establishes that adequate financial resources and freedom of expenditure (art. 9, para. 1) have to be guaranteed as well as 'financial resources [. . .] commensurate with the responsibilities' (para. 2). However, in the examined legislation, such clear equivalence between the allocation of functions and sufficient resources is hardly expressly stated. An exception is the Constitution of the Federation of BiH (as amended in 2004) which, in case of transfer of competencies, obliges higher levels of authorities to also transfer the sources of financing necessary for those operations as well as to respect a principle of solidarity. Art. 137 para. 2 of Croatia's Constitution now also states that 'revenues of local and regional units of self-government shall be proportional to their authorities', similar to the articles 63 and 64 RS Law on LSG. However, such a principle is also missing in a number of Western European Laws on LSG.

In general, the centralized decision over the allocation of public functions and central control over service delivery typically corresponds with low levels of own source revenues of local authorities. Local tax revenues as well as the income from fees and charges are comparatively low and real autonomy for self-generated revenues can hardly be expected as a short or mid-term perspective. As a general trend, financial transfers from the central government and shared resources instead of own resources of the local authorities clearly dominate: like in other transition countries, in all SEE countries, financial transfers make up the greatest share of local finances together with shared taxes (usually VAT, income taxes, business taxes, corporate taxes, etc.). The two resulting problems concern the transfer-system as well as the guarantees local authorities can rely on: the lack of a significant and stable local revenue base is often used to further argue the trend to centralize. In BiH, the Law on Distribution of Public Revenues of the Federation distinguishes municipal taxes and other municipal revenues from shared taxes, but the main problem is the implementation at cantonal level which does not guarantee these sources. Revenue-sharing practices exist in all countries (for example ministries pay salaries, while maintenance costs are covered locally), but they are usually characterized by highly discretionary decisions (Péteri 2001: 16); the same is most often true for grants. This is exactly the reason why, according to the ECLSG, the latter should not be earmarked for financing specific projects; instead block grants or even sector-specific grants are preferable (art. 9 para. 7 ECLSG). In some laws, the allocation of funds in accordance with the level of development and financial equalization procedures in support of financially weaker LSG units are foreseen (in conformity with art. 9 para. 5 ECLSG), for example art. 67 RS Law on LSG.

However, most local authorities still do not possess the capacities for increased responsibilities for fund raising, economic development and strategic planning. A common problem is the lack of investment capital. In former Yugoslavia municipalities could not borrow money. Although raising capital for investments (only) is now usually permitted, it is very difficult in the current economic situation. At the same time, the social costs of transition require increasing expenses for social and cultural assistance to citizens and tend to dominate the structure of expenses in local budgets of the area reducing the possibility of following long-term 'program objectives' rather than applying *ad hoc* policies for coping with immediate shortages (Kandeva 2001: 37). The recent reform laws contain new opportunities, but their implementation has to show whether this potential will be used.

Another crucial question for local development is the issue of property owned by LSG units. According to the previous legal situation, all local self-government property belonged to the State (see for the situation in Serbia: Ilic 2002: 715). Most of the examined countries have started with the privatization of land and the transfer of formerly state-owned property to local governments. Already by the end of the 1990s the legal basis for municipal property existed and was included in each specific country's privatization strategy. However, considerable differences in privatization policies can be observed, as the scope and the form of restitution vary by country (Péteri 2001: 17). In both entities of BiH, the assets of national- or entity-owned utilities (water, gas, electricity etc. to be reorganized in stock companies before privatization) as well as patrimony over real estate and physical infrastructure inherited by the entities or still owned by the State are issues that for long had not been resolved (Jokay 2001: 107).

## Local democracy, citizens' participation, accountability

According to the ECLSG, local institutions must be democratically constituted authorities (art. 3 para. 2). Basically, two models can be distinguished: the monistic one with an elected assembly having the power to change the situation of local government independently from its own, and the dualistic, 'parliamentary' model, with strong links between assembly and executive. However, there are strong variations of the latter, including double direct elections, whereas a 'presidential' model in its pure form is usually not adequate for the local level (Scarciglia 2001: 130f.).

All examined Constitutions and LSG Laws provide for the direct election of the representative bodies as well as for instruments of direct democracy at local level. Deliberative bodies, Councils or Assemblies, are established in all countries as the only authority that may adopt normative acts for the local sphere; consequently, they are elected in direct elections.

Originally, mayors were typically elected indirectly by the respective councils. This is still the case in BiH, where the municipal 'council' elects a 'mayor' (Federation) or the 'assembly' chooses the 'president of the executive board' (RS) by simple majority. From the municipal elections in October 2004, the Mayor replaces the Executive Board in RS and will be directly elected by the citizens. The direct election of the mayor, at least in bigger municipalities and cities, is a relatively recent tendency, common to most European countries. The result is his or her strengthened political position through direct democratic legitimacy (for example art. 45 FYROM Law on LSG, art. 40 Serbian Law on LSG). The adoption of the new Serbian Law on Local Elections in June 2002 introduced significant improvements, for example proportionality, reduction of the threshold (thus favouring minority communities) and a requirement for an increased representation of women. The first elections under this new Law were the by-elections in three municipalities in Southern Serbia in July 2003, the first multi-ethnic elections in the region in a decade and the first with direct mayoral elections (new Law on Local Government). This positive experience was repeated on a larger scale in the first Republic-wide local elections according to the new system, held in September 2004.

The Mayor is usually also the head of the local administration; however, in Serbia a municipal council elected by the assembly and presided by the Mayor ('President of the Municipality') supports him or her as a collegial body (for example art. 43, 44 Serbian Law on LSG 2002). In some countries, the Mayor is also authorized to exercise control on acts of the Council and may challenge a council decision when it is deemed to violate municipal interests or the law (for example art. 44 FYROM Law on LSG).

In order to increase democratic participation, specific advisory or consultative bodies have been introduced in some countries. An example is Serbia, where the new Law on LSG establishes a council for local self-government development and protection selected among citizens and experts (art. 127); a municipal ombudsperson may be appointed, too, to protect the collective and individual rights and interests of citizens (art. 126). These institutions might contribute positively to the improvement of the relations between public administration and citizens and offer the potential of actively involving NGOs. The RS Law on LSG also provides for the publicity of the work of LSG bodies, prescribing even the duty of regularly arranging press-conferences (art. 78).

The conditions for the exercise of direct democracy at local level vary in the different countries, but most of them comprise a considerable range of instruments such as citizens' initiatives (petitions), local meetings of citizens, public hearings and local referenda including consultative ones (for example articles 20–23 FYROM Law on LSG, articles 65 ff. Serbian Law on LSG). In FYROM, even a question of non-confidence may be raised against the Mayor upon the request of at least 20 per cent of the voters (art. 47 Law on LSG); in Serbia a recall can be initiated by at least 10 per cent of the electorate (art. 42 Law on LSG). However, for various reasons, ranging from the need for consolidating the local institutions and the power of the new ruling political parties to the identification of these instruments with the collective self-management ethos which served to the legitimacy of the old Yugoslav regime, real public participation and 'self-governance' often remain formal and rhetorical (Jokay 2001: 106).

## LSG and the ethnic question

Despite historical and recent attempts of homogenization (ranging from assimilation policies to 'ethnic cleansing'), ethnic, cultural and religious diversity is still the rule rather than the exception in all countries under review. As a consequence, nowadays all Constitutions take ethnic issues expressly into account, proclaiming equality and non-discrimination as well as providing for specific rights, especially in the fields of culture and political participation. The new 'Constitutional Charter on Human and Minority Rights and Civil Liberties' of Serbia and Montenegro even contains an article on 'identity rights' (art. 52). The single solutions regarding the local level vary very much, according to the specific situation on the ground (see for some instructive case studies: Dimitrijevic and Kovacs 2004).

According to the principle of territoriality, the autonomous provinces of Voivodina and Kosovo in Serbia had been established for accommodating the specific situation of the ethnically diverse composition of their population (24 different groups in the case of Voivodina and an Albanian majority in Kosovo). Bosnia and Herzegovina's federal structure, the recognition of the entities as well as the cantonal structure within the Federation, were the necessary preconditions for ending the war. However, this territorial compromise was in contrast with the principle of 'minority returns' aiming at re-establishing a multiethnic society by favouring the return of displaced persons and refugees to their homes as well as restitution of their property. It took five years until this contradiction could be addressed: on 1 July 2000, the Constitutional Court of BiH confirmed the 'institutional equality' of Bosniacs, Croats and Serbs, declaring all of them to be 'constituent peoples' throughout the whole territory of the State (Decision U 5/98-III): thus, the entities could not be considered as 'States' of only one group (or two of them) and respective declarations in their Constitutions were consequently declared to be in violation of the Constitution of the State of BiH. However, two more years were necessary for adopting the respective amendments of the Entities' Constitutions.[11] In accordance with these amendments, the BiH Law on Local Elections requires to thoroughly consider ethnic balances in addition to political considerations: 'the ethnic composition of the population of the municipality, canton or city shall be taken into consideration' when officials in the municipal administration are appointed or the Municipal or City Executive Board is elected. In practice, this often leads to serious difficulties in the decision-making process, as representatives from the different groups act as equal partners with the consequence that all decisions need their (informal) approval. In the Federation this has even lead to an (informal and *de facto*) duplication of the budgets as well as to parallel administrative structures (Jokay 2001: 108).

A radically different approach – 'no territorial solutions to ethnic issues' – is the basic principle laid down in the Ohrid Agreement for FYROM which tried to avoid the disintegration of the country and civil war in Summer 2001. Implementing this agreement, the Law on Territorial Division, adopted in August 2004, reduced the number of municipalities thus changing their ethnic composition with the intention of improving the participation of the Albanian population at local level; a referendum against this Law failed. In order to protect the respective group interests, a two-thirds majority for the adoption or amendments of the Laws on LSG is required in the Constitution of FYROM (art. 114 para. 3).

Besides specific provisions on the use of minority language(s) in the relations between local administration and citizens as well as in the elected and representative bodies at local level (articles 88 ff. FYROM Law on LSG), most countries have special norms for the guaranteed representation of minority-members in the local government institutions (esp. in the assembly, in Croatia such a right to representation is granted to ethnic groups and national minorities which constitute at least eight per cent of the respective electorate). After the mentioned amendments to the Entity Constitutions in 2002, in BiH proportional representation in the administration at all levels – according to the numerical strength of the respective groups in the population – is guaranteed to the three constituent peoples (that is Bosniacs, Croats and Serbs) and 'Others' according to the numerical strength of theses categories in the 1991 census, for example art. 3 RS Law on LSG (2004). A formula calling for 'an adequate national (ethnic) representation [to] be attempted [. . .] without violating the principles of professionalism' can also be found in FYROM (art. 54 para. 5 Law on LSG).

In addition, in a number of countries, Minority Councils are established as consultative bodies at local (and central) level in order to facilitate members of minorities in representing their specific interests. An example is the Commission on Inter-ethnic Relations to be established in all LG units of FYROM, in which members of different nationalities constitute the majority or a considerable number (art. 25 LSG Law). A similar body is established in Serbia's multiethnic municipalities, that is those in which one ethnic community accounts for more than 5 per cent or all ethnic communities together account for more than 10 per cent of the population. Communities accounting for more than 1 per cent of the local population are represented in the Committee for Interethnic Relations (art. 63 Serbian Law on LSG), which even has the right to initiate the procedure for the assessment of constitutionality and legality of decisions or by-laws adopted by the municipal assembly before the Constitutional Court in case of an alleged violation of the rights of ethnic or national communities.

However, the relationship between territory and national or ethnic symbols still plays an important role (emphasized by nationalistic politicians) as is demonstrated by a recent judgment of BiH's Constitutional Court: on 27 February 2004 the Court decided that prefixes to place names indicating at the ethnic character of a town or a municipality are unconstitutional, if these had been added during the war – by contrast with historical names (Judgment U 44/01). The most famous case concerned Sarajevo, claiming a part of the capital to be 'Serbian' (only). The respective list of names in the RS Law on Territorial Organization and LSG as well as title and articles 1 and 2 of the Law on City of 'Srpsko' Sarajevo had been declared unconstitutional. As the decision was not implemented by the RS legislator in the given time limit, in September 2004 the Court decided to annul these names altogether and adopted a decision on the interim names of those units until the RS legislator eliminates the established non-conformity with the BiH Constitution.

## Closer to Europe?: from legislative reform to implementation

The European Charter of Local Self-Government, which has strongly influenced the reform legislation in all analysed countries, provides a sound and sufficiently detailed legal basis for meeting the challenges of reform. Moreover, its approach is based on the voluntary self-obligation of the signatory States which leaves plenty of room for discretion, thus favouring the adherence to the commitments by conviction. The monitoring system of the ECLSG provides for the necessary degree of transparency, while the Congress of Local and Regional Authorities favours contacts and the exchange of information in order to create networks of municipalities: this opens a new, horizontal dimension to the local level in addition to its relations with the central government.[12] Associations of municipalities, cities or mayors, established in all countries, confirm the need for exchange and coordination. They are often assisted by centers and foundations for local government reform, which actively engage in the reform debate elaborating proposals and providing comparative experience (Kandeva 2001: 37), thus leading to the circulation of models and best practices (e.g. the reception of the general trend in Europe towards direct elections of the Mayor). Being involved in this process and becoming convinced of its objectives is of primary importance for the acceptance of reforms and their successful implementation: a mere importation of 'models' according to abstract 'conditionality' criteria bears the risk of (only) formal compliance through institutional 'mimicry', but does not produce sustainable reforms.

However, despite this promising approach, problems abound: over the last fifteen years, in Serbia alone, three laws regulating local self-government have been subsequently adopted. The similar situation in the other countries does not only regard the frequency in the adoption of reform laws (or amending existing ones), but also shows a certain harmonization: common traditions, comparison of best practices combined with the common objective of European integration lead to the adoption of similar solutions. But despite all efforts of bringing legislation in line with European principles of local self-government, 'good laws are not enough'. The success of reforms mainly depends on their satisfactory implementation. Due to the fact that most legislation has been adopted quite recently, it is still too early for a thorough analysis of the state of implementation. It is evident, however, that the main problems and challenges of reforming the systems of local self-government concern: the difficulties of seeking autonomy in the national system, which is often being re-defined itself; the hard financial conditions of transition, which make the improvement of quality and operational efficiency of local governments at low costs a daunting task; a necessary change of attitude and administrative culture shifting the focus on citizens; guaranteeing democratic control through participation, transparency and the fight against corruption; finding a reasonable balance between the public and private sectors.

A huge problem, due to the difficult financial situation in all transition countries, is autonomy in financial terms: a lack of financial as well as technical capacity for the actual implementation of functions is still characterizing most local authorities. At least on paper, local democracy is looking much better, and the recent direct elections of mayors in Serbia are particularly encouraging; still, it is a long way to go until decentralized and local structures might be considered counterweights in the vertical separation of powers. Of particular importance in this context is ethnic and cultural diversity. Numerous are the instruments by which participation and inclusion of members of different ethnic groups shall be facilitated, but again, their success will depend on the concrete and constructive use made of them (as the negative use of the veto for protecting 'vital interests' in BiH, during the first years of implementing the Dayton Peace Accord, has clearly demonstrated).

Although the adopted reform legislation is, at first glance, often strikingly similar, the process of local government reform in South-East Europe is a very differentiated one and, after a decade of gradual but intense reform, still far from being completed: while further decentralization is already being under way in some countries, for example, Croatia and FYROM, in others, especially in Serbia and Montenegro, much will depend on the envisaged constitutional reforms. Moreover, the established institutions of local self-government will have to further improve their efficiency and develop their responsibilities, especially in the field of public services. As the pace of this improvement partly depends on the general economic development of the countries, the realization of substantial local autonomy, in its transition from 'democratic centralism' to a parliamentary form of local government (Scarciglia, 2001, p. 131), continues to be a 'work in progress'.

## Notes

1. For a definition of 'transformation' – from a legal perspective – see De Vergottini, 1998 and Mezzetti, 2003. The differences in the Western Balkans' transition by contrast with the transition in the Central and Eastern European countries are highlighted by Batt 2004 10–19.
2. The chapter concentrates on the successor States of former Yugoslavia except Slovenia. For being currently under direct international administration, Kosovo is not included in this analysis.
3. European Treaty Series – No. 122. The Charter has been adopted in Strasbourg, 15 October 1985.
4. Cf. Rinella (1997: 53) and Sacco (1992: 151), according to whom 'the rule circulates, if the political idea circulates'. For the ECLSG see also Knemayer (2003).
5. These constitutional amendments are currently still under discussion within the Constitutional Commission of the Federation and have not been adopted so far; cf. Venice Commission, Opinions CDL-AD(2004)014 and 032 and CDL(2004)073.
6. See for a detailed description of LSG in the Yugoslavia of the nineties: Sevic (2001: 417–70).
7. As amended on 16 November 2001, following the Ohrid Framework Agreement. See, for the situation before, Todorovski (2001: 241–88).
8. In accordance with art. 4 para. 6 ECLSG, e.g. in the 2004 constitutional amendments of the Federation of BiH (Chapter VI. art. 2 d) and in three cantonal Constitutions as well as in art. 87 FYROM Law on LSG).
9. However, also within the EU there is great variety in the distribution of competencies; much of it is due to history and the (limited) role of the State in Northern Europe by contrast with the tradition of prefectorial administration in Southern Europe.
10. Art. 11 Serbian Law on Local Self-Government 2002; art. 133 Constitution of Croatia; articles 80 ff. FYROM LAW on LSG.

11. See www.ohr.int for the text of the so-called Sarajevo-Agreement (27 March 2002) as well as the constitutional amendments finally imposed by the High Representative Wolfgang Petritsch.
12. Very important to this extent is the practical support given by the network of the Association of Agencies for Local Democracy, see http://www.ldaaonline.org/.

# 6
# Institutions and Entrepreneurship: A Comparative Evaluation in SEE

*Bruno Dallago*

## Introduction

Entrepreneurs are a driving force of transformation in that they activate the new market institutions, including the new private sector; innovate products and processes, markets and social relations; assist companies privatization and restructuring; support competition and transform economic organization. However, there is no guarantee that privatization and liberalization result in entrepreneurship: it may result in 'proprietorship', that is, aversion to capital accumulation and competition and orientation towards consumption of the surplus (Scase 2003). As a consequence, entrepreneurs often make no productive contribution at all by producing goods and services that increase the overall economic value produced in the economy, and in some cases play a destructive role (Baumol 1993, 2004).

The quality of institutions is important in favouring entrepreneurs over proprietors. However, in a mutable context as that of the SEE, where institutions may not support market competition, the competitive threat to the entrepreneurs' profit may not work and the entrepreneurs' progressive role may be jeopardized. Although it is necessary to implement those '. . . institutional arrangements that encourage the exercise of entrepreneurship and that provide incentives for it to take productive directions' (Baumol 1993: 15), this approach is insufficient amid systemic transformation. Even supposing that institutions condensate history and culture, this overlooks the different variables that are important in a transformation context, including individual capabilities, the state, reform policies, the interplay between formal and informal institutions (North 1990; Pejovich 1998).

A Baumolian perspective requires assessing whether transformation can be interpreted as a move in the direction of productive entrepreneurship. Since Scase (2003) warned us that this was not so and considering that '. . . the role of SMEs varies at different stages of the transformation process as well as in different national contexts' (Smallbone and Welter 2001: 252), I will consider whether successive changes in institutions and policies represent such a desired move and consider whether the resulting entrepreneurial capabilities are supporting productive outcomes.

In spite of some progress, the situation of SMEs in SEE is unsatisfactory. SMEs are too few and weak and people in business are dissatisfied with policies and with the structures dealing with SME activity and regulation. This dissatisfaction is part of the more general concern for the dismal progress of various reforms in the area. Statistics have recorded a growing numbers of SMEs, although in relative terms the situation is disappointing compared to Western or Central Europe (Table 6.1). SMEs are seldom competitive in the market and survive protected in traditional, poor market niches. The core issue then is: how is it possible to foster entrepreneurship supporting organizational transformation *and* investment, innovation, and competitiveness?

The starting conditions in the SEE are discussed in the next section, showing that entrepreneurs did not start from scratch. The first steps of institutional reform are also discussed. The subsequent section deals with the features of the business environment and the qualities of entrepreneurs in assessing whether contextual and human factors may strengthen or counteract institutional variables. The remaining sections are devoted to the obstacles to entrepreneurship and the needs for policies; a discussion of the role of the irregular economy and its consequences for entrepreneurship, and finally in conclusion.

*Table 6.1* The number of enterprises in 2000–2002

| | *SMEs* | | *Micro enterprises* | | *Large enterprises* | | *No. of SMEs per 1000 inhabitants* |
|---|---|---|---|---|---|---|---|
| | *No.* | *Share* | *No.* | *Share* | *No.* | *Share* | |
| Albania | 56,237 | 99.6 | 54,145 | 95.8 | 253 | 0.4 | 18.1 |
| BiH | 30,000 | 99.3 | 25,600 | 84.8 | 200 | 0.7 | 7.0 |
| Bulgaria | 224,211 | 99.7 | 207,643 | 92.3 | 741 | 0.3 | 27.6 |
| Croatia | 63,135 | 99.3 | 41,988 | 66.1 | 426 | 0.7 | 13.7 |
| Macedonia | 27,938 | 99.3 | 25,985 | 92.4 | 194 | 0.7 | 14.0 |
| Moldova | 22,138 | 89.7 | 17,760 | 71.9 | 2,547* | 10.3 | 6.1 |
| Romania | 612,862 | 99.7 | 311,260 | 50.6 | 1,955 | 0.3 | 27.4 |
| SCG | 66,968 | 98.9 | 64,002 | 94.5 | 742 | 1.1 | 7.8 |
| Czech Republic | 876,990 | 99.8 | 830,601 | 94.5 | 1,671 | 0.2 | 85.1 |
| Hungary | 858,981 | 99.9 | 827,806 | 96.3 | 1,041 | 0.1 | 85.9 |
| Poland | 3,368,367 | 99.8 | 3,206,452 | 95.0 | 6,589 | 0.2 | 87.0 |
| Slovakia | 365,783 | 100.0 | 354,373 | 96.8 | 160 | 0.0 | 67.7 |
| Slovenia | 26,915 | 98.9 | 22,285 | 81.9 | 308 | 1.1 | 13.5 |
| EU-19** | 2,041,500 | 99.8 | 1,904,000 | 93.1 | 40,000 | 0.2 | 52.8 |

*Notes*: *In Moldova large enterprises have more than 50 employees.
**EU 15 + Iceland, Liechtenstein, Norway, Switzerland.
*Source*: Based on EBRD (2004b), p. 12.

## Starting conditions: transformation and entrepreneurship

By defining the rules of economic activity, institutions determine the relative returns to entrepreneurship in terms of opportunities, income and wealth, power, and prestige, thus moulding incentives to entrepreneurship. However, in the pre-transformation circumstances systemic features prevented entrepreneurship from taking the forms we are used in market economies. The little entrepreneurship that existed was concentrated in the ruling Party and perhaps in the top echelons of public administration (Grossman 1983). After economic reforms in the 1960s a part of the entrepreneurial role was delegated to firms. The situation was somehow different in the self-managed system. Here entrepreneurship was placed in the ruling party, but much was delegated to republican governments and also to firms.

The past survives in the mind and behaviour (routines) of people and organizations, in their knowledge and social and economic relations. The influence of the past constrains the possibilities and directions of change, causing learning and adaptation costs, and generating diverse transformation paths in different countries (Dallago 1996). The push to change introduces a drive to recombine new elements with pre-existing ones (Stark 1996) and perhaps gives a new sense to pre-existing elements. All this is under the influence of the economic system, which requires a certain level of interaction and complementarity among institutions (Pryor 2005a,b).

The CEECs that started transformation earlier among more favourable internal and external conditions can offer some insight into the process (Dallago and McIntyre 2003). Although there are large inter-country differences, the old economic system was generally unfavourable to the development of SMEs and systemic change alone was insufficient to generate productive entrepreneurs, due to reform and policy inconsistency and the effect of pre-existing factors. Indeed, various uncertainties and unfavourable contextual features are also noticed in these countries and the stabilization and successful development of large firms – with which SMEs can compete or enter supply relationship – are crucial factors for SME modernization and growth. Thus economic growth and growth promoting policies are important prerequisites of SME development.

The experience of CEECs shows that the systemic context has a crucial importance for the quality of SMEs. More than looking at the intention of reformers, it is important to assess the kind of reforms that they have *actually* implemented and their success in enforcing them. To this purpose it is necessary first to assess the systemic context within which SME-specific reform takes place. This appears to be satisfactory in SEE: fundamental general reforms are working or nearly so (see Introduction). However, reasons for concern arise from the incompleteness of the reform of large firms. Large-scale privatization and governance and enterprise restructuring have both a long road ahead. The systemic context for the development of SME entrepreneurship is still incomplete (EBRDb 2004).

Secondly, definitely less satisfactory is the situation concerning governance and enterprise restructuring, infrastructure reform, and reform of securities market and non-banking financial institutions, with the partial exception of Croatia, Bulgaria, and also Romania for infrastructure (Table 6.2). These EBRD indicators present a broad picture of progress in the evolution of a market economy in SEE countries. However, individual indicators are of different relevance for SMEs and entrepreneurship development. A tentative conclusion is that those institutions that are most important for supporting productive entrepreneurship are the least developed. Although small-scale privatization is practically completed in all countries, competition institutions and policies are in a dismal situation in practically all countries. Only slightly more favourable conclusions can be reached for legal effectiveness (see Introduction), infrastructure reform, and reform of non-banking financial institutions. Banking sector reform and interest rates liberalization have not yet reached a satisfactory level, particularly so for SME development.

Since reforms concerning most SMEs are still largely in the future, institutions governing the allocation of existing entrepreneurial supply are not favourable to address such supply to productive uses. The context where entrepreneurs operate is non-competitive, the legal system is ineffective, infrastructure is still largely undeveloped and unfit to support competitive market activity by providing modern transportation and communication technologies and solutions and reducing their costs.

Along with these constraints, the supply with financial services is also unfit to promote productive entrepreneurial SMEs: securities market and non-banking financial institutions are in an unsatisfactory situation and even banking-sector reform has not been completed. Finally, privatization reform, including governance and restructuring of large companies is unfinished and in various countries not really satisfactory. All this simply means that SMEs work and have real and tradable market value, not that they perform a productive function as defined above.

The outcome, then, is rather controversial. Although some basic institutions vital for a market economy are in place, the lack of perhaps the most crucial ones – in particular, competition – suggests that it may be easier for SMEs to take advantage of the working institutions – primarily, price liberalization – and to benefit without having to produce value in a competitive market.

However, it is important to realise that individual countries have rather distinct situations. In particular, the most promising situation is found in Bulgaria and Croatia. In these two countries the institutional setting is closest to the one that should foster productive entrepreneurship. In other countries, notably Serbia and Montenegro, BiH and Albania the situation is clearly less favourable. Romania and Macedonia are in between. However, in some fields – notably, legal effectiveness – the situation of these latter countries is favourable. Given this rather inconsistent picture, more information is needed to reach a strong conclusion. Variables such as the entrepreneurs' capabilities, interfirm

*Table 6.2* A comparative assessment of reforms in SEE: EBRD indices

| | *Governance and enterprise restructuring* | | *Competition policy* | | *Infrastructure reform* | *Banking sector reform and interest rates liberalisation* | | *Reform of securities market and non-banking financial institutions* | |
|---|---|---|---|---|---|---|---|---|---|
| | *1991* | *2003* | *1991* | *2003* | *2003* | *1991* | *2003* | *1991* | *2003* |
| Albania | 1.0 | 2 | 1.0 | 2− | 2 | 1.0 | 2+ | 1.0 | 2− |
| BiH | n.a. | 2 | n.a. | 1 | 2+ | na | 2+ | na | 2− |
| Bulgaria | 1.0 | 3− | 2.0 | 2+ | 3− | 1.0 | 3+ | 1.0 | 2+ |
| Croatia | 1.0 | 3− | 1.0 | 2+ | 3− | 1.0 | 4− | 1.0 | 3− |
| Macedonia | 1.0 | 2+ | 1.0 | 2 | 2 | 1.0 | 3 | 1.0 | 2− |
| Romania | 1.0 | 2 | 1.0 | 2+ | 3 | 1.0 | 3− | 1.0 | 2 |
| Yu/S&M | | 2 | | 1 | 2 | | 2+ | | 2 |
| *Unweighted average* | *1.0* | *2+* | *1.2* | *2−* | *2+* | *1.0* | *3−* | *1.0* | *2* |

*Source*: EBRD, *Transformation Report*, various issues. Ratings go from 1 (little change compared to pre-transformation situation) to 4+ (standards and performance typical of advanced market economies).

relations that form the business environment, and policies, in particular SME specific policies, are considered as determining the chances of productive outcomes.

## Business environment and entrepreneurial capabilities

The positive relation existing between long-run growth of per capita GDP and institutional quality at the beginning of the period is well known in the literature (Rodrik *et al.* 2002). Fries *et al.* (2003) found that in transformation countries there is a significant relationship on a country average basis between the quality of the business environment in 1999 and the rate of investment in the period 1999–2001. Although SEE countries had a weaker business environment than CEECs and Baltic countries and therefore had a lower investment performance, they experienced an important improvement in the business environment and therefore of investment performance in the period considered.

The quality of interfirm relations, and the firms relation with the organizations controlling the smooth and orderly working of the business environment, are very important for ensuring productive outcomes of economic activity. Trust can substantially decrease transaction costs and can provide powerful incentives. Measuring trust between firms as the level of prepayment demanded by suppliers from their customers in advance of delivery, Reiser *et al.* (2003) confirmed earlier findings that trust is higher where firms have confidence in third-party enforcement through the legal system. However, the fairness and honesty of the courts are more important determinants of inter-firm trust than the courts' efficiency or ability to enforce decisions. Also business networks are important in building trust: networks based around personal ties – family and friends – and business associations actively promote the development of trust, while business networks based on enterprise insiders and government agencies do not.

Firm origin and ownership are important for enterprise performance, although the old problem of biased selection of firms to be privatized remains open. Fries *et al.* (2003) found that new private firms have investment rates about 18 per cent higher and real revenue growth rates about 21 per cent higher than privatized firms, while state-owned firms have rates 9 per cent and 11 per cent lower, respectively. Moreover, firms reporting to have little or no market power have significantly lower rates of investment and real revenue growth than do firms with significant market power, as measured by the perceived elasticity of demand.

The Bulgarian Agency for SMEs provides some further interesting hints on the relation between entrepreneurial capabilities and the business environment. This can be interpreted as a sign of developing regional and industrial dualism in Bulgaria, similar to what has been observed in other transformation countries. Most SMEs (roughly two-thirds) produce their turnover in the municipality where they are registered. Export-orientation of SMEs is rather low and connected to the role of foreign capital and dynamic entrepreneurship. Indeed, 6 per cent of SMEs achieve at least 70 per cent of their sales abroad. The concentration of export-oriented SMEs is higher in the South-Western region, thanks to the role of the Greek capital.

A slight reverse correlation can be observed between the share of overall employment in SMEs and the level of local development. In the relatively better-off regions, SMEs use less labour-intensive techniques by investing more and attracting more FDIs. They are also more active in the national and international market and are clearly endowed with superior entrepreneurial capabilities. In 2001–2002 SME growth accounted for about 40 per cent of the increase in employment. This growth was particularly significant in half of the micro-enterprises, while the most dynamic and larger SMEs grew by investing in machinery and not by increasing employment.

The dualism hypothesis is supported by the investment behaviour of SMEs and their employment policies. In 2001 28 per cent of SMEs have invested in new equipment, but this share varies remarkably throughout regions: it is 43 per cent in the North-Eastern region and is between one-half and one-third of that in the South-East and South-West region. It varies also between micro-companies, which invest the least, and the others, nearly half of which have invested in new machinery and equipment in 2001. A predictable result was that firms with better financial indicators made greater investments in new equipment. SMEs serving local markets have also to accept higher price elasticity than export-oriented companies, although nearly 90 per cent of SMEs stated that demand for their products was determined by low prices.

The findings for Bulgaria are rather similar to those for other countries (Dallago 2003) and may perhaps be generalized: (a) newly established SMEs are more efficient because they are born in the new institutional context and embed new institutions, along with operating in more dynamic markets; (b) more open SMEs selling much of their production outside their location also invest more; and (c) smaller firms are generally more traditional and increase production by using more (unskilled) labour, while larger dynamic SMEs also invest in machinery. These achievements are primarily based on the quality of the human factor starting from entrepreneurial and networking capabilities. Institutions fostering productive entrepreneurship are then only the fundamental starting point: capabilities of the human factor are also important (ASME 2003).

## SME policies

Since entrepreneurial capabilities, institutions and contextual features are often unsatisfactory, spontaneous processes are unlikely to be sufficient and policies assume a particularly important role for economic development perspectives.

Policies for promoting entrepreneurship have many potential advantages, but also have many limits (OECD 2003). Among the latter it should be remembered that firm creation can displace existing firms, the outcome of policies depends on initial conditions and factors external to local control (for example, interest rates, macroeconomic situation), and that policy implementation and outcome are under the influence of many asymmetries and trade-offs.

Should we, therefore, assess policies performance against a benchmark of 'ideal' policies? This is hardly acceptable, since policies must be tailored to the context and the actors. Should policies be assessed against a benchmark, worked out for situations supposedly similar to the ones under scrutiny? 'Washington consensus' policies are of this type, yet far from having been successful and ripen with unforeseen and unwanted consequences (Stiglitz 1998). Should we assess policies against the specific features of the context and actors? This is obviously the best approach. However, its implementation is difficult, particularly in transformation countries and would prevent any direct comparison and general conclusion, except on how good different governments were in devising and implementing effective policies.

Should we ask the 'users' directly what do they think of policies? This 'subjective' approach may perhaps be a good compromise, since it can be hoped that users (such as businessmen) have a good knowledge of the context they are operating in and their needs and so they can evaluate properly the features and role of policies. However this approach may support the actors' entrenchment. Indeed, much depends on of those in business the capabilities. If they are entrepreneurs, chances are that their assessment reflects the usefulness of policies in promoting productive entrepreneurship. However, if they are proprietors, their assessment is likely to reflect their perception of how well and how far policies create opportunities for and protect rent-seeking.

Enterprise Policy Performance Assessments (EPPA) takes this latter perspective. These reports are prepared by the OECD and EBRD in the framework of the Stability Pact. The methodology used has been designed to 'provide insights and assessments of the performance in the implementation of policies to improve the investment environment for business'. The assessments are based on extensive interview programmes, firm surveys and findings from focus groups. In particular, the EBRD-World Bank Business Environment and Enterprise Performance Survey (BEEPS) asks enterprises to evaluate economic governance and state institutions and assess the extent to which the business environment creates obstacles to the operation and growth of their businesses. The assessment focuses on SMEs (according to EU definition) and considers six complex dimensions of good practice in the following policy areas (Table 6.3):

- the institutional framework for SME policy (institutions);
- rule of law and the regulatory environment (regulation);
- tax policy for small businesses (tax);

*Table 6.3* Average ratings of the six dimensions of good practice by SME owners and managers, 2002

| | *Institutions* | *Regulation* | *Tax* | *Finance* | *Advice* | *Incubators* | *Sample** |
|---|---|---|---|---|---|---|---|
| Albania | 2.0 | 1.8 | 1.7 | 2.3 | 2.5 | 1.5 | 151 (32-47-20) |
| BiH | 1.5 | 1.6 | 1.9 | 2.3 | 2.3 | 1.8 | 151 (50-23-27) |
| Bulgaria | 2.3 | 2.0 | 2.1 | 2.1 | 2.9 | 2.7 | 211 (46-36-18) |
| Croatia | 2.6 | 2.2 | 2.3 | 3.0 | 2.9 | 2.8 | 158 (54-25-21) |
| Macedonia | 2.1 | 1.7 | 2.0 | 2.1 | 2.6 | 2.2 | 153 (38-39-23) |
| Moldova | 2.0 | 2.1 | 2.1 | 2.4 | 2.7 | 2.5 | 153 (38.6-38.6-22.9) |
| Montenegro | 2.0 | 2.4 | 2.0 | 1.8 | 3.3 | 2.7 | n.a. |
| Romania | 1.8 | 1.8 | 1.6 | 2.0 | 2.3 | 2.1 | 217 (36-35-29) |
| Serbia | 1.1 | 1.2 | 1.6 | 1.3 | 3.1 | 0.0 | 203 (42-33-25) |
| *Unweighted average* | *1.9* | *1.9* | *1.9* | *2.1* | *2.7* | *2.0* | |

*Notes*: *Number of SMEs in the sample (% of micro enterprises, % small, % medium-sized); n.a: not applicable; ratings are: 1 = very poor; 2 = poor; 3 = satisfactory; 4 = good; and 5 = very good.
*Source*: OECD–EBRD, various issues.

- financial instruments for fostering new and small businesses (finance);
- advisory services supplied to new and small businesses (advice);
- the implementation of business incubators (incubators).

In SEE the most problematic are the first three dimensions, that is institutions, regulation, and tax. Advice is the least problematic dimension, with finance and incubators in intermediate conditions. In short, the most problematic dimensions are those which are the most critical for SMEs, those that cannot be supplied by the market.[1] This conclusion leads to the critical issue of the role, nature, and quality of the state. However, these remaining three dimensions only rate between poor and nearly satisfactory.

The situation varies through countries, with Croatia generally better off and BiH and Albania worse off, although it should be noted that in no country is the situation is good according to any of the dimensions considered. Interestingly, Montenegro is a front-runner in regulation and advice, but is a defaulter in finance. Since this kind of rating has much to do with the entrepreneurs' perceptions, that is their cognitive abilities, one should know how they evaluate their perception. Is it against a (gloomy) past or against (optimistic) expectations? Do they express disappointment because the new institutions do not work or because push rent-seekers into a competitive arena?

Table 6.4 illustrates the factors that are perceived to be obstacles to doing business. First, on average and similar to other transformation countries, obstacles are perceived to be more than minor ones. Two countries stand out: Croatia, where obstacles are considered to be on average a little less than minor ones, and Albania, where the average perception approaches that of being obstacles being moderate.

Secondly, no obstacle is considered to be a major one. The two most important obstacles (economic policy uncertainty and macroeconomic instability) are moderate ones on average. Both have to do with the broad context and reflect the unbalanced macroeconomic situation and the inability of policy makers to find a stable set of effective policy norms. However, in Macedonia, Moldova, and Albania both obstacles are perceived as rather serious.

At the other extreme, issues having to do with infrastructure (telecommunications, transportation, and electricity), property rights (access to land, title or leasing of land), and labour (labour regulations, skills and education of workers) are perceived as minor obstacles at most. Even organized and street crime are minor obstacles, although with inter-country differences. Between these two extremes there are those obstacles pertaining more directly to SMEs' activity, ranked from being moderate obstacles to minor ones: taxation, financing, corruption, contract law, competition, market regulation, licensing, in decreasing order of importance.

An indirect way to discriminate between the features of the context and governments on one side and those of enterprises and entrepreneurs on the other side is to look not at the actors' perception, which is inevitably subjective,

*Table 6.4* Perceived obstacles to doing business, 2002

| | *Unweighted average* |
|---|---|
| Economic policy uncertainty | 3.1 |
| Macroeconomic instability | 3.0 |
| Tax rates | 2.9 |
| Cost of financing | 2.8 |
| Tax administration | 2.6 |
| Corruption | 2.6 |
| Access to financing | 2.5 |
| Anti-competitive practices of other producers | 2.5 |
| Functioning of the judiciary | 2.4 |
| Contract violations by customers and suppliers | 2.3 |
| Business licensing and permits | 2.2 |
| Customs and trade regulations | 2.2 |
| Organized crime | 2.1 |
| Street crime | 2.1 |
| Skills and education of workers | 1.9 |
| Electricity | 1.7 |
| Labour regulations | 1.7 |
| Transportation | 1.7 |
| Title or leasing of land | 1.6 |
| Access to land | 1.6 |
| Telecommunications | 1.5 |
| *Unweighted average value* | *2.2* |

*Notes*: Ratings are: 1 = no obstacle; 2 = minor obstacle; 3 = moderate obstacle; 4 = major obstacle. Sample as in Table 6.3.
*Source*: OECD–EBRD, various issues.

but at the market evaluation. The dimension in which we can get the closest to obtaining such an 'objective' evaluation is financing (Volz 2004).

There are various reasons to be cautious when considering the banks' evaluation of SMEs. Banking reform in SEE is still incomplete[2] and banks, even in the most advanced transformation countries, are SMEs averse (Csaba 2003). Bank intermediation to the private sector remains exceeding low in most countries (Figure 6.1). In Croatia and also BiH the situation is somewhat better, but still far from EU benchmark. As a consequence, bank credit is a minor financial source for SMEs (on average, the fourth source of financing, after family and individual capital, repatriated capital, and micro-finance), and is valued as poor (Table 6.5).

There is lack of trust in financial market institutions: leasing, venture capital and equity funds, and credit unions are evaluated worse than commercial banks. Micro-finance, a less demanding form of financing, is valued better, although still not satisfactory. It is probably fair to say that there is mutual mistrust: SMEs do not trust banks and banks do not trust SMEs. Indirect support to this statement comes from the data shown in Table 6.6: it is consistently more difficult to obtain credit for financing new investment that for financing working capital.

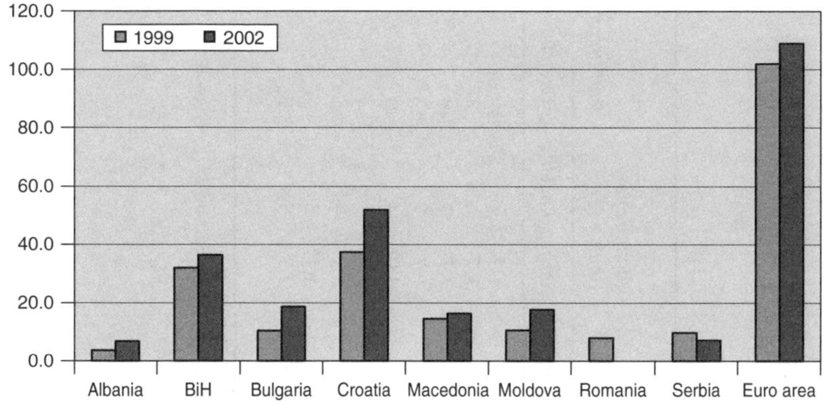


*Source*: OECD–EBRD, Various issues.

*Figure 6.1* Domestic credit to the private sector (% of GDP)

A prudent conclusion, then, is that banks are not eager to lend to SMEs and when doing so they prefer low-risk lending (for working capital). SMEs may be unable to convince banks to finance their investments for different reasons. First is the level of collateral: 124 per cent of the value of the loan on average (EBRD 2004). Secondly, SMEs prefer cheaper, less complex and softer sources of finance (own sources, family's and friends' sources), in particular for establishing SMEs. Thirdly, SMEs are unable to present bankable projects for new investment. This may be because the SMEs aren't capable or because of their aversion to risk and development. In either case the weak level of productive entrepreneurial capabilities of the average SME may require specific support: forcing improvement of context and policies may not be sufficient if people in business are averse to act as entrepreneurs. The fact that advice receives the highest score among the dimensions of good practice by SME owners and managers (Table 6.3) in all SEE countries, with partial exception of Croatia, may be seen as an indirect proof that this is what SMEs need most to overcome are contextual uncertainty and weak capabilities.

## A difficult guest: the irregular economy

So far we have examined the role of institutions and policies for entrepreneurship as if only formal institutions and consistent enforcement exist. It is time to ease these constraints. Informal institutions are hardly policy variables, or at least they are not in the short term. When formal and informal institutions are misaligned, a conflict between formal institutions and actual incentives to economic actors follows. This conflict generates the irregular economy.[3] By

*Table 6.5* Relative importance of main financial sources accessed by SMEs, 2002

| | *Family or individual capital* | | *Repatriated capital* | | *Micro-finance* | | *Commercial bank loans* | | *Leasing* | | *Venture capital/equity funds* | | *Credit unions* | |
|---|---|---|---|---|---|---|---|---|---|---|---|---|---|---|
| | *Rating* | *Ranking* | *Rating* | *Ranking* | *Rating* | *Ranking* | *Rating* | *Ranking* | *Rating* | *Ranking* | *Rating* | *Ranking* | *Rating* | *Ranking* |
| Albania | 2.8 | 1 | 2.2 | 3 | 2.3 | 2 | 2.0 | 4 | 1.5 | 6 | 1.4 | 7 | 1.9 | 5 |
| BiH | 3.6 | 1 | 2.5 | 2 | 2.4 | 3 | 2.2 | 4 | 1.7 | 5 | 1.7 | 6 | 1.3 | 7 |
| Bulgaria | 4.1 | 1 | 1.8 | 6 | 2.4 | 3 | 2.2 | 4 | 2.7 | 2 | 1.7 | 7 | 1.8 | 5 |
| Croatia | 3.5 | 1 | 2.2 | 6 | 2.4 | 4 | 2.7 | 3 | 2.9 | 2 | 1.7 | 7 | 2.2 | 5 |
| Macedonia | 4.2 | 1 | 3.3 | 3 | 3.5 | 2 | 1.3 | 7 | 2.6 | 5 | 3.0 | 4 | 2.0 | 6 |
| Moldova | 3.4 | 1 | 2.7 | 2 | 2.5 | 3 | 2.4 | 4 | 2.0 | 7 | 2.4 | 5 | 2.2 | 6 |
| Montenegro | 1.8 | 3 | 2.9 | 1 | 2.7 | 2 | 1.8 | 3 | n.a | – | n.a | – | n.a. | – |
| Romania | 4.7 | 1 | 0.1 | 6 | 2.3 | 3 | 1.5 | 4 | 1.2 | 5 | 4.1* | 2 | – | – |
| *Unweighted average* | *3.5* | *1.3* | *2.2* | *3.6* | *2.6* | *2.8* | *2.0* | *4.1* | *2.1* | *4.6* | *2.3* | *5.4* | *1.9* | *5.7* |

*Notes*: *Capital from 'mother' company; n.a: not applicable; ratings are: 1 = very poor; 2 = poor; 3 = satisfactory; 4 = good; and 5 = very good.
*Source*: OECD–EBRD, various issues.

*Table 6.6* SME's perception of ease of obtaining loan for working capital/Investment needs, 2002 (%)*

| | *Impossible* | | *Very difficult* | | *Fairly difficult* | | *Fairly easy* | | *Very easy* | |
|---|---|---|---|---|---|---|---|---|---|---|
| | *Working capital* | *New investment* | *Working capital* | *New investment* | *Working capital* | *New investment* | *Working capital* | *New investment* | *Working capital* | *New investment* |
| Albania | 2 | 10.5 | 18 | 25.6 | 34 | 31.6 | 35 | 21.7 | 3 | 2.0 |
| BiH | 3 | 6 | 15 | 22 | 27 | 31 | 34 | 23 | 7 | 4 |
| Bulgaria | 7 | 12 | 41 | 40 | 27 | 27 | 14 | 11 | 4 | 3 |
| Croatia | 7.0 | 6.3 | 10.8 | 17.7 | 16.5 | 24.1 | 33.5 | 22.8 | 20.3 | 15.8 |
| Macedonia | 1 | 12 | 21 | 35 | 27 | 27 | 39 | 11 | 3 | 3 |
| Moldova | 1 | 12 | 21 | 35 | 27 | 27 | 39 | 11 | 3 | 3 |
| Romania | 6.9 | 10.6 | 17.1 | 21.7 | 21.7 | 27.2 | 28.6 | 24.4 | 19.4 | 10.1 |
| Serbia | 2.0 | 8.4 | 7.9 | 15.3 | 18.2 | 20.7 | 29.1 | 15.3 | 20.2 | 9.9 |
| *Unweighted average* | *3.7* | *9.7* | *19.0* | *26.5* | *24.8* | *27.0* | *31.5* | *17.5* | *10.0* | *6.4* |

*Note*: *Totals not equally 100% are due to unavailable answers.
*Source*: OECD–EBRD, various issues.

violating (formal) institutions, the violator may either save on transaction costs (for example, contract implementation costs) or may gain from the infringement of property rights by appropriating income or assets that belong to another legitimate owner (for example, tax or social security evasion). When this event occurs, the conflicting incentives thus generated increase the costs of maintaining and enforcing the institutional environment.

While, logically, the distinction between the irregular and the formal economy is clear, it is more difficult to separate statistically the two and distinguish them statistically from measurement errors and weakness. Although the absolute value of quantitative estimates may be questioned, there is no doubt that the irregular economy in SEE countries, although widespread before transformation, boomed during the last decade and a half (Schneider 2002; Vitosha Research 2004). Although EPPA reports do not consider explicitly the irregular economy, they take some important components into account, such as corruption, anti-competitive practices of other producers, contract violation by customers and suppliers (cf. Table 6.4).

Corruption and state capture are important components of the irregular economy that are widespread in SEE countries, with important inter-country diversities (Table 6.7). Based on the data supplied by the BEEPS surveys in 1999 and 2002, Steves and Rousso (2003) analysed the anti-corruption activities of 24 transformation countries in the period 1999–2002, including SEE countries. These activities are divided into omnibus anti-corruption programmes, legislative reform aimed at tackling corruption, and adherence to international anti-corruption conventions. The authors found that countries with low levels of administrative corruption were more likely to adopt intensive anti-corruption programmes than countries with high levels of administrative corruption, independent of the level of state capture, particularly in SEE.

Among SEE countries, high intensity reformers include Albania, Croatia, Bulgaria and Romania. These countries have high scores across all three indices. The group of medium-high intensity anti-corruption countries includes Moldova, and S&M. These countries have relatively high scores on the legal and international conventions indices and average scores on omnibus activities. However, for S&M scores are high on new legislative reforms and low on the conventions index. The medium-low reform group includes BiH, and FYR Macedonia. The countries in this group score low on omnibus reforms and closer to average on the legal and conventions indices. No SEE country is included in the low reform group of countries.

Across the transformation countries, omnibus anti-corruption programmes and membership in international anti-corruption conventions have not led to reductions in the level of either administrative corruption or state capture – at least in the relatively short period considered – while new or amended laws aimed at tackling corruption have led to reductions in administrative corruption, but not in levels of state capture. Another interesting finding is that perceptions of corruption – measured by the degree to which firms consider

*Table 6.7* Bribes and kickbacks paid and captor firms in 2002 (%)

| | *Bribes and kickbacks* | | | | | | *State capture* | | |
|---|---|---|---|---|---|---|---|---|---|
| | *Share of firms paying bribe tax*[1] | *Average bribe tax rate*[2] | *Average bribe tax*[3] | *Share of firms paying kickbacks*[1] | *Average kickback tax rate*[2] | *Average kickback tax*[3] | *Proportion of captor firms (laws and regulations)*[4] | *Proportion of firms affected by capture (laws and regulations)*[5] | *Proportion of firms affected by capture (courts)*[6] |
| Albania | 77.1 | 4.6 | 3.3 | 68.8 | 9.6 | 6.0 | 12.4 | 34.1 | 44.7 |
| BiH | 42.3 | 3.0 | 0.9 | 35.7 | 7.8 | 1.2 | 7.8 | 35.9 | 38.5 |
| Bulgaria | 51.2 | 4.2 | 1.9 | 37.2 | 8.5 | 2.5 | 10.0 | 38.8 | 45.6 |
| Croatia | 24.6 | 2.6 | 0.6 | 11.2 | 7.9 | 0.9 | 11.2 | 18.2 | 22.5 |
| Macedonia | 61.2 | 1.5 | 0.8 | 44.1 | 10.2 | 2.9 | 13.5 | 33.6 | 36.5 |
| Moldova | 53.4 | 4.0 | 2.1 | 14.9 | 5.0 | 0.7 | 8.6 | 28.8 | 43.7 |
| Romania | 54.9 | 4.7 | 2.6 | 26.3 | 8.1 | 2.1 | 4.7 | 21.4 | 24.3 |
| S&M | 54.0 | 4.0 | 1.5 | 52.0 | 6.8 | 1.8 | 11.2 | 25.7 | 25.2 |
| *Unweighted average* | *52.3* | *3.6* | *1.7* | *36.3* | *8.0* | *2.3* | *9.9* | *29.6* | *35.1* |

*Notes*: [1]Share of firms in each country paying at least some bribes and kickbacks in % of responding firms.
[2]The proportion of sales and of government contracts, respectively, paid in bribes and kickbacks averaged for all firms that made such payments.
[3]Calculated as unweighted averages of all responses, whether or not bribes and kickbacks were paid.
[4]Calculated as interaction of two questions: (a) one that asks firms to report if they attempted to influence the government and (b) a second that asks whether firms like theirs make any unofficial payments in attempt to influence the content of laws and regulations.
[5]Proportion of firms affected by capture (law and regulations is measured by a proportion of firms that perceive at least minor impact by unofficial payments to affect either parlamentarians or government officials and that are not themselves captor firms.
[6]Measured by a proportion of firms that perceive at least minor impact by private payments to affect decisions of either criminal or commercial courts.
*Source*: Fries *et al.* (2003), p. 25.

corruption being an obstacle to the operation and growth of their business – are positively correlated with the intensity of anti-corruption programmes. One plausible explanation is that by launching high-profile anti-corruption initiatives, governments may heighten business people's perceptions of the problem rather than reduce the impact of corruption on firms.

Albania and Macedonia offer two interesting opposing cases. Albania is the only country in which both state capture *and* administrative corruption and also the frequency of bribes have increased in the 1999–2002 period. FYR Macedonia has not developed any major component of omnibus anti-corruption strategies, but it was successful in bringing down levels of administrative corruption (although levels of state capture increased over this period).

Fries *et al.* (2003) find a strong association between business obstacles, added costs and constraints on business (such as corruption), private security protection or reliance on internal sources of finance. There also is a significant positive association between firms that engage in state capture and their average investment and real revenue growth rates. In the case of the 26 transformation countries considered, the authors found that those firms engaged in state capture have investment rates about 10 per cent higher and real revenue growth rates about 15 per cent higher than do other firms. However, those firms that reported being affected by state capture have slightly lower rates of productivity and sales growth than do other firms. Predictably, state capture is a means for those firms that engage in it, probably large firms, to strengthen their market position, at the expense of other firms, probably SMEs.

The research on the irregular economy in SEE suggests that much of it has an unproductive character and distorts competition. The irregular economy supplies economic actors with additional means and ways to pursue their economic goals (survival, profit, market share, rents) thus giving unfair competitive advantages to those who use it (Pinto 2004). The ability of firms to make use of the irregular economy allows them to decrease asymmetrically transaction costs and increase improperly their market opportunities. These firms are advantaged not because they are better in decreasing their costs through investment and productive innovation, but because they find unfair ways to avoid those costs. When capturing the state or evading taxes, the captor or escaper obtains unfair advantages in the form of unlawful transfers and other privileges. In all these cases entrepreneurship is unproductive or even destructive.

However, a firm may use the irregular economy to avoid unjustified costs that state capture by its competitors imposes. The irregular economy may also be a powerful mechanism supporting the firm's adaptation into a rapidly changing, highly unstable and unpredictable environment. Finally, there may be an irregular economy that changes with the firm life-cycle. The irregular economy, although unlawful, may help the growth of truly productive entrepreneurs in an environment that is hostile. Since marginal costs of using irregularities tend to increase when the firm grows and becomes more visible and reputation may have a market value, the firm may progressively abandon the irregular economy. Indeed, in a competitive context most firms are irregular only in part and their use of irregularities is often a counter-cyclical device.

## Conclusions

Reforming (formal) institution is fundamental for having entrepreneurship playing a productive role. Although starting conditions were not particularly favourable, the situation changed with transformation. However, reforms have not been particularly desirable and effective to streamline institutions in a productive sense. This concerns both general policies and SME-specific policies. The former have made the context often unfavourable to SMEs. The latter have too often promoted SMEs independently of their character. Consequently, SMEs are too few, too small, and too unproductive. The widespread irregular economy has weakened the virtues of regular institutions and offered alternative ways to survive and prosper. This outcome is explained in part with entrepreneurial capabilities, that depend on the entrepreneurs' origin and nature, and the lack of competition. However, another important explanation lies in the undeveloped features and role of the state (Smallbone 2005).

The above conclusions stress the complexity of transformation. Stabilizing and privatizing the economy and even setting (formal) institutions right are insufficient. Institutional reform should also take informal institutions into consideration and align the two, so that incentives are not contradictory, and should also discount for the irregular economy. This can be done by developing the role of the state according to the requirements of emerging market economies; devising and enforcing (productive) entrepreneurship-friendly regulation, entrepreneurial capacity building and education, and market capacity; avoiding crowding-out market-based institutions with undue interference; stimulating and supporting the cooperation and coordination of local actors, also with national and international ones.

An obvious attack against the irregular economy may be too costly during transformation and perhaps not even possible or socially advantageous. Formal institutions are still too weak and perhaps it is not even useful to oblige actors to strictly and immediately follow them. In addition, the irregular economy may provide a useful mechanism of adaptation and self-protection. However, particularly in its unproductive components, it may cause a permanent damage to the economic system of a country. If so, entrepreneurship will be unproductive and will contribute to the low competitiveness of the economy.

In these circumstances there is an important case for allocating resources to having the entire institutional setting right. This concerns formal institutions, informal institutions and the irregular economy, and particularly their interrelationship. The irregular economy has filled the institutional void that derived from the collapse of the old economic system. There is now need for a patient reform activity that aligns formal and informal institutions, fights the most unfavourable components of the irregular economy (usually the distributive ones) and progressively addresses the others towards formal institutions.

The nature of this interrelationship influences the outcome of the entrepreneurial game, that is whether entrepreneurs adapt to the new context and whether their activity is productive or unproductive or destructive. Concentrating only on formal institutions and disregarding their misalignments with informal institutions will lead to unforeseen consequences, undesired outcomes and higher costs of economic activity.

The situation in various SEE countries is still far from these requirements, although the situation varies from country to country and although promising progress has taken place. In general, SEE countries have plenty of entrepreneurial capabilities. However, much of these capabilities are allocated to uses that are socially and economically unproductive. Reallocating and upgrading them along productive lines requires rethinking policies implemented so far and accelerating some processes critical for rebuilding the economic and social fabric.

## Notes

1. The issues researched institution are: (a) institutions responsible for SME policy/strategy development; (b) government-approved strategy; (c) structured action plan for implementation of strategy; (d) existence of an institution responsible for policy/strategy of implementation; and (e) existence of budget for implementation of SME strategy.
2. The average EBRD evaluation of 2.8 means that there has been substantial progress in establishing bank solvency and of a framework for prudential supervision and regulation; full interest rate liberalization with little preferential access to cheap refinancing; significant lending to private enterprises and significant presence of private banks.
3. Also known as underground or black economy. I use the term irregular economy to stress its institutional origin.

# 7

# Elites in the Making, and Their Organizational Behaviour: Cases in Russia and the Balkans

*Bruno Grancelli and Antonio M. Chiesi*

## Introduction: beyond the debate on elite reproduction vs circulation

Postcommunist transformation has been aptly summarized as a process of 'making capitalism without capitalists' whereby the key players are former communist technocrats and (sometimes) dissident intellectuals, and not a propertied bourgeoisie (Eyal *et al.* 2000: 1). This phenomenon was conceptualized at the outset as 'political capitalism' (Hankiss 1990; Sztaniszkis 1991), but later on that concept turned out to be of limited heuristic value. Indeed a number of investigations on the reproduction–circulation of elites has revealed that a good deal of former nomenklatura members are among the losers in the transition for the conversion of their political capital into economic wealth was often unsuccessful (Szeleny and Szeleny 1995; Higley *et al.* 1998; Eyal *et al.* 2000). On the other hand, a high number of the former elite have been able to keep power, privilege and prestige also under the new regime, especially in Russia (Kryshtanovskaya and White 1996; Lazic 2000; Steen, and Gel'man 2003). The different degree of elite reproduction and circulation in the countries of CEE has been explained through the degree of cooptation of the intelligentsia or the formation of a counter-elite during the communist regime or the current stage of democratic consolidation (Szeleny and Szeleny 1995; Adam and Tomšič 2002); the political changes of the perestrojka years (Lane and Ross 1997); the impact of nationalist movements on elite selection, as in the former Yugoslavia (Lazic 2000). All these research show that nomenklatura is the past which is going to reproduce itself in the present to different extent. But the point is: what past, and what reproduction?

According to Eyal and Townsley (1995) the first issue to be tackled is that of continuities and changes in the class structure after the fall of communism and the second is whether the formation of nomenklatura had been an episode (however long lasting) in the history of Eastern Europe or if it was part of a wider historical legacy. Starting from the much cited essay of Konrad and Szeleny (1979), they state that, with the end of Stalinism, the possible games for 'the intellectuals on the road to power' were either an ideological compliance towards the party's leading role, on the one hand, or a culture of critical discourse, on the other. The outcome of such an analysis is that neither bureaucrats nor intellectuals had been playing the two games quoted above. In other words, under the previous regime there was not any clear cut division between a traditional Nomeklatura on one side and an intelligentsia with a 'class project' on the other: both groups defined one another through a long lasting interaction process moulded both by the worldviews of intellectuals, the social capital and the recruiting practices of the Nomeklatura (Eyal and Townsley 1995). The very mechanism at play was a strategy of a social group able to keep a quasi-monopoly of access to elite positions through marriages, sociability, bureaucratic patronage and entry barriers. This upper class did not become a hegemonic class, though. The intelligentsia should have become so in its road to power if its privileges had been legitimized by universalistic criteria. But I was not so. This is then the old picture of an upper class that reproduced itself without bothering much either of official ideology or meritocratic criteria of promotion (Eyal and Towsley 1995; Hanley *et al.* 1995; Eyal *et al.* 2000).

But nowadays, after 15 years of postcommunist transformation the central issue is to what extent the post-1989 elite may still be considered as the Nomeklatura successor, and an upper class in the sense referred to above. The answer which emerged in the debate among 'elitist' and 'transitologist' scholars of a decade ago was positive, especially for the countries of interest here, namely Russia and the Balkans: the concept of upper class maintains its validity insofar as in all socialist countries, with the exception of Poland, and partly Hungary, a counter-elite could not form outside the communist party. But if it is true that communist elites were embedded in the history of these countries, as the persisting difficulties in the emergence of a counter-elite seem to demonstrate, then the dichotomy reproduction/circulation would loose much of its significance in that circulation at individual level might just be the reproduction of advantages and privileges as during the previous regime, while forms of reproduction might be based on meritocratic criteria (Eyal and Townsley 1995).

This adaptation of most of the former economic elite based on the possession of human capital gets confirmation from research whereby the reproduction/circulation issue has been framed within specific organizational environments such as that, for instance, on the career patterns of a group of former *kombinat* directors in the former GDR (Steger and Lang 2003). But adaptation is not necessarily based on the possession of human capital in that what matters also are the forms of social capital in use under the old regime. In other words, the dichotomies old-new elites and reproduction-circulation are going to loose much sense. What has coalesced at sub-state level is an amalgam of political, administrative and business elites overwhelmingly from the communist era that used their networks to colonize the new elected assemblies, to 'regroup' and consolidate their control over the local economy, and in doing so displayed political pragmatism combined with *enrichissez-vous* practices (Steen and Gel'man 2003).

Indeed in the Balkans, and in Russia (as a control case), new institutional arrangements are nowadays in place. The basic issue though is the capacity of the 'elite amalgam' quoted above to meet the challenges of societal modernization and economic change. In this respect, understanding just who the elites are, and where do they come from, is not enough to tackle this issue: we also need to explore values, motivations, behavioural patterns, and networks of the key actors in the transformation process (Steen and Gel'man 2003). The evidence on these issues is really scarce and unsystematic but, if appropriately framed, it can yield useful insights for further research anyhow.

A note on this possible framework cannot but start from the generally acknowledged fact that while the influence of experts, EU institutions, professional press and competition have changed the cognitive patterns of local key actors, all this does not greatly impinge on their actual behaviour. According to Jeffrey Hass this gap between the public discourse and the individual behaviour may be solved not just through competition as by enforcement mechanisms devised by the state that may be isomorphic (people with new cultural capital that rise through the ranks) and/or coercive (pressure on organizations through resource dependency). In other words, what is deemed important is not so much the direct role of social capital in economic development as the state capacity to enforce new rules and cultural constraints. Within this framework, the issue of local development is explicitly put aside for regional governments 'tend to influence incentive more than perceptions,' and this is seen as not so important for an analysis that should be centred not so much on policies as on the way economic principles are created and activities carried out (Hass 1999).

But one may ask: why should perceptions be more important than incentives for understanding economic activities? Why should we not focus on the links between the social/cultural capital of the key actors of economic change where the central state is not so developmental? A proper answer to these questions has been provided by those scholars who point to the risk of an 'institutional disjuncture' between imposed institutions and the norms and practices of key actors whose behaviour is still largely path dependent. In other words, a risk do indeed exist that institutional rationalization gets out of touch with the social capital of the broader society. In fact, it is worth remembering that those of interest here are 'hour-glass societies' in which social ties are strong both at the base (families and friends) and at the top (bond of trust among key actors in the polity-economy) while the links between these two spheres are limited, weak and full of distrust . In societies such as these the newly created institutions are largely unable to deliver appropriate performance levels with negative consequences in terms of legitimacy and stability (Fedderke *et al.* 1999). Thus the basic research questions becomes: what are the actors who should straddle the divide between the two level of the hour-glass-society?

The research hypothesis is that they are, to a large extent, all those young people who have got new cultural capital abroad and are working in private and public organizations on which the processes of local development are based. What kind of human capital do they have? To what extent are they able to promote learning and organizational innovation? Where are they? How much does the gap between perceptions and actual behaviour applies to them? And, finally, what kind of incentive do they have to work at home instead of emigrating?

This paper provides some evidence and preliminary remarks on these issues and is based both on secondary sources and semi-structured interviews with a small sample of 22 young managers and official from the Balkans who have been attending the Master on Comparative Local Development at the University of Trento in the last two years. The first section highlights few basic features of organizational environments whereby different groups of the upper class (established or in the making) are playing their games, namely the state apparatus, local administration and enterprises (multinational and local). The second section points to continuities and changes in the organizational behaviour of key actors with reference to the spread of a culture of resource-dependency which, however, do not prevent the emergence of some positive trends in local development.

## Elites in the making in different organizational environments

Area studies on different aspects of postcommunist transformations reveals some common trends despite the diversities between nations and regions. Worth recalling are, for instance, the 'revolution of deputies' (Szeleny *et al.* 1995), the correlation between the degree of elite circulation with the pace and quality of institutional change so that where the extant indicators are low, the outsiders tend to enter public administration more than business (Lane and Ross 1997). As for the economic elite, the gathered data seem to validate the hypothesis that enterprise managers appear as a bloc hostile to radical reforms and favourable, instead, to a gradual (and interstitial) formation of market institutions (Grancelli 1997). However, despite multiple signs of elite reproduction, cultural capital and individual skills (and not just know who) are of growing importance. But not the same importance in different regions, sectors, administrations and firms, and this should be taken into due account.

### The weak state syndrome

The country which has been singled out here is Romania for it is scoring consistently poorly in the IMF and European Commission's annual reports, but also because of the availability of high quality investigations by some of its analysts. A consensus exists, at home and abroad, that the weak state syndrome is particularly remarkable in Romania where the government show an insufficient capacity to design, adopt and implement public policies, irrespective to their nature (Jonită 2003).

All the indicators referred to here are arranged in a scale from 1 to 7 with the poor performances being closer to 1. If one takes the 'state burden', Romania score last insofar as its tax and tariff system is the more complex and distortive in a sample that includes three Western countries (USA, Italy and Greece), and 10 former socialist countries. The same applies to government regulation whose quality is the lowest in Eastern Europe in that the distribution of subsidies is the highest (an index between 1 and 2), the anti-monopoly policy rather ineffective, business has very few possibilities of challenging government action, and the accounting standards are the worst in the sample.

The index of clientelism has been constructed by assessing the degree to which government officials favour well connected firms and individuals along with the criteria of assignment of management positions. Clientelism seems rampant in Romania (a bit more than 2), but it also high in Slovakia, Poland, Bulgaria, and the Czech republic (with their indexes between 2 and 3, close to that of Italy). The lowest degree of clientelism, according to these measures, exists in Estonia, Slovenia and Lithuania.

Unfortunately, if one takes the whole picture in the Balkans one may note a worsening of the governance indexes, at least between 1998 and 2001. Kaufmann *et al.* (2002), for instance, arranged the quality of governance score between 1.5 and −1.5. The countries that in 1998 were at zero level or below were Croatia, Bulgaria, Romania, Albania, Yugoslavia (−1.2). In 2001, a slight improvement was apparent in Croatia and Bulgaria but not in Romania. Yugoslavia also improved its negative score and got at approximately the same level as Russia (−07/08). As for Romania, these authors specifically pointed to highly negative indexes on: government effectiveness (close to −0.6, that is, the minimum), control of corruption (−0.5), regulatory quality (from 0.2 to near −0.3). A slight improvement emerged in the rule of law (from −01 to 05) while the only very positive index was that of 'voice and accountability' which got close to the maximum of 0.6.

Thus the quality of regulations and the supply of public good such as law and order, protection of property rights, impartial and competent judiciary is quite poor in the Balkan and make up the weak state syndrome which, unfortunately, seems to be worsening just in the crucial period that should lead to the accession to the EU. Romania, again, is a case in point within an asymmetric relationship between Government and donors with the overarching goal of accession, on the one hand, and a fixed time span to achieve it on the other. The problems of administrative capacity emerges quite clearly even here in terms of inadequate information, rigidities and delays in procedures from disbursement (Jonita 2003).

But the point is that the admittance of countries at the stage of development that Romania and other countries in the Balkans have reached at present poses problems not just of institutional reforms but economic and social development as well. And what still is far from clear is whether the improvement of administrative capacities is a question of human resources rather than organization and, as a consequence, if the priority should be investment in structures, in institution building or in the formation of new cultural capital among managers and administrators (Watson 2002). This is certainly a basic dilemma that can be properly addressed only if some more evidence (however scattered) on transformations within three typical organizational environments is brought into the picture, namely local administration, enterprises, and Non-Governmental Organization (NGO).

### Local governments, decentralization, and mayors' strategies

Researches on local administration are not so numerous, at least in the Balkans (Bird *et al.* 1995; Baldersheim 1996), and often merely describe programmes of institution building (sponsored by the EU) without telling much about their implementation. Thus we do not know much on the difference in performance among the different regions of a given country and the combination of factors that may explain it. A good exception is the research of Sorin Jonită and Ciprian Fortusnic (2002) on the strategies, attitudes and effectiveness in the Romanian local administration in front of the privatization and decentralization processes set in motion by the reform of 1998–99. The fieldwork was conducted in mid-1999 with interviews to 425 mayors aimed at evaluating the factors which explain attitudes and performance such as the socio-economic conditions in rural and urban municipalities, ideological affiliations, and the local political culture. Also tested was the effect of age, education and previous administrative experience to see whether a cohort effect may be noticed, that is, whether younger generations, brought up in a new social climate and better educated, will display different patterns of behaviour and policy preferences.

What emerged in this research is that these factors left a large residual which the authors explained by another independent variable they called fiscal optimism which resulted as the best predictor for the local government strategies, even if its sources are very difficult to identify. Anyhow this factor was able to predict if mayors will pursue active or passive policies, if they rely on local tax revenues or expect transfers from the government. The typology which emerged from this investigation identified four types of possible strategies:

Neoliberalism (5 per cent of the sample): 'reduce expenditure and rely on your own resources'; Welfarism (16 per cent), that is a 'tax and spend attitude'; Passive-realism (11 per cent): 'reduce expenditure and ask for help', and the most widespread strategy of Passive-wishful thinking (68 per cent), that is, 'expand the budget and ask for help'.

Also interesting is the construction of the index of institutional innovation on the basis of questions concerning cooperation with other local governments, promotion of structural changes in the local administration; forms of partnership with the private sector; new taxes introduced or new sources of revenue identified, and whether or not welfare aid is conditional on community work.

On this points, the result is that whenever it comes to 'hard' budgetary issue the explanatory power of fiscal optimism is the highest one. However, as far as 'soft' aspects of innovation are concerned, they are somewhat influenced by local political culture. In fact a higher degree of institutional reformism and inter-municipality cooperation seems to be stronger in areas where the proportion of Hungarians is higher (Jonitǎ and Fortusnic 2000). Yet, even the mayor who reorganized their administration seem to have done it without firing personnel except, perhaps in the few big towns to a limited extent. The problem is, on the contrary to fill vacant positions which is the same across regions, type of socio-economic environment and budgetary expectations. This applies more specifically to big towns and in crisis-torn regions, even if for different reasons: in the first case, hiring qualified staff is difficult for the availability of better alternatives; in the second isolation and harsh conditions are the explanatory variables (Jonitǎ and Fortusnic 2000).

As for the attitude toward corruption, mayors were asked if they think there are corrupt officials in their administration, and if so whether measures have been taken against the persons found guilty. Three out of four mayors of the cities with population over 100,000 admitted the presence of the problem, and one out of four of those bigger than 35,000 punished corrupt civil servants. Corruption appeared less widespread in rural areas due, perhaps, to less possibilities for embezzlement, and a lower demand for 'corrupt services'. The evidence, however, was not sufficient to check the validity of the widespread belief that the Northern and Western part of Romania are more 'institutionally clean' than the others.

The data revealed instead a role of political affiliation in the fight against corruption: 30 per cent of right wing mayors got the highest score while the same applied to only 2.5 per cent of left wing mayor. This may partly explained by the fact that right wing parties tend to have more urban mayors than the leftist ones, yet the correlation between ideology and fight against corruption seem to be stronger (Jonitǎ and Fortusnic 2000).

These authors conclude that the use of fiscal optimism as an *ad-hoc* explanatory factor of the local government performance seems to depend more on the way mayors perceive the environment than on the real socio-economic conditions to be addressed within the framework of the new laws on privatization and decentralization. This attitude does not correlate with mayors' demographic, political affiliation or the local contexts. And it seems to be quite evenly distributed all over the country. Fiscal optimism may be a measure of personal skills and determination to cope with the changing contextual conditions. Thus the good news is that there seems to be room for a proactive behaviour in spite of the adverse conditions, even if this attitude usually correlates negatively with the willingness to privatize the local public services for fear of loosing sources of revenues. The bad news is that the cohort effect must be rejected for all the factors investigated in the study point to the fact that younger or better educated mayors do not make any difference when it comes to resource management, institutional innovation, effectiveness or good communication: 'This is bad omens for the optimistic theory of generation change and shows that other factors than the mere demographics of the political representatives should be taken into consideration if a real reform of the political class is the pursued goal' (Jonită and Fortusnic 1999: 20).

This is however an investigation on mayors, not their staff. When human resources have been mentioned it was only to compare the ratio of inhabitants to local government employees and the proportion of vacant administrative positions. A rough idea of the typical patterns of Human Resource Management in public and private organizations may be conveyed by some answers to a questionnaire from a very small sample of 22 participants in the Master on Local Development for the Balkans, at the University of Trento. A questionnaire which largely draws from the tool kit on training needs assessment and program design in transition countries prepared by the European Training Foundation in Torino (2002).

The basic point which gets confirmation from the replies is that it is difficult to expect quick changes in the state of affairs in countries with a strong centralistic traditions. Path-dependency is still very strong in the Balkans, both at central and local level: rigidity and bureaucratic centralism, decision-making process not based on factual data, patron-client relationship between politicians and administrators, a lot of direct and indirect control on subordinates, risk aversion and a lot of corruption. And all this despite the huge amount of training courses for public officials.

Two kinds of consequences of this lack of significant changes have been reported by two respondents from the Master program of Trento University. First, both organizational elites and 'lower participants,' chosen on the basis of political affiliation, are worried first of all of their tenure, try to carve a 'niche' for themselves, and sometimes display an 'autistic' behaviour of sort. Second, the recruitment procedures, which begin with universalistic criteria and end up, more often than not, with clientelistic and/or nepotistic choices.

This picture is largely confirmed by an investigation on the training needs in five Bulgarian state institutions carried out in 1999 within a PHARE programme. The results may be summarized as follows (Beninski 2000). Decision making processes did not imply any form of involvement of subordinates, and was rather clumsy and slow. State officials appeared generally well prepared, even if most of them pointed to the need to improve their qualification in order to comply with all the clauses of the Acquis communautaire. Communication problems emerged not so much within individual departments as in the administration as a whole. Meetings used to be conducted in a rather unproductive way so that the planning of activities appeared more the result of individual choices than a matter of managerial decision making. Job evaluation was more formal than real and was disconnected from the remuneration criteria. Finally the idea of team work was accepted by the majority of respondents, but only if applied in their office, not the whole organization. Asked for the reasons of this persisting state of affairs, our Master students pointed especially to the lack of previous knowledge, the scarce communication between superiors and subordinates, and a preference for the old Soviet-style administrative methods.

The legacy of state socialism is stronger in the public administration, and this is well known so much that when it comes to technical assistance programs, some of the most qualified local scholars claim that institution building in the public sector should have a priority over capacity building in the private one. The motive behind this claim is that, in spite of the many current difficulties, most people do possess the knowledge and resources necessary to improve their condition once the right institutions are put into operation. A widespread pessimism in former Soviet-type societies is often blamed on the mindset of Homo Sovieticus, on cultural cleavages or material deprivation while it is the rules of the game which are circumvented: 'When these are fixed, we usually see rational behaviour and self-reliance emerging with remarkable speed' (Jonită 2003b: 2). How much 'usual' this case might be is a matter of further investigation in different organizations and local environments. However the 'right institution' seems, almost always, to be a foreign owned (or sponsored) organization. Thus, it may be useful to refer to one kind of such institutions, namely NGOs.

Here a question to begin with might be: where do NGO activists come from? Here the evidence available is mainly anecdotal, but the paradox seems to be that they come to a non negligible extent from the Government itself. In fact, the persisting problem is not so much in recruiting as in retaining high-quality staff because of the already mentioned reasons: low salaries, poor working conditions and a Soviet-style bureaucratic culture. Thus the impression of an author who investigated the relationships of the Romanian public service with Western donors is that, '[it] functions as an apprenticeship for entry to the pool of highly skilled labour, mostly in Bucharest, upon which the private or external institutional sectors draws. Government service provides the opportunity to network, to develop expertise and improve language skills and these, in their turn, enhance an individual's market value. Obviously, only the best staff are likely to leave the security of public service in this way, but these are the people upon whom the system depends' (Watson 2002: 14).

If this impression is empirically founded, a question arises: what is the calculus of these people who get involved in programs of aid and technical assistance? How do they interact with other actors and institutions in the local environment? Unfortunately, there is a lot of description of activities in this field, and very little evidence on the behaviour of those who carry out these activities. An exception is the thought provoking study on the way NGOs 'are selling civil society' in the post-Soviet context (Henderson 2002).

The calculus of local staff which emerges from this research has to do with the fact that the local context is marked by extreme uncertainty and scarcity, and may be summarized in the following points. First, the main motive of these (young) people becomes surviving in a risky environment; producing results for the founders rather than making a real impact on the local community; hoarding information, duplicate each other projects, arguing among themselves instead of disseminating results and rendering their organizations self-sustainable. Consequently, what emerges is not networking but the propensity to work in closets by groups that often tend to reinvent the wheel and individuals members who often choose to leave the group, form their own organizations and establish separate relationships with donors within a logic of 'principled clientelism'. Second, the long established dualism between centre, which gets the bulk of funds, and periphery tends to be reproduced which breed resentments in the regions. Third, a civic community is actually growing, but is made mainly of young people more comfortable at international conferences with fellow Western audiences than at home working on local communities. Fourth, the evaluation of output often recalls Soviet times for it is based on the 'quantitative principle,' and the formal compliance with the stated objectives (Henderson 2002).

However, a note of partial optimism should also be drawn: some functions of advocacy and interests articulation are nonetheless being performed by local NGO activists (Henderson 2002). And students from the Balkans also added some points of further elaboration on this research which focused only on the Russian case. Firstly, the rough competition on the input side may stem from the share amount of funds that flow both to Russia as a whole and to individual aid projects. Secondly, while it is true that the management style of NGO is often quite 'familistic', this applies only to the smaller and local organizations. Thirdly, the amount of cooperation among NGO in the Balkans seems higher than in Russia both for the pressure of donors institutions, and the awareness that the flow of help is going to be reduced and redefined in the process of Europeanization.

Be that as it may, the risk exists that those managed by NGO may be depicted in terms not so dissimilar from the followings: '[programs] that make available to the existing Romanian public institutions substantial resources to play with, rather than use this resources in order to reform the institutions and make them more efficient – a tendency that suit well the Romanian authorities and aggravates the problem of clientelism' (Jonită 2003: 3). Hence, institutional building effort may also result (according to the same author) into a shopping sprees by public administrations or training abroad by those employees with the right connections.

## HRM in foreign owned firms: implications for local development

The first striking evidence on Human Resource Management in firms of Eastern Europe and the Balkans, seems to be a prevailing tendency not so much to convergence as to divergence from Western practices. The structural reasons of this are certainly to be found in the downsizing of many big firms in a process of privatization which went along with a lack of investment funds (Koubek 2000). Yet another significant reason lies in the management style that prevail in local firms, focused on 'hard' factors such as production and finance to the neglect of 'soft' factors such as HRM (Todeva 1996; Grancelli 1997; Savitt 1998;

Catana and Catana 2002; Mikl-Horke 2004). As a consequence, human resource practices still largely bear an administrative character so that the evaluation of functions, when it is done, is more formal than real, is based merely on quantitative indicators and it is carried out with reference to compensation and not to verify the training needs and to draw career plans.

This kind of HRM has little to do with what is badly needed, namely the formation of a new organizational leadership (Koubek 2000). Hence, the condition of junior enterprise managers appears not so brilliant in that they are recruited from outside in a situation whereby middle management is promoted from within and the mobility of personnel is generally quite limited and not on the rising.

Within this framework, some typical attitudes and behaviours of junior managers in local and multinational enterprises may be highlighted by a comparison with students of business schools, on the one hand, and expatriate managers on the other. An investigation conducted in Bulgaria is revealing for it compares attitudes and behaviour of 50 students in the business school of Sofia University with those of 50 middle managers of Bulgarian enterprises, mostly subsidiaries of multinational firms (Minkov 2000). The three classical dimensions of cultural analysis reveal the persistent strength of the personal factor in organizational behaviour and professional relationships. Thus the indicators of 'power distance' show that the attitude toward those who make mistakes or are not competitive and the individual stance in commercial transactions, depend heavily on the presence or absence of friendship relations. The fact that personal relationship come first also get confirmed along the second dimension of individualism/collectivism in that those who already have got a work experience show a greater inclination toward a Japanese style collectivism, that is, they express a scant appreciation for individual incentives in favour of a collective redistribution of enterprise profits (Minkov 2000).

As for the third dimension of 'uncertainty avoidance', two results are worth mentioning which show that the discriminating factor is the work experience. In fact, when students were invited to choose between the Anglo-Saxon and the Japanese model of management, they usually expressed a preference for the first one, that is, a model made of low guarantee of employment, frequent evaluation of performance, pressure for short-term results, and chances of quick promotion. On the contrary middle managers, who usually did not show great expectations, tended to ask more information on the organizational framework of an hypothetical promotion. The second significant result is that uncertainty avoidance has to do with the belief that work rules must exist and being binding for all, but this belief was much less firm if the circumventing of rules would involve respondents or their friends (Minkov 2000).

Uncertainty avoidance seems to be also widespread among top managers in privatized enterprises along with: (a) the tendency to use the key words of strategic management without the capacity of understanding its methods and imposing them to stakeholders; (b) the imitation and manipulation of Western decision making techniques not accompanied by a sufficient capacity to interpret environmental pressure to change, to focus on technology on 'soft factors' such as HRM (Todeva 1996; Catana and Catana 2002).

Similar evidence, along these three cultural dimensions may be found in research in which the behavioural patterns of Russian managers are compared with those of expatriates. In this case, the usually good level of education and training is accompanied by orientations to work that have been summarized as follows. First, a scarce separation between personal and professional relations. Secondly, a low degree of loyalty to the firms along with monetary motivations and a resentment for salary differentials between expatriates and locals. Third an indulgency for 'tolerable' ethical breaches and the dark sides of Russian business (possibly justified by the differentials quoted above). Fourth, a good deal of sciovinism expressed in the tendency to refuse solutions to a given problem without proposing alternatives ('In Russia it does not work'): a tendency that often goes along with a propensity to stick to the assigned tasks (Camiah and Hollinshead 2003).

That this is a quite typical situation may be confirmed by similar investigation in Slovenian firms whose environment is the most advanced and dynamic in the area (Pučko and Čater 2001). First, organizational changes such as strategic business units, profit centres, lean organization, flexible networks are applied by just few big firms. Second, significant deficiencies manifest itself in finance, marketing, strategic management, and in a HRM still largely oriented by the traditional legalistic/administrative approaches which goes along with obsolete remuneration and incentive practices.

Thus the question arises: within this organizational environment in which the 'mimicry' of Western methods is quite widespread and the soft factors of management are quite neglected, what are the typical behavioural patterns of junior managers? Two forms of adaptation are worth mentioning. The first seems to be quite typical in local subsidiaries of multinational firms, and the second seems to often hidden behind the request of 'practical' approaches by people attending management training courses at home and abroad.

A dualistic situation has been noted in multinational firms. On the one hand there are those which strive to productivity increases through the ultra-specialization of relatively low paid local managers; on the other there are firms who try to reach the same objective through an increase in the flexibility of junior managers. In the first case, management training is not a priority so that the narrow specialization of these managers makes it difficult for them to find better employment opportunities. In the second case the result is the same insofar as the adopted forms of flexibility are too typical of a given firms and are of no great value in the managerial labour market. The consequence is that these two forms of internal labour markets represents an hindrance to inter-company mobility as a mean of promotion. That is why many junior managers are looking for master programs abroad: academic education is seen as a substitutive channel for vertical mobility. Unfortunately, this signal an element of cultural continuity even if the organizational environment has radically changed, namely the search for certification, for administrative recognition, and not the business school that can provide the better training (Cornuel and Kletz 2001).

The cultural legacy emerges in a Rumanian research on the attitudes to training on the part of young and 'inherited' managers (Catana and Catana 2002). The latter often express a refusal of the idea of being trained for they think of being enough prepared to the market economy. Yet that is a conviction that stems from the knowledge of a given set of management techniques, but not the socio-cultural environment they are embedded in. The young, on the contrary, have less managerial experience but a higher level of education. For them what may indeed be useful is a training based on case studies and experiential learning with and emphasis on factors such as team building, management by objectives, contribution/reward, and so on. However, this possibility sometimes does not materialize because of environmental conditionings that are sometimes addressed in a quite different way from those expected in the Terms of Reference of European training programs. In other words, if asked about the reasons of mismanagement, these young people usually point to the organizational environment and its turbulence (lack of financial resources, technological gap, inadequacy of policies, and so on). And this kind of reply is in itself a sign of continuity with the past when all organizational troubles used to be explained as a consequence of the uncertainty on the input side stemming from the plan (Grancelli 1988). But the continuity is not only attitudinal: it is behavioural as well in that the ways of coping with objective difficulties are indeed forms of opportunistic adaptations to them. For instance, the legislation on financial matters is complex, contradictory and thus difficult to interpret and apply correctly. Thus, an interest arises in some trainees towards forms of training that can put them in condition to skillfully operate in the grey area between legality and illegality in order to quickly raise their earnings. Clearly this form of self-interest seeking with guile is not much congruent with approaches to training that are long, too theoretical and not so flexible as Western programs sometimes actually are (Grancelli 2002; Catana and Catana 2002).

Be that as it may, two concluding remarks are in order. The first is that the human capital acquired within Western training programmes is usually a key which opens up a professional career in those sectors which were almost nonexistent in Soviet management, such as marketing or finance, or that used to be carried out by expatriates during the first stage of postcommunist transformation (Danis 2003). The second may be expressed in form of hypothesis for further research, that is, the mixture of personal and professional relations may be a precondition for entrepreneurship development possibly starting from forms of outsourcing from foreign-owned (or local) firms. Indeed, this is what is going to happen in a number of regions of the Balkans (especially of Romania) through the processes of outsourcing which involve foreign owned firms and networks of local subcontractors (Majocchi 2004), and that requires further investigation.

## Conclusions

The evidence provided so far, however scattered, may show that it is pointless to address the issue of elite reproduction and circulation without bringing external actors into the picture as it is the case with elitist approaches. Local scholars are more aware of the importance of exogenous factors, but seem inclined to think that European programs of technical assistance should prioritize institution building over capacity building in the private sector for the legacies of the past regime are particularly strong in the state administration (Jonită 2003). Yet if we focus instead on the elite in the making in more dynamic organizational contexts what emerge is that the issue is not so much the priority as the coordination of the two processes. As Slavo Radosevic points out, it is not much a question of EU funds as of European networks that involve local partners. The real priority is the design of a comparative research on local development in which the analytical priority is given to its micro-determinants for the policy implications of this research are: (a) how the policy practice of local and national governments is going to support the emergence of network organizers oriented to change and not to status quo and partial reforms in which 'winners take all', and how much is that policy conducive to an alignment of local and foreign networks (Windolf 1998; Radosevic 2002).

If one specifically refers to the Balkans, what emerges is that national determinants of development are quite weak for the research institutions of the previous regime are still there but appear as almost-empty boxes. On the other hands, sectoral determinants are also weak for the national economies cannot create a sufficient demands for the restructuring of industrial branches; a problem worsened by processes of insiders privatizations which brought about not organizational restructuring as an increase of power for local notables. Hence, given the weakness of these determinants, the research should focus on the micro level, that is, on the involvement of foreign MNCs and local firms in the processes of innovation and networks alignment. Innovation initiatives in the Balkans show some typical problems such as short-term funding of standalone organizations, supply-push nature of programs, and the donor's tendency to avoid the messy world of local institutions . That is why the analysis of restructuring process in areas more in need of innovation cannot skip over the changes in the quality of social capital. This implies, however, a focus not so much on logistic of networks and associational activities as proxies for social capital as on its intrinsic and extrinsic contents. In other words, an investment in network building seems to be lacking in many local development projects. Yet this is an investment that should be done in that it implies the enhancement of local leadership within a process which connects agents both within the public and private sectors: a process based on the awareness local power structures are status quo oriented more often than not (Radosevic 2002; Steen and Gel'man 2003).

In conclusion, the risk indeed exists that, 'the growing EU assistance, if not restructured, will create a culture of dependency in the public sector and parts of the private one similar to the cargo cult among the people of the Pacific islands. We have the bad experience of Southern Italy or Greece to witness that this kind of development is not a far-off perspective' (Jonită 2003a: 4).

But before jumping to the conclusion that we are witnessing the birth of a new variant of *compradore intellectuals* (Eyal and Townsley 1996: 174), we need more cross-regional and cross-sectoral comparisons of the kind hinted to above, and we should not ignore the organizational dimension.

# 8

# International Aid, Policy Transfer and Local Economic Development in North Montenegro

*Will Bartlett*

## Introduction

Early attempts to theorize the relationship between international aid and economic growth of poor countries assumed that aid inflows would fill a savings 'gap' and would lead to increased levels of investment that would boost growth and lift poor countries out of underdevelopment and poverty. In the 1990s a number of empirical studies cast doubt on this optimistic picture and appeared to show that there was little relationship between aid and economic growth (Boone 1996). This was explained by the argument that aid donations tend to be converted into higher public or private consumption rather than being channeled into increased investment. Subsequently, Burnside and Dollar (2000) showed that the effect of aid on growth depended on the macroeconomic policies of the recipient countries. In countries with 'good' fiscal, monetary and trade policies, aid was shown to have a positive effect on growth. This gave rise to the argument that aid should be targeted on countries that followed so-called 'good' policies. As Easterly (2003) has shown, donor governments have adopted this framework to target growth where it is expected to be most effective. Critics of the approach have argued that there are diminishing returns to aid even in countries which pursue good policies (Dalgaard and Hansen 2001; Hansen and Tarp 2001). This implies that even where good policies are adopted, there is a point beyond which aid loses its effectiveness. This could be explained by the limitation on the absorptive capacity of the recipient country to use aid donations effectively because of various factors such as weak public administration. Easterly *et al.* (2004), among others, further challenged the Burnside and Dollar findings by replicating their econometric estimations using additional data and different definitions of aid and policy. In the revised regressions the link between aid and good policies disappeared.

Collier and Hoeffler (2004) have extended the debate by considering the impact of aid in post-conflict societies. They found that aid can be especially effective in such situations, especially where governments' sources of revenue have collapsed, and infrastructure has been destroyed. The contribution that aid can make to growth through rebuilding infrastructure in such circumstances has been demonstrated by their econometric research findings. Collier and Dollar (2002), using an improved measure of policy, broadened the analysis in another direction. They showed that aid can be more effective in high-poverty countries, and argued that aid allocation should be influenced by consideration of the depth of poverty as well as by the policy orientation of the government.

Knack (2001) found that there is a complex relationship between aid and corruption, bureaucratic quality and the rule of law. Corruption can reduce the effectiveness of aid, while increased aid is unlikely to reduce corruption. In such a situation, where there is corruption, Collier and Dollar (2004) propose that aid should work *around* the government, for example by financing local NGOs. Alternatively donors should work *through* the government, establish goals (as with the Millennium Development Goals) and take a more proactive stance in determining the poverty reduction policies that a government should follow when using the aid provided. Collier and Dollar argue that these approaches of working around or through the government are likely to be most effective in countries that have an above-median policy environment and greater-than-median inequality. Working through the government rather than around it may in itself help to improve the public administration. But working around the government, through local NGOs, can undermine democratic accountability.

Most of this analysis is based upon an approach in which aid is conceived of simply as a financial flow from a donor government to a recipient government. Although the approach gives a useful insight into the conditions in which aid flows might have a positive economic effect in the recipient country, there are a number of problems with the approach that limit its usefulness for assessing the impact of international aid on local economic development. First, the approach is focused on the aggregate level, and does not investigate the differences in the effects of aid programmes in different localities within a country. Secondly, it assumes that 'policy' within the recipient country is a given, exogenous, factor that is not influenced by the flow of aid and the political conditions attached to it. Thirdly, the approach does not take into account the specific interests and motivations of the various actors involved in the aid process, and it neglects the institutional and political dimension of the relationship between international aid and economic development. There are two strands of literature which cast light on these problematic areas of the conventional econometric approach: the policy transfer literature and the principal agent literature.

One of the main drawbacks of the Burnside and Dollar approach and the literature that has followed from that has been the assumption that policy, good or bad, in the recipient country is a given, exogenous factor. An alternative view of the policy process that has been put forward by political scientists in recent years is that governments frequently draw lessons from experiences in other countries in developing their own policies (Rose 1993), or that policy may be transferred across national settings either voluntarily or on a more coercive basis. This policy transfer approach has been developed more systematically recently by Dolowitz and Marsh (1996, 2000) and Stone (2004). They argue that policy transfer can take place through a variety of channels, at various levels of government, and through a variety of different agents of transfer, including central government, local government, international aid agencies and NGOs. The debate centres on the identification of different patterns of policy transfer and the agents and networks through which the transfer takes effect. The contrast with the aid literature discussed above could not be starker. Here, policy formulation is conceived as an endogenous process. Bringing the two sides together it is easy to see that policy is unlikely to be a purely exogenous factor but is more likely to be embodied in the flows of aid from donor to recipient. This immediately draws attention to the private interests, motives, aims and purposes of the actors involved in the donor–recipient relationship.

A recent approach to the analysis of the effectiveness of aid that encompasses the aims and purposes of the actors involved is based upon the 'principal agent' model (Martins *et al.* 2003). In this model the *principal* is the policy maker in the donor country who contracts with various agents to manage the delivery and implementation of aid projects in pursuit of varied objectives. Although the purpose is sometimes altruistic, donors often offer aid in order to advance their own country's political interests or pursue particular foreign policies. The *agent* is the implementing body that carries out the aid programme or project. This may be a private profit making company or an NGO. These agents in turn interact with policy makers in the receiving country at the level of central government and/or local government. Where there is an information asymmetry, the agent may pursue his or her own interests rather than those of the principal. The model points to the complexities of the institutional arrangement through which aid is structured. It suggests that there is unlikely to be a simple one-to-one correlation between the amount of aid and the outcome in terms of economic performance either at national or local level. It suggests that in place of an econometric analysis using aggregate data, a case study approach is needed which would investigate the detailed interaction between the various principles and agents and identify the interactions and outcomes of individual cases with their own institutional, historical and political specificities.

Methodologically, the in-depth case study is an appropriate research design when 'how' and 'why' questions are being asked (Yin 2003). In a later section of this chapter I apply this approach to a particular example of the impact of international aid on local economic development in North Montenegro. But first, in the next section, I present a brief overview sketch of the recent developments in the field of international donor assistance to South-East Europe.

## International aid flows to the post-socialist countries of South-East Europe

The total flow of international aid to the countries of South-East Europe amounted to 6.4 billion Euros in 2001 and has gradually increased to an estimated 7.7 billion Euros in 2005. Among the donors, the proportion of aid originating from the bilateral donors and from the EC has fallen from 3.9 billion Euros in 2001 to an estimated 3 billion Euros in 2005, while the International Financial Institutions (IFIs) have increased their aid flows (including concessional loans) from 2.6 billion Euros in 2001 to an estimated 4.7 billion Euros in 2005 (see Table 8.1).

Flows of international aid to South-East Europe in the form of grants have declined from 61 Euros per capita in 2001 to an estimated 51 Euros per capita in 2005, a decline of over 16 per cent, while per capita aid in the form of concessional loans increased from 49 Euros in 2001 to an estimated 81 Euros in 2005, an increase of 64 per cent. As can be seen from Table 8.2, the aid flows to the Western Balkan countries in the form of grants has declined sharply since 2001 as the bilateral donors in particular have wound down their assistance efforts in response to increased economic and political stability in the

*Table 8.1* International aid flows to SEE, 2001–2005 (billion Euros)

| | *2001* | *2002* | *2003* | *2004*[a] | *2005*[a] |
|---|---|---|---|---|---|
| Bilateral donors & EU | 3.9 | 3.7 | 3.2 | 3.3 | 3.0 |
| IFIs | 2.6 | 3.0 | 3.3 | 3.7 | 4.7 |
| *Total* | 6.4 | 6.7 | 6.5 | 7.0 | 7.7 |

*Note*: [a]estimate.
*Source*: European Commission and World Bank (2004).

*Table 8.2* Per capita international aid flows to SEE, 2001–2005 (Euros)

| | | *2001* | *2002* | *2003* | *2004*[a] | *2005*[a] | *% growth 2001–2005* |
|---|---|---|---|---|---|---|---|
| Western Balkan countries | Grants | 82 | 83 | 62 | 57 | 44 | −47 |
| | Loans | 66 | 75 | 58 | 80 | 83 | 27 |
| Bulgaria and Romania | Grants | 36 | 38 | 40 | 53 | 58 | 60 |
| | Loans | 42 | 47 | 71 | 64 | 86 | 104 |
| All SEE | Grants | 61 | 58 | 51 | 54 | 51 | −16 |
| | Loans | 49 | 57 | 61 | 67 | 81 | 64 |

*Note*: [a]estimate.
*Source*: European Commission and World Bank (2004).

region, and as the need for aid in other parts of the world has become more urgent. International aid flows in the form of concessional loans has increased to partly offset the decline in grant aid. The picture is quite different in the accession countries of Bulgaria and Romania where per capita pre-accession assistance from the EU has increased in terms of both grants and concessional loan.

These data underscore the fact that the major donor organizations in South-East Europe are the EU and the World Bank, and that EU assistance is increasingly oriented towards the goal of EU accession of the post-socialist Balkan states (see EC and World Bank 2004). Bulgaria, Croatia and Romania are currently candidates for EU membership, while the other countries of the Western Balkans are clearly on a path in the same direction. Bulgaria and Romania have been in receipt of pre-accession assistance through the PHARE programme, while the Western Balkan countries have been in receipt of development assistance through the CARDS programme which is increasingly geared towards priorities such as the implementation of the *acquis communautaire*, the reform of the judiciary, the reform of public administration, and security and cross-border issues. Local economic development is fairly low down the agenda of EU assistance policies except as part of the support for public administration reform. Decentralization of social and municipal services does feature in some CARDS projects, but the main focus tends to be on the reform and improvement of the efficiency of the central government.

The World Bank has a more specifically developmental agenda. Several of the Balkan states have been supported in the development of Poverty Reduction Strategy Papers (PRSP) which set out a pro-poor development agenda for the countries concerned. The first of these was the Albanian National Strategy for Social and Economic Development (NSSED), which is now in its second phase. This has been followed by PRSP policy documents in S&M (2003), and in BiH (2004). However, these tend to be focused on sectoral development and do not set out a specific set of proposals to promote local economic development.

Local economic development policies do figure in two of the other international donor organizations. The EBRD has a programme to support the development of the local municipal infrastructure, while the United Nations Development Programme (UNDP) supports a variety of programmes and projects at the local level. For example UNDP Albania has pioneered the development of regional development plans. The UNDP has carried many projects with a local focus including a major programme of assistance to Southern Serbia and organized a major conference on local economic development in Belgrade in 2002.

Bilateral agencies also tend to focus at least some of their efforts on development projects at a local level, if for no other reason than their smaller capacity limits the scope of their operations. Major bilateral donors from the European states such as Department for International Development (DfID) (UK),

Kredit fuer Wiederaufbau (KfW) (Germany), Swedish International Development Cooperation Agency (SIDA) (Sweden), as well as other countries. UK's DfID is beginning to disengage with the Balkan region as resources have been drawn to Afghanistan and Iraq in pursuit of the latest geo-political imperative (DfID 2004).

The USAID programme is one of the largest bilateral programmes and has had a strong focus on local economic development, especially through the development of municipal government (including programmes of local municipal development projects in Croatia and Macedonia, and other similar projects elsewhere in SEE).

Inevitably perhaps, NGOs have been the organizational form that has been most heavily engaged at local level, with their emphasis on short term emergency relief and small scale of operations. While having a significant impact in some instances, generally speaking their capacity to carry out long-term developmental interventions at a local level has been rather low. In recent years the most effective NGO activity has been in the provision of microfinance. This provides small scale financial resources to individual entrepreneurs, often to women, in an effort to kick-start business activity in deprived rural or urban areas where the conventional sources of finance are scarce. However, micro-loans typically carry high rates of interest that encourage short-term investments with high rates of return. The effect is often to stimulate retail trade and services rather than more competitive industries capable of selling products outside the locality.

## Local economic development in Montenegro

The Montenegrin economy suffered a series of severe shocks in the 1990s including the loss of markets following the break-up of Yugoslavia, the imposition of UN sanctions against the rump Yugoslavia (composed of Serbia and Montenegro), and the negative effects of the Kosovo war in 1999 (Djurić 2003). The imposition of sanctions in particular encouraged the growth of the grey economy and organized criminal groups that profited from sanctions-busting, smuggling and the war situation. The perverse macroeconomic policies of the government in Belgrade led to hyperinflation in 1994 and to the destruction of the savings capital of the middle classes and general impoverishment of the population while enriching the political and economic elite. The Dayton peace agreement of 1995 led to a brief respite until the outbreak of the Kosovo war of 1999.

In 1998 the main political party of former communists split into two wings. The DPS, led by Milo Djukanović was in favour of liberal reforms and independence from Serbia (Bieber 2003). The SNP, led by Momir Bulatović, was in favour of continued ties with Serbia. The DPS, in coalition with two smaller parties the SDP and the NS, won the parliamentary elections in 1998. The SNP became the main opposition party with its power base in North

Montenegro,[1] the region closest to Serbia. The region came to be viewed as politically suspect by the central government, which adversely affected the government's commitment to its economic and social development.

Because of its independent political stance, the Djukanović government secured substantial economic and political support from the international community, which viewed the republic as a bastion of anti-Milošević sentiment and was willing to support political and economic liberalization with substantial inflows of aid funding and advisers. In 2000, the USA and the EU provided combined international aid to Montenegro amounting to $90m (Bieber 2003).[2] This aid and subsequent aid flows to Montenegro have been closely connected to international policy for the region. After the transition to democracy in 2000, the EU aimed to hold Serbia and Montenegro together to avoid spill-over of separatism to other neighbouring countries. Since 2004, the EU has adopted a 'twin-track' approach under which trade, economic and sector policies will be covered separately for Montenegro, while defence issues will be addressed at the level of the state union of Serbia and Montenegro.

At a macroeconomic policy level the main advice offered to the government by the international donors was to liberalize the economy and open it up to international trade as widely as possible. This policy was implemented swiftly because the Serbian government had imposed a trade blockade on Montenegro, which led to widespread food shortages. Securing food imports from the EU, Slovenia and Croatia was a short term expedient to substitute for the loss of food imports from Serbia. The EU established a Food Security Unit within the Ministry of Finance in Podgorica, which advised the Montenegrin government on the implementation of the free trade regime, the liberalization of prices and the reduction and elimination of subsidies to farmers and to state owned enterprises. This placed a final twist of the screw on the state owned enterprises in the North, which entered into a phase of terminal collapse leading to the present situation in which most factories in the region have either closed down or have almost entirely ceased operating on a day to day basis. Most of the old socially owned companies in the region, now effectively owned by the state,[3] are either closed down or operate well below full capacity.

Agriculture also suffered from a lack of subsidies and so when the border with Serbia was again reopened following the toppling of the Milošević regime at the end of 2000 and the entry of a democratically minded government in Belgrade, the agricultural economy in the North was unable to compete with cheap subsidized imports of food and milk products from Serbia. In addition over the years of war and sanctions the practice of smuggling, illegal economic activity, tax avoidance and other practices that have led to the weakening of the developmental capacity of the state have multiplied. Today the population of the region perceives that corruption, the grey economy, and the politicization of officials are the main causes of poverty. According to a recent newspaper report:

> A meeting of the citizens of Mojkovac, Kolašin and Berane declared that the main causes of poverty in these municipalities are corruption, the grey economy, the politicization of officials, and the priority of politics over economics. The meeting was organized together with members of the Network for the Promotion of Nongovernmental Organisations (MANS). . . . The inhabitants of Mojkovac and Berane believe that corruption is the biggest cause of poverty not only in these municipalities but in the whole of Montenegro . . . other causes of poverty include tax avoidance and late payment of salaries . . . the citizens further believe that the state credit policy does not meet their needs.[4]

The high level of uncertainty that this has induced has further led to a great difficulty in attracting both domestic and foreign investment. In consequence unemployment is high and incomes are low. Many people get by on a subsistence income from small-scale family farming. Others receive remittance incomes from relatives working overseas. Yet others are employed in a variety of state or local government activities, and others subsist from the grey economy. Perhaps the worst off are those who have lost their jobs in collapsed industries, and neither own land nor have relatives abroad. These people are the urban poor who live in the main towns, or who have moved to other parts of Montenegro. Other groups in severe poverty include the many tens of thousands of refugees and displaced persons who live in Montenegro.

The North suffers from higher unemployment and greater incidence of poverty than other parts of the country. Table 8.3 shows that in 2002 the absolute poverty rate in the North, where 34 per cent of the population reside, was 14.9 per cent compared to a national average of 9.4 per cent. In terms of absolute poverty rates, more than half (54 per cent) of those in poverty live in the North. Many others live close to poverty. A high share (45 per cent) of the population in the North is economically vulnerable, and lives on an income less than 50 per cent above the poverty line. There is a widespread

*Table 8.3* Poverty rates in Montenegro in 2002 (%)

| | *Montenegro* | *North* | *Centre* | *South* |
|---|---|---|---|---|
| Absolute poverty rate | 9.4 | 14.9 | 6.5 | 6.8 |
| % of total number of poor | 100.0 | 54.0 | 30.5 | 15.5 |
| Economic vulnerability | 36.4 | 44.8 | 33.2 | 29.8 |
| Population share | 100.0 | 33.8 | 43.3 | 23.7 |

*Source*: Radevic and Beegle (2002: 13).

perception that politicians in the capital have neglected North Montenegro and that local authorities have been starved of funds for carrying out even basic infrastructure repairs, and have weak capacity to design their own local economic development projects. There is little doubt that the region needs substantial development assistance from the government and international donor agencies if it is to succeed in escaping from the current levels of underdevelopment and poverty, and move from stagnation to self-sustained economic growth and social development.

## Government policies towards the North

In 1998, the government of the Federal Republic of Yugoslavia (consisting of the republics of S&M) drafted a regional development policy that recognized the North Montenegro municipalities of Andrijevica, Berane, Bijelo Polje and Rožaje as 'underdeveloped', and the municipality of Plav as 'highly underdeveloped'. On that basis, and using additional data from the municipalities, the Montenegrin Secretariat for Regional Development set out its regional policy in 2000 (RoM 2000). The policy emphasizes three key steps for regional development including infrastructure and environmental protection; strategic regional development of mountainous regions; and smaller local investment projects. In the North it identified the priorities as infrastructure development, the development of small and medium sized enterprises, the promotion of vocational education, the improved use of natural resources especially wood processing, and the development of agro-tourism. Since that time however relatively little has been done to implement the policy or to achieve its objectives. The region has continued to experience severe economic decline and social dislocation (Djurović *et al.* 2002). Indeed, from discussions with officials and politicians in local municipalities, the perception appears to be that the central government has exercised a regime of benign neglect, allowing the regional economy to decay over the past twelve years.[5] The government adopted an Agenda for Economic Reform in 2003, which gave little attention to the Northern region from a development perspective. The government also set out a PRSP in collaboration with the World Bank in 2003, but also with little in the way of specific orientation to local economic development.

One of the main instruments of local economic development in Montenegro has been the Development Fund, financed by revenues from privatization and the sale of shares in companies under state ownership.[6] The Fund's strategic priority is to develop the SME sector in Montenegro and to that purpose it has established a credit scheme to finance the expansion plans of SMEs that employ at least ten workers. From 1998 to 2003 the Fund financed 329 SME projects with a total value of 40 million Euros, to which its contribution was 9.5 million Euros. The Fund estimated that it created 5,500 new jobs through these projects at a cost of 1,700 Euros per job created.[7] The average size of loans was 30,000–35,000 Euros, and over 80 per cent of loans were made to companies operating in the manufacturing sector. Loans were given at a 4–12 per cent rate of interest with a one-year grace period and a three-year payback period. The main criteria for awarding a loan included both the profitability of the project; the creation of at least five new jobs; the export of at least 20 per cent of output; and the use of improved technology. The achieved payback rate of the loans was however rather low at 80 per cent. The Development Fund has been a key agent in the delivery of the government's economic development programmes for SMEs for whom its credit fund is the only source of long-term development finance in the country. However, the regional distribution of the funds is heavily skewed towards just two municipalities: Podgorica and Plevlja.[8] Little of this resource goes to companies operating in other municipalities in the North.

The Employment Bureau is the other major government agency with a developmental impact. It runs a programme to promote self-employment and small business start-ups among the unemployed. It provides micro-credits of up to 3,000 Euros per person employed with a limit of 15,000 Euros on a long-term low-interest basis to unemployed people to start up their own businesses, on condition that they employ up to five workers. In contrast to the Development Fund scheme, the credits are evenly distributed between the municipalities. Since the start of the scheme over 1,000 projects have been funded in the North, which have created over 1,500 jobs. Credits are repayable over three years at an interest rate of 3 per cent per year with a one-year grace period. Because of the low interest rate the scheme runs at a loss since only 60 per cent of beneficiaries make regular repayments and the penalty rate of interest is relatively low. It is likely, though undocumented, that many of the loans find their way into financing consumption expenditure. There is no monitoring or follow-up of the continuity of the jobs created.

While the Development Fund and the Employment Bureau are home-grown institutions, the government has drawn on international experience and advice to establish two new government agencies. The first is the Agency for Small and Medium Sized Enterprises (SMEDA). This agency develops business advisory services to SMEs throughout the country. Thus far it has established five Local Business Centres (LBCs), two of which are located in the northern municipalities of Bijelo Polje and Rožaje, with plans for a third in Berane. The second is the Agency for Reconstruction and Foreign Investment, which is responsible for promoting foreign direct investment into the country. This agency actively invites foreign investors to purchase shares in state-owned companies through a publicity campaign. The publicity campaign has focused noticeably more on the state assets in the coastal tourism industry than on the collapsed industrial companies and hotels in the North.

Various line ministries also have responsibilities with implications for local economic development. The Ministry of Agriculture supports the development of family farming. Its priorities are the development of rural infrastructure, technical services and social support for farmers. In 2002 the Ministry of Tourism prepared a project for the development of the Northeast region of 'Prokletija'.[9] The ministry considers that the biggest tourism opportunities for the North are in eco-tourism and skiing. The ministry has drawn up a master plan for the development of tourism in the whole country.[10] The Ministry of Education aims at the development of vocational training and has supported a Regional Training Centre (for the wood processing industry) in Berane.

## International donor activities in Montenegro

As with the other countries of the Western Balkans, the EC aid programme to Montenegro has focused largely on the improvement of public administration, reform of the judiciary and on security, giving relatively little attention to local economic development with the exception of cross border projects (see CEC 2002, 2004). The European Agency for Reconstruction (EAR) is the implementing body for the CARDS programme in Kosovo, Macedonia, and Serbia-Montenegro. The EAR has established an office in Podgorica, and has carried out several projects that have had an impact in North Montenegro including vocational training, the rehabilitation of a secondary school, and a turn-around management project for enterprise restructuring. The latter has provided assistance to several medium-sized companies in Bijelo Polje including Vunko, a wool-processing company, and Mladost, a shoe company. It is also involved in a turn-around management project in the wood-processing sector and has produced an assessment of the wood processing industry.[11]

Other European institutions have been involved in the provision of financial support to Montenegro. The European Investment Bank began its operations in Montenegro in 2001 and has financed several major infrastructure projects including the rehabilitation of the Port of Bar, the repair and reconstruction of the main north-south highway, and the rehabilitation of the railway system. The European Bank for Reconstruction and Development has financed projects to the value of 22 million Euros in Montenegro (EBRD 2004a). In the tourism sector, EBRD gives priority to the development of the coastal region, and major projects financed have included an environmental project to reduce pollution in Kotor Bay, an important coastal tourist attraction.

The World Bank has been a major donor in Montenegro since Serbia and Montenegro were admitted to the organization in 2001. The main ongoing support is for a (second) structural adjustment loan approved in September 2004 amounting to US$18 million, designed to support key reforms to promote growth and fiscal consolidation.

The UNDP has designed a number of project proposals for the development of North Montenegro. It argues that there should be a reorientation towards the service sector and tourism, and has proposed several projects in the fields of sustainable forestry, eco-tourism, and energy efficiency and in developing mini hydro power stations at municipal level.

The main bilateral donors to Montenegro are the United States and Germany. Since 2001 the US has allocated US$200 million to Montenegro mainly managed by USAID. A key activity has been the Local Governance and Community Development programme with a budget of US$13.6 million in 2004. This has encompassed two sub-programmes. The first is called Community Revitalization through Democratic Action (CRDA), which has focused on improving economic and social infrastructure working through local municipal development advisory councils. The second is called Good Local Governance (GLG) to support fiscal decentralization and improved delivery of public services at local level. The other key activity has been the Economic Reform, Restructuring and Policy programme, with a budget of US$8.5 million in 2004. This has been geared to building capacity in the central government and financial institutions to support private sector development.

Following its early focus on humanitarian support, the German KfW has targeted infrastructure development, support to the financial sector and to SME development. It has established a 'European Fund for Montenegro', which manages donor credit lines on behalf of the EAR, and German, Swiss and Austrian donors to support the micro-enterprise and SME sectors. The German aid agency GTZ has also proposed a strategy for mass tourism that involves creating 150,000 new beds, and improving water supply and other infrastructure services, which however focuses exclusively on the coastal areas.

This section has demonstrated that, as in other countries in South-East Europe, numerous donor organizations have active programmes of economic assistance in Montenegro. The international assistance is closely tied in with policy advice and policy transfer to the government. New government agencies have been established following donor advice. The larger multilateral institutions such as the World Bank and the European Union have an even stronger influence and are able to ensure that what they see as 'good' policies are adopted by the government by the use of financial leverage and conditions attached to the achievement of wider goals such as progress with EU integration. At the same time the government has its own development agenda and priorities. The international donors contract with various agents to carry out the assistance programmes, and to interface with counterparts within the government. This complex web of interactions produces outcomes at local level that give shape to the specific character of local economic development in the different localities within the country. In the next section I outline two examples of the effects of international aid and policy transfer on local economic development in the region of North Montenegro.

## International assistance and policy transfer

The first example concerns the financing of economic development in the region. An important element holding back the economic development of the North is the lack of formal banking facilities. The Montenegrin Commercial

Bank, Opportunity Bank (Berane) and Euromarket Banka (Rožaje) are the only local bank branches in the region. Various micro-credit institutions have been established by bilateral aid agencies and NGOs to fill this gap. Micro-credit can be a useful intervention tool in areas where there is a lack of normal banking institutions, and in poor localities where micro-credit funds can be targeted at economically and socially disadvantaged groups. One example of a donor financed micro-credit organization that operates in the North is an NGO called AgroInvest. It operates a 'character-based lending' programme which aims to establish close links to the community. From a technical point of view it has been highly successful with a very low default level and a strong record of repayments by its clients. The provision of micro-credit by such organizations is a perfect example of policy transfer embedded within the provision of international aid.

Nevertheless micro-finance also has a number of drawbacks as a development tool. In the first place, such loans tend to be offered at very high interest rates with short repayment periods. This tends to favour projects with a high short-term return, and is therefore biased towards quick turnover traders rather than long-term manufacturing development projects. The pressure for quick turnover also rewards entrepreneurs who exploit loopholes in the law. As one local expert observed:

> Many clients of the micro-credit funds are people who have seen a profitable opportunity to exploit the forest and make a quick return.

Therefore, the provision of micro-credit (which is in high demand) needs to be supplemented by the provision of additional long-term development finance. As described above, in contrast to donor-driven finance schemes, the government has established its own institutions to provide development finance through the Development Fund and the Employment Bureau. Such state provision is however vulnerable to capture by interest groups. This appears to have been the case with the Development Fund scheme, which has had little impact in the North (apart from one municipality). State run programmes may also suffer from inefficient operating practices as in the case of the Employment Bureau scheme, which has inefficiently low repayment rates compared to the achievements of NGO micro-credit schemes such as AgroInvest.

The second example concerns the development of agricultural policy. In 2000 the European Union provided economic aid to farmers in the North through a donation of one thousand dairy cows from Schleswig-Holstein in northern Germany. The aid was provided with the aim of building political support for the new anti-Milošević Djukanović government that was supported by the West. The Ministry of Agriculture was concerned about the lack of milk processing capacity and requested one of the bilateral donor agencies to carry out a feasibility study to establish a dairy in North Montenegro. The report set out a plan to construct a new dairy in one of the major towns in the region. The aims of the project were to (a) support the development of the dairy sector in North Montenegro (b) to increase profitability and sustainability of dairy farming and (c) to develop profitable milk processing enterprises. The report pointed out that although the region is highly suitable for dairy farming, most of the dairy farms are small subsistence farms which have just one or two cows, and which do not produce a marketable surplus of milk. There are relatively few farms (3 per cent) that have more than four cows and which would be in a position to supply the dairy. The report warned that there might be bottlenecks in the delivery of milk to the newly established dairy.

The dairy was eventually established and started operating in March 2003 providing jobs to 35 employees. The Montenegrin government provided premises, and the donor provided equipment and expertise. The dairy soon ran into a number of serious problems. In Montenegro milk could be sold at the market for 50 cents per litre, or turned into *kajmak* cheese. Although supplying milk to the dairy was a secure way to sell milk with a guaranteed demand, many farmers still preferred to take their milk to their local market, or to supply it directly to the customers at home. Since the dairy offered the farmers only 27 cents per litre it faced a supply shortage. To solve the problem the dairy management decided to import milk from Serbia, where farmers were subsidized and protected by the government, and milk cost only 25 cents per litre. The dairy was able to operate at full capacity (15,000 litres) only by importing 5,000 litres of milk a week from Serbia.

The problems facing the dairy illustrate the dangers of relying on a single large-scale project. The benefits of the project were narrowly focused on the relatively small number of new employees, whilst local farmers were disappointed with the prices offered to them. The dairy needed to import subsidized milk from Serbia to operate efficiently, and the intended beneficiaries – the local dairy farmers – did not benefit as much as expected from the project. The case study illustrates the way in which the motives and intentions of the donors and recipients, principals and agents, can interact to produce below optimal outcomes, and reduce the effectiveness of aid interventions.

## Conclusions

The economics literature on aid and economic development is undecided about the macroeconomic impact of international assistance. Some studies appear to show that there is little relationship between aid and growth, and that much of the financial transfers associated with aid flow into consumption rather than investment. Other studies indicate that the impact of aid is conditional on the policies followed by the recipient government. Some studies also argue that aid is more effective in post-conflict situations, or where poverty is severe. The findings are controversial and depend sensitively on the definitions and the sampling frames that are used to generate the empirical regression results. In this chapter I have argued that a number of additional factors should be taken into account in considering the impact of international aid on local economic development. These are (a) the role of policy transfer which links aid flows to policy advice and makes policy an endogenous factor, (b) the aims and purposes of the actors in the 'principal agent' chain of aid donations, and (c) the specificity of institutions in the localities and neighbourhoods to which aid is provided. These considerations point to the need for in-depth case studies of the impact of international aid on local economic development.

In this chapter I have taken as an example the case of North Montenegro, an historically underdeveloped area in one of the poorest countries in SEE. International donor activities have for the most part mirrored the central government's neglect of the North. Where international donors have provided aid it has often been in pursuit of agendas that bear little relationship to the real developmental needs of the region. The EU intervention in 2000 to distribute dairy cattle to farmers was essentially guided by the political motive to bolster the electoral support for the pro-independence parties. Subsequent policy advice to liberalize the trade regime undermined the local economy of the North, already weakened by years of sanctions and isolation from neighbouring and international markets.

Micro-credit programmes that have been sponsored by bilateral donors and NGOs have been technically efficient in terms of loan recovery rates but have provided incentives for projects with quick returns rather than long-term development. Financial assistance provided by government schemes has suffered from the problems of capture by interest groups and from administrative inefficiency. Local economic development is caught in the gap between these two approaches. In another example considered, the construction of a dairy was heavily influenced by the determination of the donor to provide a beacon of commercial rationality with the result that the original aims of the project to provide income to local farmers was undermined by the commercial incentive for the dairy to import cheap subsidized milk from Serbia.

These cases provide examples in which the interaction of the aims and purposes of the various actors in the donor-recipient chain have led to sub-optimal or even perverse outcomes. This does not mean that there have not also been success stories. The example of a USAID-funded Community Revitalisation programme could be mentioned as one of the more successful projects in the region; but even that, based upon the policy transfer of notions of community involvement from the US context and on the development of *ad-hoc* municipal councils, could be criticized for by-passing institutions of local democracy and representation.[12]

Overall the findings reported in this chapter point to the complexities of the relationships involved in local economic development and clearly indicate that neither international aid nor policy transfer are likely to provide easy solutions to the endemic problems of poverty and underdevelopment in the backward regions of the transition economies of South-East Europe.

## Notes

1. The region of North Montenegro includes the municipalities of Pljevlja, Bijelo Polje, Berane, Rozaje, and Plav. These municipalities are part of the old Ottoman district of Sandzak, which straddles the Montenegrin–Serbian border. The Sandzak still retains vestiges of this older identity and a number of political parties and newspapers are devoted to its rehabilitation as a distinct region.
2. Elections held in 2002 gave a narrow parliamentary majority to the DPS-SDP coalition. The pro-Serbia parties gained a majority of the votes in some of the municipalities in the North, including Andrijevica (66.7 per cent) and Pljevlja (58.3 per cent). Other northern municipalities have large minorities of Bosniak Muslims (Rožaje) and Albanians (Plav) (see Sistek and Dimitrovova 2003). These groups tend to support the pro-independence parties, and the pro-Yugoslav vote was just 5 per cent in Rožaje and 20 per cent in Plav. Despite their political orientation, those two municipalities have also been relatively neglected by the central government.
3. 'Privatization' in Montenegro has taken the perverse form of effective nationalization, of formerly socially owned enterprises.
4. 'Korupcija, siva ekonomija i politizacija kadrova' [Corruption, the grey economy and the politicisation of officials] A.P. in the newspaper *Publika*, 5/4/03, p. 10.
5. The author carried out fieldwork on behalf of a bilateral aid agency in North Montenegro in March 2003. The discussion draws on interviews carried out with local officials and aid workers and on documentation collected at that time and subsequently.
6. Through the 'privatization' process of the early 1990s the Development Fund became a shareholder in 371 companies, which were thus converted from socially ownership into state owned companies.
7. Inevitably the estimation of gross job creation overestimates net job creation due to the impact of deadweight loss and displacement effects.
8. See Development Fund of Montenegro 'Annual Report' 2002 (p.10).
9. See 'Program integralnog razvoja područja Crnogorskih Prokletija', Podgorica: Ministarstvo Turizma Crne Gore, April 2001.
10. See 'Touristic Masterplan for Montenegro – Executive Summary'.
11. See Birchmore *et al.* (2002).
12. Recall the Collier and Dollar critique of 'working around' the government set out on pp. 2–3 above.

# 9

# Rediscovering the Value of the Co-operative Sector in SEE: History, Current Developments and Some Ideas for the Future

*Milford Bateman*[1]

## Introduction

Co-operatives are enterprises/institutions owned and controlled by their members, who may be their workers, customers, service users, or simply concerned individuals within the community. Ownership and control is determined not by capital invested, but by membership of the co-operative and a system of 'one person-one vote'. Co-operatives offer to both members and to the wider community alike many important economic and non-economic advantages. As the ILO has long concluded (ILO 1981, 2002; Parnell 2001; Birchall 2001, 2003), for a number of reasons co-operatives are vital community-based institutions: they create new and sustain existing jobs, help to establish and underpin economic and political democracy, promote greater equality of wealth and power, help to ensure greater personal dignity and self-respect in the workplace, underpin employment security and continuity, facilitate market access and higher returns for small-scale agricultural/rural producers and artisans, and help build crucially important reserves of solidarity and trust (social capital) in the community.

By the end of the 20th century, in spite of much hostility from established business traditions and elites, the co-operative movement had made significant progress right across the world. Very many individual co-operative experiments had managed to achieve considerable local success (Birchall 1997; Parnell 2001). It was also possible to point to an increasing number of highly efficient local/regional co-operative systems, notably the famous Mondragon Co-operative complex in the Basque region of northern Spain (Foote-Whyte and Foote-Whyte 1988) and important regional clusters of co-operatives in the northern Italian regions, such as in Emilia-Romagna (Holmstrom 1989; Brusco and Pezzini 1990). In developing countries, too, the co-operative movement has played a central role in successful local and regional economic development, most notably in India (especially in the state of Kerala – Parayil, 2000), South Korea, Taiwan, Brazil and China since 1980 (Hirschman 1985;

Ranis and Stewart 1993; Girardin and Ping 1997; Harper 1991; Harper and Roy 2000). Most recently, co-operatives are said to represent one of the best possible local collective defences against the destructive economic and social effects of globalization (Shuman 2000; Gunn 2004). For example, the EC now sees the co-operative sector playing a crucial role in protecting and extending the European social economy model (EC 2001b), while the UN and many EU governments portray co-operatives as vital poverty reduction tools that can help achieve the Millennium Development Goals (Stiglitz 2004; Co-operative College 2005).

This chapter explores the potential role that co-operatives can play in the still ongoing reconstruction and development of SEE. Particular emphasis is placed upon the situation in the Republic of Croatia, where a major data gathering and policy formulation exercise was carried out in 2003 (Bateman and Maleković 2003). The chapter starts with an appreciation of the rich history of co-operative development in South East Europe. This includes paying some attention to the 'worker self-management' system pioneered in Yugoslavia between 1950 and 1990, which was tantamount to an economy-wide network of worker co-operatives. I then examine the main problematic issues and barriers relating to co-operative development in Croatia, which are largely generalizable right across South East Europe. In the final section I provide some brief recommendations with regard to the most urgent policy interventions now required.

## Background to co-operative development in SEE

After getting started in Western Europe in the late 18th and early 19th century (Birchall 1997), the co-operative concept very quickly emerged further East. It then moved south to almost all developing countries (then colonies) as well. The co-operative concept reached South-East Europe as early as the mid-1850s. By the mid to late 1800s an extensive network of agricultural and financial co-operatives was in operation in the Balkans, particularly extensive and efficient in Slovenia (Čuješ 1980). These new co-operatives provided very many obvious benefits for the rural areas and they became the most popular and well supported community-based institutions of the time. Through their co-operatives many individuals and communities were able to organize most of the important aspects of life, particularly the provision of affordable financial services and market access. By 1930 the co-operative sector in Yugoslavia was flourishing and it had the largest co-operative assets of all countries in SEE (Lampe 1996: 1691). Notwithstanding a number of setbacks, such as the after-effects of the worldwide Great Depression, prior to the Second World War the co-operative movement in South-East Europe had clearly become an integral part of the economic and social structure, and for sure an institution of absolutely pivotal importance to the region's rural communities (Lampe 1996).

As in the Soviet Union after 1917, however, in the centrally planned economies that arose in South-East Europe after the end of the Second World War in 1945 – Bulgaria, Romania, Albania, Yugoslavia (until 1950) – genuine co-operatives were rapidly emasculated and incorporated into the overall central planning framework (Balawyder 1980). Just as much as their capitalist elite counterparts in Western Europe, the new communist elites in Eastern Europe also feared genuine cooperatives and independent worker-based activity and empowerment. Successful co-operative development might suggest to the wider population a more efficient and more popular alternative to the prevailing system of 'top down' central planning. The communist authorities therefore took steps to suppress co-operative ideals and concepts, and to prevent any genuine co-operatives emerging in practice. Even though a Soviet-ized version of the co-operative concept was allowed to emerge under communism in SEE – so-called 'state co-operatives' – their dictatorial management structures, lack of democracy, unmotivated workers and low productivity only served to further discredit the term 'co-operative' among the wider population.

After several years of attempting to establish a functioning Soviet-style central planning system, Yugoslavia broke away from Soviet ideology and control and effectively converted the entire industrial structure into 'worker co-operatives'. The new system of 'worker self-management' came into being in 1950. Responsibility for an industrial unit was transferred over to its employees, who were thenceforth given substantial autonomy to manage their enterprise through an elected Workers Council (Singleton 1985). At the same time, the property and assets of state enterprises became so-called 'social property' – that is, it could be used by the employees in the new worker self-managed units as they saw fit, but it could not be sold, transferred to another party, or otherwise disposed of. This replicated a form of pure common ownership co-operative, neither private nor state ownership, found in many western countries. In the agricultural sector, the old agricultural co-operatives were modified somewhat and partially incorporated into the worker self-management system.

The first years after the new worker self-management system was introduced were difficult. Initially, the state retained considerable influence over the strategic policy of each new worker self-managed unit, though the Workers Council was still able and willing to argue its corner successfully on many issues of importance to the enterprise and its employees. In the early 1960s, the autonomy enjoyed by each worker self-managed unit was extended quite considerably within the emerging semi-market economy, leading to the period of so-called 'market socialism' (Estrin 1983). As the Yugoslav economy entered the 1970s, however, a number of adverse developments took place that undermined the worker self-management system. *Inter alia* it was felt that too many elected managers were using manipulation, deception and corrupt links to local politicians in order to stay in power and personally enrich themselves at the expense of regular employees. Growing regional disparities in income and wealth were also severely undermining the cohesiveness of the Federation (Pleština 1992). A series of decentralizing reforms aimed at addressing these and other problems were implemented. However, the reforms only exacerbated the lack of democracy and accountability and, combined with a world oil price hike in 1979, actually had the effect of quickly pushing the Yugoslav economy into crisis. Horvat and others continued to make the case for genuine worker co-operative structures to be allowed to emerge from the impending collapse of Yugoslav communism (Horvat 1982), joined by many more as Yugoslavia itself began to collapse (Ellerman 1990; Estrin 1991), but these efforts were largely in vain. Starting in 1989, the Yugoslav worker self-management system was legislated out of existence and consigned to the history books.[2]

Looking back, and especially if we apply fairly the hindsight offered to us by more than 15 years of what is increasingly being perceived as a failed transition in SEE (see below), the Yugoslav system of worker self-management was actually something of a comparative success story. For sure the first two decades of worker self-management in Yugoslavia were instrumental in helping Yugoslavia quickly recover and grow under enormously difficult post-war conditions (Waterston 1962). Indeed, in the 1950s and 1960s, the Yugoslav worker self-managed economy emerged as one of the world's fastest growing economies, and for several years over this period the fastest growing economy in the world (World Bank 1975; Ottolenghi and Steinherr 1993). Living standards in parts of the northern Republics of Slovenia and Croatia rose in the 1970s to near Western European levels, allowing the traditionally always poorer southern Republics and regions (especially Kosovo) to benefit from the 1960s onwards from a substantial flow of EU-style regional development aid. Overall, the worker self-management system clearly underpinned successful growth and development in a number of very important inter-related ways, especially in terms of higher productivity and investment (Horvat 1976, 2000). One other important aspect was the way that it also undoubtedly generated high levels of trust, participation, motivation, inclusion, volunteerism and goodwill (Barratt-Brown 1996). These important solidarity factors – what we now refer to as 'social capital' – played a pivotal economic and social development role not unlike that in Northern Italy's successful post-war 'consensus-driven' development experience (Putnam 1993).

The period 1988 to 2000 saw at least four virtually identical neoliberal reform packages introduced in the region under the auspices of the World Bank and IMF.[3] The predicted outcome of each of these neoliberal reform packages was for a rapid, broad based and sustainable recovery (Sachs 1990; World Bank 1991, 1997, 2000a; World Bank *et al.* 1996). Yet rather than being associated with sustainable growth and development, the World Bank/IMF-piloted transition to capitalism in South-East Europe instead precipitated economic and social collapse.

As a result of the emerging failure of the neoliberal project in South-East Europe, and because of several other developments (e.g. the World Bank's recent 'discovery' that social capital is perhaps the 'missing link' in development – Grootaert 1997), the real possibility finally began to arise of there being meaningful international and government support for alternative community-driven local economic development initiatives such as co-operatives. The word 'co-operative' even began to appear in important World Bank documents, such as in the prestigious *World Development Report* (World Bank 2001). From the late 1990s onwards a number of fairly substantive co-operative development programmes were indeed established in SEE.

## Co-operative development in Croatia

The co-operative movement in Croatia began to emerge more or less in parallel with the first pioneering experiments in Western Europe in the mid-1800s. Following the lines of the first co-operative structures established in Rochdale in 1844, in 1862 in present day Croatia a number of co-operatives (*Zadruge*) were established in Pitomača and on the island of Korčula. Many more co-operatives became established in this region in line with the expansion of the sector in Italy under the influence of the Republican leader and co-operative advocate Giuseppe Mazzini. In 1895 in Dalmatia and Istria, a Slovene, Janez Krek, launched a parish-based co-operative network which, by as early as 1912, involved more than 400 functioning credit co-operatives with 115,000 members and 170 agricultural co-operatives (Lampe 1996: 75). Agricultural co-operatives were particularly quick to get started in Croatia. Financial co-operatives based upon the Raiffeisen model also continued to grow in the wake of the growing credit needs of the expanding agricultural co-operative sector, and they quickly began to displace the networks of private money-lenders that traditionally had always stunted rural development in the region (Tomašević 1955). By 1930 in Croatia low interest loans from the financial co-operative sector accounted for upwards of 15 per cent of total agricultural debt (Lampe and Jackson 1982: 375) – considerably less than Slovenia's equivalent co-operative sector agricultural debt of 30 per cent, but nevertheless an indication of just how many rural areas across Croatia were increasingly able to access low interest rate credit. Worker and artisan co-operatives also began to emerge thanks to the Italian and Austro-Hungarian influence in Croatia, and also because the local conditions of high unemployment, very low wages, and strong local traditions of co-operation naturally led on to such 'bottom up' collective structures. Consumer co-operatives also began to emerge to provide higher quality and cheaper services in remote areas, especially on the islands. Partly in order to avoid the clutches of commercial middlemen operating in the grain industry, the Croatian Peasant Party (HSS) had established in the 1930s a co-operative network (*Gospodarska Sloga*) that by 1940 had grown to involve more than one third of all Croatian farming households (Lampe 1996: 170).

Immediately after 1945 an attempt was made to collectivize the agricultural sector. Long-standing agricultural co-operatives were quickly taken over, private land was confiscated and central planning introduced. The collectivization drive was a huge mistake and it was abandoned only a few years later (Horvat 1976). State financial support was offered to the agricultural co-operative sector from the late 1950s onwards, and the routine state purchasing of the often very varied outputs of the private farming sector largely removed many traditional rural insecurities. However, constant interference by the state became an enduring feature. For example, machinery and equipment could be taken from one co-operative to another without any warning. More urbanized delegates were often imposed on the co-operative's Council in order to avoid them becoming too reliant on peasant representatives from the rural communities, or so-called 'peasantizing' (*seljakovanje*). Self-initiation of new co-operatives – so-called 'wild' co-operatives – was discouraged as much as possible. However, the agricultural co-operative sector plunged into crisis in the mid-1960s as the reduction in state aid reduced farmers' motivation for wanting to join an organization that was now operating on strongly commercial lines. When these more commercial imperatives were introduced, in line with the general marketization of the Yugoslav economy then underway, many farmers began to resent the high prices charged for processing, packaging and selling on of their outputs (Horvat 1976: 155). Moreover, the major restructuring of worker-self-management in the mid-1970s even more firmly established the employees of agricultural co-operatives in a powerful position *vis-à-vis* members, further reducing the level of member motivation and participation.

By 1990, the worker self-management system was no more, while in the agricultural sector there were fewer than 300 weakly functioning agricultural co-operatives, involving some 20,000 members, 10,000 employees and around 100,000 voluntary co-operators (mainly small private farms).[4] The agricultural co-operative sector in Croatia went into another crisis shortly after independence in 1991 when the old agricultural co-operatives were sold off to the highest bidder or, more commonly, taken over by the senior managers of the co-operative. This episode was not confined to the co-operative sector, but was instead just one facet of the problematic privatization process that got underway in Croatia as a whole after 1991 (Bartlett 2003).

Moreover, government policy after independence in 1991 was to work against co-operatives. Co-operatives hinted to some of old style collective/socialist structures and values, an association particularly anathema to the new right wing government under President Franjo Tudjman, as well as to the World Bank and IMF and key western governments. The result was that rather than allow the main functioning agricultural co-operatives to restructure into genuine Western European-style co-operatives, the first Croatian government instead worked hard to dissolve most of them. Just as with regard to the wider socially owned enterprise sector, most of the largest and best agricultural co-operatives were 'restructured' and the resulting assets carefully distributed to favoured groups and individuals. The nature of the intended goal of this global project – termed the '200 families project' – was the transfer of Croatia's inherited commonly owned asset base into the hands of around 200 of the most 'reputable' and 'loyal' individuals and their families (Bartlett 2003). Co-operatives and co-operative ownership were clearly antithetical concepts with regard to the overt effort to rapidly reconstitute a domestic capitalist elite.

The economic and social urgency of there being a genuine co-operative sector in Croatia was only finally recognized when the first post-Tudjman government came to power in 2000. A new vision of rural development resulted in the formation of a new Co-operatives Department within the new Ministry of SMEs and Crafts. Co-operative development was seen as a key instrument that could assist in the promotion of sustainable local economies, balanced rural development and the recovery of the 'Areas of Special State Concern' (the former conflict regions). The new Croatian government was also instrumental in establishing the Croatian Co-operative Federation (HZS). This new institution was meant to replace the old Croatian Co-operative Alliance (HSZ), which had discredited itself both by its inactivity and, probably more so, by its open support for the conversion of the largest agricultural co-operatives into private companies. To support the activities of the new HZS, the new Croatian government first gave it the legal right to the mandatory membership fees previously collected by the Croatian Chamber of Crafts. Additional 'pump priming' financial support was also provided with which the HZS was supposed to develop its membership base and provide some services to its newly re-registered members. The EU also helped by financing the preparation of the 'Co-operative Development Strategy for Croatia' by a team of international and local consultants (Bateman and Maleković 2003). This helped the HZS assume a more visible policy-making role in the co-operative movement, including with regard to drawing up a new Law on Co-operatives to replace the 1995 Law on Co-operatives. Additional EU financial support was also offered for a number of agricultural co-operative development programmes in the war-affected regions. Subsequently, following a strategic review of the sustainable development needs of the post-conflict regions (Bateman, 2004b), the World Bank and EU combined to offer a sizeable financial and technical support package that very much included the agricultural co-operative sector. The World Bank's Post-Conflict Facility also financed and provided technical support for a sizeable co-operative development project in the Krajina region. Other foreign assistance bodies, such as the USAID and GTZ, also began to support co-operative development more actively; again, particularly in the post-conflict regions. The most recent data on the current structure and numbers of co-operatives are given in the following table, Table 9.1.

Table 9.1 indicates a number of important things. The lack of worker co-operatives is a stark reminder of the complete break with the worker

*Table 9.1* Number and type of co-operatives registered as active in Croatia as of January 2005

| *Type* | *No.* |
|---|---|
| Agricultural | 338 |
| Crafts | 79 |
| Financial | 44 |
| Housing | 10 |
| Consumer | n.a. |
| Worker | n.a. |
| Total | 495 |

*Note*: n.a.: not applicable.
*Source*: Based on data supplied by the Croatian Co-operative Federation (HZS), 2005.

self-management system. The absence of consumer co-operatives, traditionally one of the strongest aspects of the co-operative movement in the region, is also noticeable. Financial co-operatives are reasonably well represented, as are the traditionally strong rural-based craft co-operatives, though both sectors remain very weak and under-capitalized. The bulk of functioning co-operatives in Croatia today are found in the agricultural sector, with 338 active agricultural co-operatives considered to be operating in 2005 out of a total of just under 500 registered agricultural co-operatives. As we will see below, however, many of these active agricultural co-operatives are very small indeed, some with no more than a handful of members. The decline of the agricultural co-operative sector is shown in more stark detail in Table 9.2, which shows that the number of registered agricultural co-operatives in Croatia declined quite rapidly from 1989 onwards, until eventually stabilizing at the end of the 1990s. Thanks to the new initiatives indicated above, the co-operative sector has staged a very limited recovery in the last five years or so.

Although the last five years has brought some more positive developments, particularly in terms of technical and financial support, overall the current situation of the co-operative sector in Croatia looks rather bleak: declining numbers, weak existing co-operatives, few new genuine co-operatives being established, non-existent support structures, and confusion in the co-operative sector as to its real direction and purpose. There are clearly a number of serious barriers to sustainable co-operative development in Croatia, and it is to an examination of these that we turn in the next section.

## Key co-operative development issues in Croatia

Given the growing willingness to provide financial and technical support for co-operative development in Croatia, it became increasingly important to

*Table 9.2* Number of registered agricultural co-operatives in Croatia in selected years

| Year | 1989 | 1995 | 2000 | Change 1995–2000 (%) | 2004 | Change 1995–2004 (%) | Change 2000–2004 (%) |
|---|---|---|---|---|---|---|---|
| Co-ops | 2200 | 1,212 | 787 | −35 | 495 | −59 | −37 |
| Employees | – | 5,090 | 2,762 | −46 | 3,143 | −38 | +14 |
| Members | – | 20,650 | 13,063 | −37 | 14,335 | −31 | +10 |

*Source*: Based on Croatian Co-operative Federation (HZS), 2005.

understand the key internal and external factors that affect co-operative development (Davis 1999). Accordingly, as part of the preparatory work for the National Co-operative Development Strategy for Croatia, a data collection exercise was undertaken in 2003 (Bateman and Maleković, 2003). From the interview and data collection programme it was possible to distil the following core problematic issues.

### Competitive pressure from the informal sector ('grey economy')

The massive rise in the informal sector since 1990 is one of the most marked features of the transition in South-East Europe (Bateman 2004a). In Croatia it is currently estimated that the informal sector accounts for over 30 per cent of the total output of the Croatian economy, somewhat smaller than most other South-East European countries, but a very large part of the Croatian economy nevertheless (Bateman 2004a).The informal sector impacts very negatively upon the co-operative sector in a number of ways. By their very nature, co-operatives tend to operate in the formal sector. Co-operatives are reluctant to avoid their responsibilities towards the wider community and the state, such as paying taxes, providing good working conditions, paying social benefits, and so on. This naturally puts them in an unfavourable and unfair competitive position compared with the many informal enterprises that do not share such a responsible approach. To the extent that the informal sector achieves greater competitiveness through its refusal to abide by the formal norms of economic life, the emerging co-operative sector cannot hope to compete. Accordingly, when the traditional agricultural supply chains and state co-operative structures largely collapsed after 1990, it was not surprising that networks of informal intermediaries quickly emerged to organize the agricultural supply chain, from basic producer right through to final retailer. These intermediaries generally involve irregular collection and cash-in-hand payments. Many intermediaries actually offer a poor overall service to the farmers that choose to work with them, but because immediate cash is offered, they still have little trouble finding potential suppliers. Many small farmers are *de facto* forced to remain within the informal economy simply in order to survive in the short term. They are forced to ignore the longer run negative consequences to themselves and to the wider communities that arise. As a result of the informal sector's power to take advantage of the situation and reduce margins and prices to rock bottom levels, many other farmers in Croatia have been forced to cease farming altogether. This has resulted *inter alia* in much of the prime cultivable land in Croatia no longer under crop.[5] The overall end result is that a large share of agricultural output in Croatia is produced, processed, packaged and sold through informal private sector intermediaries, rather than through the farmer owned and controlled co-operative structures that are traditionally far more advantageous to the farmer.

### Open membership

Open membership is one of the core principles of a genuine co-operative (ICA 1996). Existing members must allow for those they work with to become members. This stipulation exists to avoid the co-operative degenerating into a two-tier body not unlike a conventional investor-driven enterprise – that is, freely using the contribution from large numbers of non-members, but channeling most of the benefits to members. Worse, when existing members depart the co-operative for whatever reason – a better-paying job, retirement, death, and so forth – the co-operative will eventually effectively convert into a private company.

There is very strong evidence to suggest that very many of the agricultural co-operatives established in Croatia over the last decade deliberately restrict membership rights to a select few, usually the founder-members. For example, the ratio between members and non-members would appear to be very high, around 1 to 20, which is much higher than in most other EU agricultural co-operatives. When questioned, founder-members tend to justify the situation in a number of ways. Most often they argue that it is actually the case that many non-members are simply disinterested in membership. A persistent variation on this theme is that because the co-operative (deliberately) offers the same level of services to both members and non-members alike, there is no reason to want to join the co-operative as a member.[6] Second, founder-members also very often argue that the co-operative will not be managed properly by involving in it a group of rural people with admittedly little formal education and business experience. Many non-members highlighted the fact that they would like to join the co-operative with which they work on a daily basis, but are denied the chance on a number of spurious reasons. Sometimes the membership fee is simply far too high. Many non-members were also correct in their firm belief that it was actually the *policy* of the co-operative to restrict membership to the founders or a select few of the subsequent members. On closer examination of the internal rules of a number of agricultural co-operatives, the founder-members were found to have deliberately and permanently placed control in their own hands. This was most often done by inserting into the Internal Rules a clause allocating to founder-members a permanent 'right' to constitute the Management Board (*Nadzorni Odbor*), perhaps together with one or two other members they handpick themselves. Although this contradicts the ethos of the co-operative concept, such types of abuse of the Internal Rules have emerged as a slightly more formal way of skirting around the weak legal requirements and regulations governing the co-operative movement in Croatia.

**'Pseudo-co-operatives'**

Due to the lack of transparency in the privatization process, a significant number of the oldest and most successful agricultural co-operatives in Croatia ended up in the hands of just a few of their former senior managers. In the privatization law of 1991, co-operative property was not recognized: only state and private property forms were accorded legal status. The decision to denote co-operative property and assets as state property meant that co-operative assets could then be sold off to interested parties, including former employee/members. Recognizing this loophole, many senior managers in the largest agricultural co-operatives began to push from within to take control of the co-operative. Many long-standing members were gradually pushed out and their membership rights cancelled, sometimes in return for a token financial payment. As intended, the co-operative was slowly converted into a company owned by the senior managers. The co-operative could then either distribute all profit to the small number of members/owners, or else they could eventually sell the co-operative for an immediate financial gain for themselves. Such co-operatives were denoted as 'pseudo-co-operatives' (Bateman and Maleković 2003). Over the 1990s most of the largest and most successful co-operatives in Croatia were gradually transformed into private companies in this manner. For the reasons noted above, the Croatian government was uninterested to intervene to halt this process of privatization. Even worse, the co-operative sector's then apex membership body – the (HSZ) – actually *assisted* in the dismantling of the largest agricultural co-operatives, providing political and other forms of protection for many of the largest 'pseudo-co-operatives' in return for their continued financial contributions.

A further variation on the 'pseudo-co-operative' theme emerged in the early 1990s in the shape of many so-called 'family co-operatives' (*obiteljske zadruge*). Typically, the organization of 'family co-operatives' involves a small group of entrepreneurs bringing together a number of families into a horizontal 'co-operative' structure. This 'family co-operative' structure then contractually agrees to undertake a particular task within the agricultural supply chain, such as milk production, bull fattening and so on. The 'family co-operative' structure is highly functional in establishing higher levels of self-organization, solidarity and collective effort, which ultimately leads to higher productivity (Blinder 1990). At the same time as establishing the 'family co-operative' structure, however, the small group of entrepreneurs purposely positions itself in the supply chain either vertically above or below the 'family co-operative' in a company or even another co-operative structure. For example, the 'family co-operative' is put under contract to sell all its output through the entrepreneurs, or perhaps contractually it must buy all of a particular key input through them. The result is that the actual power and independence the 'family co-operative' enjoys in practice is quite minimal: in fact, as intended, power and control deliberately rests with the entrepreneurs. The bulk of the value added created in the supply chain by the 'family co-operative', *pointedly including the additional value generated by the co-operative-induced higher productivity*, is then largely, if not entirely, appropriated by the initiating entrepreneurs. Rather than a reflection of 19th century solidarity and mutual support within the community, therefore, the 21st century version of the 'family co-operative' concept was more often than not just a subtle form of manipulation and exploitation, thus further discrediting the co-operative concept in Croatia as a result.

## Co-operative degeneration

In line with most EU countries, the 1995 Co-operative Act specified that in Croatia a co-operative's assets were held in common ownership rather than individual ownership. Thus, according to Article 19 of the 1995 Law, a departing co-operative member had no right to demand his/her proportionate share of the co-operative's entire value. This provision was meant to ensure that the co-operative would not be subject to the gradual leakage of its asset base by having to constantly pay off departing members. Without such a clause, a co-operative would inevitably be de-capitalized over time, and thus become less competitive *vis-à-vis* the conventional investor-driven enterprise sector. If a large section of the membership happened to depart simultaneously, moreover, then the co-operative would clearly risk going bankrupt. However, the common ownership rule was removed in the amendments to the 1995 Co-operative Act passed in early 2002. Article 15 of the Decree issued in February 2002, removed the offending Article (Article 19 paragraph 2) stipulating common ownership. Article 15 also removed the restriction on members pushing to wind up a co-operative in order to distribute the assets. Article 15 also added a new paragraph to the 1995 Co-operatives Act specifying that on departure a member is entitled to a proportionate share of the assets commensurate with the members' contribution over the time period as a member of the co-operative. These amendments passed in 2002 were added in good faith in order to encourage greater membership of co-operatives in the short term. But the practical result was not more newly established co-operatives, but more pressure from some co-operative members to take out of the co-operative as much value as possible. Over the longer term the new ownership structure and member rights in Croatia have had the widely anticipated effect of undermining the longer-term viability of the co-operative movement. Constantly reallocating capital assets to departing members will undermine any co-operative structure, particularly in today's increasingly competitive business environment where enterprises must constantly invest in order to survive and expand.

**Lack of specialization**

Many of the co-operatives that existed prior to 1991 were of the so-called 'general co-operative' variety (*opće zadruge*). These types of co-operatives usually sold the entire diversified output of the small farmers, and also provided inputs at lower prices. They established a solid and reasonably efficient link between the supply potential of the rural regions and demand from the urban areas. Such forms of co-operative were popular with the farming communities both before and during the worker self-management period. As everywhere else, farming communities desire above all to have higher incomes and security of income, and the co-operative structures at this time helped to provide both.

Local attempts to rebuild the co-operative sector in Croatia after 1990 often failed to understand the inherent inefficiency of the 'general co-operative' structure in the new market and political realities. In particular, global competition, the introduction of free trade regimes and the extreme competitive threat arising from several countries and regions where agriculture is highly subsidized (for example, the EU)[7], means that such very small-scale agricultural structures cannot realistically hope to compete and retain market share in Croatia. It is clearly imperative that more specialized co-operatives are promoted as one way of encouraging a greater degree of specialization in the agricultural sector as a whole. The need for more specialization appears to have been largely accepted by the Ministry of Agriculture and extension services, but less so by the farming community. Many co-operative member-farmers in Croatia still wish to reserve the right to decide what outputs to produce, but nevertheless expect that their co-operative will buy up and attempt to sell on whatever it is that they decide to produce. Crucially, a lack of specialization implies very little use of state-of-the-art machinery and equipment, the deployment of new agricultural technologies, and a need for skilled labour.

**Lack of financial support**

Even more than with regard to the SME sector in general, private financial institutions in Croatia are quite unwilling to offer support to co-operatives. The largely foreign-owned commercial banking sector in Croatia has very little interest in supporting *any* domestic enterprise projects, preferring to support trade and consumer credit in the main. The Croatian Bank for Reconstruction and Development (HBOR) mainly intermediates its funding support through the commercial banks, thus also ending up largely reflecting short term commercial priorities rather than the need to promote sustainable development. The few micro-finance institutions that work in Croatia have mainly supported unsustainable development trajectories: first, a wave of small-scale traders and retailers, and then, when this first wave began to collapse, a second wave of equally unsustainable small-scale household agricultural activities, such as three cow milk farms. The commercial imperatives inherent in most of these micro-finance institutions means that they generally support only simple, short-term oriented business ventures (Bateman 2003, 2004b). Good initial intentions to do otherwise are quickly lost to commercial imperatives that help to ensure institutional survival, and thus also, not unimportantly, the employment opportunities of those involved. A long mooted 'Bank for SMEs', which would include a mandate to support co-operative development in Croatia, still remains to be established. In the meantime, the Croatian government has managed to establish a financial support programme for co-operatives involving very modest funding (only around 3,000 Euros) to assist with registration and set up costs. But because there is no matching institutional support (see next section) it was overwhelmingly taken up by conventional businesses pretending to be co-operatives (Bateman 2004b). Finally, the local network of 70 savings and loans co-operatives in Croatia has a poor reputation for efficiency and security, but anyway their very small asset base precludes significant support for co-operative development. In short, therefore, there remains a crucial 'funding gap' in Croatia for co-operative development.

### Unfavourable tax treatment

The co-operative sector in Croatia does not benefit from any forms of favourable tax treatment. Co-operatives are obliged to pay income tax, corporate tax and VAT in exactly the same manner as investor-driven companies. Worse, unlike in most EU countries, co-operative members in Croatia are subject to tax from any dealings they have *within* the co-operative. In practise, this means that VAT is levied on all transactions between members and their co-operative, which clearly undermines much of the rationale for joining the co-operative in the first place. For example, when passing on to members the raw materials purchased by the co-operative (fertilizer, seeds, etc.) it is necessary to levy VAT on the agreed price. An even more serious problem arises with regard to agricultural co-operatives and the agricultural cycle. Not only are all transactions between members and their co-operative subject to VAT, but any VAT liability incurred is also deemed payable at the time of the transaction. Yet if the raw materials purchased – for example, grapes or fruit bushes – are associated with the production and/or sale of a product some time into the future – fruit, wine – the VAT recouped in the final sale price may be received several years after the initial VAT payment was made. This represents a significant additional financial burden for the co-operative's members. The taxation system also fails to discriminate between co-operative members and non-members (*kooperanti*) who work with the co-operative on a purely market basis. Legal contracts are required for both members and non-members alike. It is also a clear discouragement to even simply work with the co-operative as a non-member, because it is perfectly possible to purchase items on the 'grey economy' where VAT is avoided.

### Lack of dedicated advice and support

Croatia has a number of representative bodies for the co-operative sector at the national and regional level, and even a number at the local level (such as in Zadar county). The two main national apex organizations for the co-operative sector, the HSZ, and the Croatian Agricultural Co-operative Alliance (HPZS), are joined by six regional associations operating across Croatia. However, in the very depressed conditions prevailing in Croatia, and in rural areas in particular, the membership base simply cannot pay anything other than a token membership fee, which in most cases barely covers the cost of maintaining irregular postal or telephone contact with them. The result is that all of the main co-operative representative bodies in Croatia are struggling to keep themselves afloat and they are currently able to offer only a very limited service to existing members. Moreover, there are obvious moral and practical problems expecting very poor co-operative members to financially support specifically development activities undertaken by their representative bodies. And even though some international donors are willing to offer financial support in order to support the advisory services offered by some co-operative membership bodies, this largely only postpones their core financial/capacity problem rather than solves it. Finally, exactly the same institutional sustainability conundrum prevails in the mainstream enterprise development support bodies in Croatia, such as the Entrepreneurship Centres, Local Economic Development Agencies (LEDAs), which are also under significant pressure to raise cash from selling their services. They are therefore equally unlikely to be responsive to the urgent support needs of new and emerging co-operatives (Bateman 2004b).

## Policy implications for SEE

The analysis above has identified some of most serious barriers to sustainable co-operative development in Croatia. Many of these barriers are also clearly generalizable to SEE as a whole. In this final section, therefore, we briefly introduce a number of the most important interventions urgently required in order to promote the sustainable development of the co-operative sector.

The first over-arching policy intervention requirement is to establish a dedicated institutional support structure for the co-operative sector. There is very little recent experience anywhere in the world of market automaticity processes being responsible for establishing a flourishing co-operative enterprise sector. Instead, some form of dedicated and pro-active institutional capacity is almost always required. Perhaps the most appropriate institution to kick-start co-operative development is to establish a dedicated national Co-operative Development Agency (CDA), or several regional-level CDAs. Such a CDA should operate as a public or para-statal agency and would be charged with facilitating co-operative development as a core component of both an economic and social development strategy. Ideally, in order to get down to the grassroots level, it would operate with a local sub-office structure, or else work in very close co-operation with economic and agriculture development departments based within most local governments in South-East Europe. A number of smaller European countries have achieved important results with a national CDA format, including Portugal and several of the Scandinavian countries.

The second major institutional support intervention required addresses the obvious lack of appropriate financial support for the co-operative sector. There is an urgent need for a dedicated Co-operative Bank in each of the South-East European countries. Such a bank would be able to invest into the long-term development of the co-operative sector while, perhaps later on, also providing savings services to co-operative members and anyone with an interest in the co-operative movement. Such an institution needs to learn from other experiences; for example, from the excellent experience of post-1945 Finland where the government helped to establish and capitalize via the state treasury a network of co-operative banks. These subsequently played a major role in the successful development of the very strong co-operative sector seen today (McIntyre 2003). In Italy, too, its post-1945 reconstruction strategy gave a central role to co-operatives at the national level. A special branch of the *Banca Nazionale del Lavoro* was established in order to provide affordable financial support packages for the wide variety of co-operatives (Bartlett and Pridham 1991). The Mondragon co-operative group's *Caja Laboral Popular* (Peoples Bank) is the best example of a dedicated co-operative development bank that has achieved spectacular success in establishing viable co-operatives using savings generated largely within a regional co-operative group itself.

Alongside new national or regional co-operative banks there is also an important role for the existing financial co-operative sector to play in supporting co-operative development and co-operative members in rural areas. These relatively small-scale financial institutions should be given much greater technical and financial support in order that they can provide existing co-operatives and their members with modest and affordable loan arrangements. These loan arrangements can be used for a variety of small-scale investment purposes, such as equipment and stock purchase, irrigation equipment, power generation services (for example, wind and solar power) and so on. Importantly, the provision of small and affordable loans can also help co-operative members avoid the clutches of informal lenders or informal agricultural intermediaries. Moreover, and notwithstanding some important risk diversification arguments, it is eminently preferable in SEE if scarce locally mobilized resources be invested back into the local community itself, rather than transferred out to other (possibly much richer) areas in search of higher returns.

A third major policy initiative is needed to firmly deal with the continued existence of the 'pseudo-co-operative' phenomenon. Two key actions are required. The first is to encourage a gradual phasing-out of a co-operative's employee-members in line with an agreed timetable, possibly using some financial incentives of one kind or another to compensate for the financial benefits they were otherwise expecting to reap from taking over and selling off the co-operative's assets. Perhaps a one-off tax-free payment, rather like a redundancy payment, could be paid over in order to permanently lodge the co-operative's assets under common ownership. Here, therefore, it will also be important when revising most of the current Co-operative Laws in the region to promote the growth of current and future co-operatives on the basis of common ownership, rather than full individual ownership as at present. Full and partial common ownership co-operative structures are familiar within most of the EU and are quite unproblematic, so there is no shortage of guidance and experience in terms of the legal changes that are required in the region.

Closely related to the evolution of many 'pseudo-co-operatives' is the widespread abuse in many co-operatives of the open membership stipulation. Enforcement of the open membership rule is best ensured by a combination of 'carrot and stick' measures. On the 'stick' side, a much more robust legal and regulatory framework is urgently required. Especially when linked to favourable tax treatment, the need to assess what is a genuine co-operative, and what is not, is of major importance. Perhaps the best way to enforce the open membership stipulation is for the co-operative movements own apex bodies to play a central role. The respective national co-operative bodies in the region should be strengthened and encouraged to build a co-operative auditing capacity, which will allow them to ensure that most of the recognized (that is ICA) rules are adhered to in the co-operative sector. This is the situation in many Scandinavian countries, for example, where open membership is strictly enforced by the national co-operative apex body. One way this is done is by offering legal and other support to non-members who approach it for help when full membership has been consistently refused (FDCAC 1993). In addition, a set of 'model rules' should be drawn up in order to better deter a co-operative's founder members from inserting unethical rules into a co-operative's constitution.

On the 'carrot' side, the above analysis should have made it clear that there are strong reasons why co-operatives should be afforded more favourable tax and other financial incentives than investor-driven enterprises. One of the most urgent reasons is the need to encourage informal sector entities – artisans, small farmers, and so on – to gradually formalize their activities through membership of a relevant co-operative. Membership of a co-operative can provide a major opportunity for these informal sector entities to reap economies of scale and scope, as well as tap into the many forms of technical and financial support only available to formally registered entities (for example, loans and grants, training, public sector contracts), all of which will help to offset the many 'benefits' of remaining hidden in the informal sector (Bateman 2004c). Accordingly, many EU countries, most notably Italy, have established special tax breaks, financial programmes and technical support measures for genuine co-operatives. The countries of South-East Europe need to follow this lead as soon as possible.

A fourth intervention relates to the accepted need to promote greater specialization of production in co-operatives. Greater specialization is needed in the co-operative sector in order to ensure higher productivity, lower costs, higher quality, and a better application of appropriate technology and technical support. One method used to encourage this is to establish sectoral development programmes targeting key agricultural co-operative products, such as wine, olives, herbs, and so on. Already a number of these programmes have been established in SEE particularly in relation to the organic products concept. To overcome traditional risk diversification arguments, it is also important to support a co-operative to integrate downstream into processing and retailing areas. For example the establishment or purchase of processing capacities by an agricultural co-operative or group of co-operatives (that is, a secondary co-operative) should be encouraged wherever there are reasonable grounds for commercial viability. The EU experience, notably in Denmark, shows that agricultural co-operatives can best establish their own commercial viability and security by owning – singly or jointly with other co-operatives – their own processing capacities (FDCAC 1993). Slovenia's strategy of privatizing most food processing capacities into the full and part ownership of the country's agricultural co-operatives, which has very clearly been instrumental in the growing strength of the co-operative sector and farmer-members, is another obvious regional example to examine (Bateman and Maleković 2003). Another tried-and-tested methodology is to encourage specialization through government purchasing policies. Government contracts to provide food for schools, hospitals, government offices and so on, can be linked to the purchase of quality outputs from specialized co-operatives. Finally, the role of 'demonstration projects' could also be important here in showing others how it is possible to improve productivity via greater specialization.

A fifth, and final, policy intervention relates to the need to promote the common ownership of co-operative assets. The category of common ownership or indivisible assets needs to be restated and re-established as preferable for the co-operative sector. Without such a condition, the co-operative sector in SEE stands ready to repeat many negative experiences across the world associated with individual asset ownership, especially co-operative decapitalization. In some countries in the region, such as in Croatia, the first requirement is clearly to urgently redraft the Law on Co-operatives to re-state a common ownership provision. All countries in the region should endeavour to establish a Law on Co-operatives that provides for reinvested profit to be divided between investment back into the co-operative, which becomes co-operative (common ownership) property, and cash or deferred bonus payments to members. Second, the Internal Rules (perhaps via the Model Rules concept mentioned above) can be drafted to stipulate a particular division of the profits in advance, in order to discourage a damaging annual 'short termist versus long-termist' debate over the distribution of any profit. Third, and as noted above, the government should seek to encourage reinvestment back into all co-operatives through various forms of tax relief. For example, in Italy tax relief is provided on profit re-invested back into a co-operatives' asset base and which also becomes co-operative property.

## Notes

1. This work represents the author's personal viewpoint. I would like to thank several anonymous referees for their comments and suggestions. Bruno Dallago offered valuable comments on the first draft of the chapter, and I must also add that he was extremely patient. Of course, responsibility for all mistakes and misunderstandings remains solely with the author.
2. Virtually alone among the Yugoslav successor states, and in contravention of all the advice being given to it by the IFIs and foreign advisors, the Slovenian government felt obliged to reconstitute much of its worker self-managed enterprise sector into a substantial employee-owned enterprise sector (Mencinger 1996). Its subsequent good performance would seem to suggest that this was the optimum policy (see also Uvalić and Vaughn-Whitehead 1997).
3. These were: the 1988 IMF reform package in Yugoslavia, the 1990/91 post-independence/post-communist transition policy reforms in the Yugoslav successor states, the reconstruction and development package in Bosnia and Croatia in 1996 following the Dayton Peace agreement, and finally the reconstruction and development policy package in Serbia, Kosovo and Macedonia following the NATO military action against Serbia in 1999 (Bateman 2004a).
4. Information supplied by the Croatian Agricultural Co-operative Association (HPZS) (2003).
5. In 1991 the share of uncultivated arable land was nearly 27 per cent of the total agricultural area (UN FAO and MAF, 2003: 33).
6. Horvat (1976: 137) pointed out that this problem existed even under communism, noting that in the agricultural co-operatives across Yugoslavia in the 1960s and 1970s '. . . formal membership became practically pointless, for the co-operatives ceased to differentiate between members and cooperants'.
7. All of the CEE Countries registered a deterioration in their agricultural trade balance with the EU after 1989, some very significantly (see EC 2002).

# 10

# De-localization, Investments and Knowledge Transfer: The Case of 'Triveneto' Industrial SMEs' De-localization in Romania

*Italo Trevisan*

## Introduction

Italian companies have been very active in CEEC, to the point that Italy comes only after Germany among the exporters to these countries (excluding the Easternmost ones). Since SMEs are the load-bearing structure of the Italian economy and are amazingly dynamic and competitive worldwide (Di Matteo and Piacentini 2003), in the countries where Italy has a large share of that country's imports, they are the leading force of Italian presence.

Such a presence can be seen in the trade of goods and services as well as in the establishment of local subsidiaries. The foreign direct investments made in the CEEC by most SMEs are mostly the result of a de-localization strategy (Innocenti 2003). This strategy involves most often a part only of the productive process (Corò and Grandinetti 1999), so it is possible to say that an international production network is taking shape between Italy and some CEEC, mostly because of international vertical integration (or rather disintegration coupled to networking) by Italian SMEs. This results in stronger and continuous operational contacts between Italian firms and foreign ones. Another peculiarity of the presence of Italian SMEs in CEEC is that they tend to reproduce abroad the typical district structure that characterizes the Italian manufacturing structure (Turato 2001).

These two factors contribute to make the link with Italian SMEs an important component in the development process of the transition countries. In Italy, specialized manufacturing districts – often eccentric to the main industrial areas – played a determinant role in the economic and social development of whole regions that had been left behind in the first process of industrialization of the country. It is possible that, if the process of economic integration with the rest of Europe in a transition country has as one of its main actors the SMEs of Italian industrial districts, the development of that country becomes characterized by a locally ingrained and SMEs-led economic development that spreads to other areas of the country, while causing only relatively minor disruption to the social fabric of those areas. This chapter identifies Romania as one of the countries where this type of development has the greatest chance of happening.

After presenting the methodology and the data used, the first part of the chapter will discuss the Italian industrial district (area sistema), its reproducibility, and present the Veronese footwear district.

The second part will examine the trade, in particular Outward Processing Traffic (OPT) flows, between Italy and the transition countries, identifying Romania as Italy's most significant trading partner among them and gauging how important is de-localization in the overall trade with these countries. More detailed attention will then be given to Romanian trade with Italy, to evaluate whether it is possible to speak of an international production network taking shape between Italy and Romania and in which industries it is happening.

The last part will discuss whether the SMEs de-localization towards Romania can lead to the replication of the area sistema model, and will take the de-localization of the Veneto SMEs and the Veronese footwear district as an example of this process.

## Methodology and data used

The discussion about the Italian industrial district, its 'reproducibility' and trade flows is based on a review of the relevant literature and an analysis of secondary data on international trade. These data seldom have the degree of detail required to show the quantitative dimension of the link between SMEs from industrial districts and transition countries: therefore, it was necessary to apply a certain degree of deduction to the quantitative data and to acquire information about the qualitative aspects of the de-localization process through questionnaires to a number of footwear firms and interviews to relevant individuals in the Verona footwear district. As their number was rather small (nine questionnaires plus six interviews), no generalization is possible. The privileged witnesses interviewed were SMEs owners involved in the de-localization process in Romania, managers of banks present in the CEEC and managers or representatives of business associations (often SME owners themselves).

In order to verify the existence of an international production network between two countries, it is necessary to assess the extent of de-localization of production between them. There are different ways to measure the international de-localization of production. Data on trade between two countries may be used, but it is difficult to isolate fully movements of goods due to the de-localization of production from the normal trade (Sanguigni 1995). OPT data are better: OPT is the consequence of de-localization that affects only part of the production process and results in a double flow of goods: first of basic materials or components from the de-localizing firm to the processing one, then of the processed components back to the first firm. OPT flows can originate payments of various duties and taxes in each leg of the traffic. According to Regulation 636 of 16 March 1982, EU firms are partially exempt from custom duties that fall only on the value added by the processing carried out abroad (Crescini and Mistri 1996: 29). However, to claim the exemption, the company must meet certain conditions that have a cost and are time consuming. Therefore the convenience of conforming to these requirements is directly proportional to the incidence of the levy (Brunetti 1995: 70–1).

Through OPT data it is possible to distinguish the movements of products (temporary exports) that concern goods exported to be further processed in the third country as well as the subsequent imports (re-imports) of those goods. The main problem for using the OPT data for the SEEC, is that OPT is losing importance: since 1997, between EU and CEEC, Association Agreements have been signed that provide for the gradual phasing out of custom duties on the goods traded. After 1997, then, these data, although very reliable, cover less and less of the real exchange of goods due to international division of production. They offer only a limited view of the international production network: they record only the goods that are partly processed abroad and do not include components made abroad for assembly at home, nor the full production abroad (for the home firm) of goods from material supplied from home. Machinery that is physically transferred abroad in order to start or expand production facilities abroad is not counted in OPT, nor is, obviously, processing traffic of goods that are classified as final in order to avoid the hassles of the procedure for being included in the OPT.

Since the very detailed data required to isolate such movements are seldom available, a certain amount of deduction and estimate is called for. As in an international production network, control in terms of ownership is not necessary, also data on FDI have a limited use since they will lead to an underestimating the real international production process.

To be able to say that flows are a consequence of international vertical integration of a production process, that is, to verify the existence of an international production network, three conditions must be satisfied (Schiattarella 1999):

- export flows of intermediate goods must be balanced by imports of products that are downstream in the production process;
- the value of upstream goods (exported) must be reasonably lower than that of downstream goods (imported);
- there must be stronger flows along the filière in comparison with other flows.

## Industrial district and 'area sistema'

Many Italian industrial districts show characteristics that make them something peculiar. Although they started, similarly to any industrial district, as areas of industrial monoculture, they have developed to a degree of complexity and interaction among firms belonging to different, albeit related, industries. Industrial districts can be classified according to the degree of their organizational and structural complexity (Garofoli 1983).

At the lowest level of complexity there is the *area monoculturale semplice* (simple monoculture area). This is the typical *industrial district*: an area characterized by a large concentration of firms, some large, but mostly small and medium-sized, belonging to one industry, that specialize in some phases of the production. There are no meaningful structured relationships among the firms, locked in a tough competition, and the larger firms have a guiding role that strongly limits the independence of the smaller ones: its essence is the subdivision of labour and the specialization in the production process.

The *sistema produttivo locale* (local production system), too, is characterized by SMEs operating in the same industry and specialized in some parts of the production process. There is strong horizontal competition but intra-industry relationships are by far more developed. Relationships and groupings of firms are changeable and often it is difficult to identify firms that have a leading role or the capacity to influence the operations of the others. Spontaneous local development springs from the build up of a critical mass of factors leading to entrepreneurial activation. Leading companies start to appear from within the ranks of the local firms and they tend to remain of middle size, the critical mass being reached through groups of SMEs, generally family run.

The higher degree of structural complexity is attained in the *area sistema* (AS, integrated industrial system). The firms are mostly small, although some of the most successful firms can reach larger size (seldom above 500 employees) and assume a leading role in shaping the strategy of the firms in the area. The division of tasks goes beyond the original industry and involves correlated and supporting industries. Relationships among firms are often characterized by strategic collaboration (without dampening the strong local competition) and are both intra-industry and inter-industry; the latter involve both upstream (for example, specialized machinery production) and downstream (for example, marketing services) industries. The result is an aggregation of strength and capabilities due to strong functional links between the dominant (manufacturing) industry and the set of activities that supply it with operational or strategic inputs.

The AS are the last step in the evolution of Italian industrial districts, reached only by the most successful ones.[1] This evolution, in front of significant changes in the competitive structure of the world economy, was instrumental for keeping their competitiveness in the world markets. Despite often being in a peripheral position to the main poles of industrial development (Becattini 2002), AS have been repeatedly successful in nurturing entrepreneurial development and local economic growth. This makes them a unique and very interesting example for fostering economic development of specific geographical areas.

SMEs and SME clusters are at the basis of a bottom-up type of growth that has local roots and, therefore, can become ingrained in the local community (Bianchi *et al.* 1997). The AS appears to be a dynamic model, able to adapt to a changing situation. Such ability makes it legitimate to wonder whether the AS model can be 'exported' to environments that are different from the ones where it evolved, what adaptations are necessary and in which conditions this move can be successful.

## Characteristics and reproducibility of an 'area sistema'

Because of the peculiarities of the *area sistema*, the reproduction of this model is linked to the possibility to recreate or re-adapt its essential elements in the new environment. If any were missing, as it is rather likely, it would be necessary either to build them up from scratch or to identify some local characteristics that can be used in their place.

According to literature (Gandolfi 1988; Tripodi 2000), the essential elements of an AS are:

- a small and clearly demarcated territory, with some definite characteristic that set it apart from neighbouring areas;
- the presence of a community, sharing a homogeneous system of values in terms of work ethic, family values, a sense of belonging (Becattini 1990);
- a large number of small and medium-sized enterprises, specialized in one or few phases of the production process;
- the presence of strong, as a rule informal, links among the firms, creating an atypical system of relations, where cooperation and competition coexist;
- widespread competency and know-how among the local population, mostly of a technical type, related to the dominant industry of the area;
- the involvement, not necessarily from the beginning, of institutional players; this involvement is expression of the full participation of all the components of the local community to the working of the AS.

The systemic nature of the AS consists of the co-presence, interaction and integration of elements of disparate nature, and explains its complexity (see Becattini 2004: 78–9). Some of these elements, such as territory, concentration of SMEs, institutional players, are tangible and, hence, easier to reproduce; while others that are at least as essential for the AS, such as a value sharing community, the network of informal links among firms and the specialized and localized know-how, are intangible and, because of their immateriality, are much more difficult to re-create. Furthermore, the AS is not simply a grouping of elements: the interaction that makes those elements work successfully is essential; and also this mechanism of interaction must be activated when the replication of the model is attempted.

The issue of the reproducibility of an AS has long been debated in the literature (Becattini and Rullani 1993; Bagella and Pietrobelli 1995; Baragani 1996; Mistri 1998; Tripodi 2000) and for long the consensus pointed to a negative answer, because of the peculiar conditions that caused the development of each area and made each area a unique case. However, the fact itself, that so many districts appeared in the Italian productive system and so many of them successfully evolved to the level of an AS, each thanks to its unique combination of factors, leads to conclude that there is a relatively large number of factor combinations that can result in the development of such a system. Indeed, recently the possibility to replicate the AS model in other countries has been seriously considered both in the literature (Baragani 1996; Majocchi 2000; Tripodi 2000) and in the operational practice. Therefore, the AS can be used as a reference to identify the fundamental characteristics that can stimulate local development in areas that are economically weak.

When looking at the conditions for the development of an AS, it is necessary to distinguish between *essential* and *ancillary* conditions (Turato 2001). Among the former, two appear of the utmost importance: a) the vocation of the territory in the leading industry of the AS; and b) the presence of a sociocultural context conducive to the materialization of the entrepreneurial potential of the area. Among the latter are the availability of good infrastructure, simplified access to financial resources through a local credit system (Becattini 2004), specific vocational training.

When an area presents the above mentioned characteristics, the possibility of its having an SME-led locally rooted development, and so reproducing the AS model, depends on some critical factor that can act as a primer to propel and guide the local entrepreneurial potential. Although this priming factor can vary according to the characteristics of the area and of the actors, local development can basically be of two types (Marelli *et al.* 1992):

- *endogenous*, when the priming factor has origin within the area;
- *exogenous*, when it is linked to the appearance in the area of an external force.

When the development has endogenous origin, usually the priming factor is one or a few local firms, which, through their growth and decentralization processes, put into motion the local entrepreneurial potential. When it has exogenous origin, it is usually the result of an external company moving in and creating a spillover effect involving local actors. Although at times this can start the development of a district-like network of businesses, quite often such a move tends to create mostly a sub-contracting pattern that seldom can develop into a vibrant local business community.[2] Another possible external primer is a group of firms that settles in a specific geographic area, eventually transferring therein the network of relations they already have in their original place. This is the replication of the AS. The biggest problem of an exogenous development is the integration between external firms and the various local actors. Only when it is effective the incomers can stimulate locally ingrained growth. The most likely such case is the grafting of a group of companies, belonging to an AS.

This type of exogenous factor appeared with the start of the delocalization process of the AS (in the early 1990s) that produced, first, the *pocket multinationals* – when isolated companies from an AS established themselves abroad – and, then, the clustering of SMEs in a delimited area – when a number of companies from an AS ended up establishing their activity in the same part of a foreign country. The process has been haphazard and is essentially too recent to allow any firm conclusion[3] about the possibility of success of the duplication of an AS.

Since an AS is a system wherein specific working mechanisms take shape that make it successful by influencing both the area itself and each firm in the area, it appears essential to encourage local forces and foster local entrepreneurial potential, in order to harness them for developing the area and embedding in it these mechanisms. Within this context, the value system of the area becomes determinant, because only where values sustaining economic initiative, innovation and change are, albeit weakly, present in the community, this development has a chance to take root.

It is debatable whether some automatic process of cause and effect can be relied upon to take place to establish local development. Many argue (for example, Bianchi *et al.* 1997) that it is not possible, because the number and diversity of the actors involved and of the factors necessary require some guiding hand. However, despite the constructive involvement of institutional actors in the workings of an AS, a common feature in the development of these areas in Italy is the absence, in the initial phase, of any co-ordinated attempt at guiding it. Most Italian industrial districts have developed without any action of institutional parties, which appeared in the action later, usually after a first crisis. Up to a point, in the Italian case, once the basic conditions were present and the priming party exerted its influence, things evolved without external action: the guiding hand was the initiative of local entrepreneurs; or sometimes it was the local banks that in their advisory role helped to steer the growth of the local firms and in the aggregate contributed to establish the industrial district. An important role was certainly played by institutional actors, but in the development from industrial district to AS, once the former had already been established.

When discussing the reproducibility of an AS, one must take into consideration that the establishment of many Italian industrial districts took place before the mid-1980s, when a greater degree of protection prevailed, and globalization and its extreme competitiveness were still to be felt. This may point to an additional and perhaps insurmountable obstacle to the reproduction of the AS model in SEEC countries. However, the fact that AS developed in later years, some of them in Southern Italy, may lead to the conclusion that even in a globalized world the establishment and successful development of an AS is still possible, albeit more difficult than in earlier times. This greater difficulty may lead to argue that, in the existing situation, the presence of a guiding hand, in the shape of institutional actors implementing local development policy decisions, becomes essential for the success of the district. Since attempts at replication of the AS model are still in their infancy at best, there is no factual evidence in this regard. Considering the recent experience of Southern Italy (Viesti 2000), institutions and policies are an important factor of strength of the district but are never the priming factor of their birth, and come into play, mainly as facilitators, only after the district is established.

## The Veronese footwear district

The Veronese district is one of the three footwear districts of Veneto (the other ones being the Montebelluna sports footwear district, and the Riviera del Brenta district). The district is located in a group of towns to the west of the city of Verona, which itself is part of the district not only because a number of footwear firms are there but, more importantly, because there are located firms in supporting industries such as modelling, certification and software for the footwear industry. The main product is the normal walking shoe, mainly for men. The product is aimed at the middle segments of the market; consequently it has a limited innovative content, average quality and middle price. Therefore, most of the firms are volume producers[4] and as such are more sensitive to price competition from low cost countries than the firms in the other footwear districts of Veneto.

The Veronese district makes up about 10 per cent of the whole Italian footwear industry and Verona is in fourth place among the 104 Italian provinces in footwear exports.[5] In 2002, there were 539 firms belonging to the principal industry (footwear), and about 200 in supporting manufacturing industries. There were also about 50 firms specialized in services to the footwear industry. A further component of the district is a sizeable support in logistics and related services that developed as a consequence of the large recourse to de-localization.

The production amounts to about 40 million pairs. Most of the firms are small, specialized in one (or a few) phase of the production process, and supply the main final shoe producers and marketers. There is a certain concentration in terms of size: about 10 per cent of the firms (52) account for almost 90 per cent of the turnover.

The period from 1995 to 2002 saw a difficult restructuring when many smaller firms could not withstand the highly competitive environment caused by globalization. The district as a whole, however, is still competitive: a turnover of about 1,000 million Euros, more than half of which from exports, testifies its strength.

The institutional structuring of the district is recent and received a strong impulse by national and regional legislation of the late nineties. Regione Veneto, after having identified a number of *productive districts*, in 2003 established the rules for their institutional recognition and for the implementation of the so-called *'patti di sviluppo'* (development pacts). Through the pacts, the districts benefit from regional support and firms that sign on to the pact can take part in projects financed by the Region.

In the Veronese footwear district, 120 firms with a total of 3,592 employees, practically all the larger ones, have signed on to the pact. However, the firms themselves with the institutional support of the Industrialists' Association started the initiative most relevant to the internationalization process: the Consorzio Shoes Export Verona, established in 2000 for supporting the internationalization of Veronese footwear firms. Yet its effect on the de-localization strategies of the firms has been limited: certainly, there was no attempt at drawing the strategic lines of the internationalization of the district or at guiding the decisions of the firms.

In 2003, the Veronese footwear district exports amounted to 581 million Euros (28 per cent of the footwear exports of Veneto) and its imports to 419 million Euros (34.6 per cent of the regional total). While the exports, albeit concentrated in Western Europe, were to all the world, almost half of its imports came from Romania, which clearly appears as the most important de-localization country for the firms of the district. As indicated by the higher proportion of regional imports, the district is the main de-localizing footwear district of Veneto; the fact that imports are 72 per cent of exports, while for the Veneto footwear industry as a whole they are 52 per cent is another clue to the relevance of its de-localization. Such greater incidence of imports is a sign of the existence of an international production network.

Since most of the smaller firms are highly specialized in a few phases of the production process, initially the de-localization was undertaken mostly by the bigger ones. Indeed, some of the decrease in the number of smaller firms is due to their shift to suppliers abroad. However, such a pressure motivated the smaller firms to follow suit. Therefore, currently almost all the firms with more than ten employees have de-localized their production, mostly in the CEEC.

The production phases that have been de-localized first are those with higher intensity of labour: shearing (*tranceria*) and sewing (*giunteria*) are now de-localized by almost all the firms (there are a few that as a matter of policy do not de-localize); lately also *il fondo*, the final phase of the production process, is increasingly de-localized (CCIAA VR, 2004: 8). Since in the latter case the goods cannot be labelled 'made in Italy', this points to a change of strategy on the part of the de-localizing firms: those products, besides being marketed to complement the product range for the lower market segments in rich countries (where they compete with imports from developing countries but making use of a push marketing strategy whereby the intermediaries – who know the

Italian connection of the products – can extol their style and quality to the consumers), constitute the spearhead for attacking the market in developing and transition countries where the 'made in Italy' footwear can only aim at a still small, albeit growing, niche market.

## Outward processing trade between Italy and CEE countries

Italy is almost always (excluding the easternmost countries) among the first three CEEC commercial partners and, in 2003, was the main exporter to three countries in SEE (Albania, Romania, Croatia) and a close second to two other (Bulgaria and S&M).

Italian exports to many CEEC have increased at a faster pace than those of other countries. In all CEEC the trend is towards an increase of the weight of imports from the two most important Western European countries, Italy and Germany. The partners where the growth of Italian export is strongest is Romania, where they grew, in the period 1995 to 2003, from 1,080 to 3,873 million Euros pushing the share of Italian exports from 13 per cent to 20.1 per cent, overcoming Germany as the main exporter to that country.

Unfortunately, OPT data from ICE and ISTAT show *temporary exports* and *re-imports* only for macro-regions, while details for specific industries are available only for total flows. Table 10.1 shows the amount of *temporary exports* from Italy to the CEEC countries and their proportion of the total exports to the region, from 1993 to 2003. While total exports show a veritable spurt from the year 2000 onwards, *temporary exports* kept growing until that year and then started falling. As a consequence, their proportion of total exports, which grew considerably after 1997, started swiftly falling, to reach the lowest point in 2003.

Imports and *re-imports* had a similar development. The latter started to decrease in value in 2002 but their proportion of total import, which reached a very high 8.65 per cent in 1998, had started its significantly downward trend already in 2000, in conjunction with a considerable surge of total imports.

From the mid-1990s, Italian OPT with the CEEC increased, as proportion of total trade and not only in value terms, which strongly points to the existence of an international production network; and one of the conditions mentioned earlier as necessary for having such a network, that the value of upstream goods (exported) must be reasonably lower than that of downstream goods (imported), appears to be satisfied for all the years taken into consideration, bar the first one.

OPT flows start falling after 2000. This fall is linked to the gradual phasing out of custom duties on the goods traded between Italy and the CEEC, following the signature of the Association Agreements. The fall was not immediate, probably because for a few years the advantages of the OPT regime vs. normal trade were still worth having. The fact that temporary exports started to fall one year earlier than *re-imports* may be due to the timing of the two

*Table 10.1* Italian OPT to CEEC (in million Euros) and their trend (1995 = 100)

| *Year* | *1993* | *1995* | *1997* | *1999* | *2001* | *2002* | *2003* |
|---|---|---|---|---|---|---|---|
| Temporary exports | 341 | 632 | 853 | 1,060 | 1,177 | 1,046 | 1,016 |
| Total exports | 7,102 | 12,929 | 17,116 | 16,238 | 25,354 | 26,510 | 28,026 |
| Temporary/total (%) | 4.80 | 4.89 | 4.98 | 6.53 | 4.64 | 3.95 | 3.62 |
| Temporary exports | 54.0 | 100.00 | 135.0 | 167.7 | 186.2 | 165.5 | 160.6 |
| *Total exports* | 54.9 | 100.00 | 132.4 | 125.6 | 196.1 | 205.0 | 216.8 |
| Re-imports | 288 | 676 | 1,029 | 1,195 | 1,312 | 1,169 | 1,046 |
| Total imports | 7,336 | 12,293 | 12,686 | 14,892 | 24,591 | 25,180 | 26,119 |
| Re-import/total (%) | 3.93 | 5.50 | 8.11 | 8.02 | 5.34 | 4.64 | 4.00 |
| Re-imports | 42.6 | 100.00 | 152.2 | 176.8 | 194.1 | 172.9 | 154.7 |
| *Total imports* | 59.7 | 100.00 | 103.2 | 121.1 | 200.0 | 204.8 | 212.5 |

*Source*: Based on data supplied by the Istituto peril Commercio Estero (ICE).

flows, so that goods temporarily exported in the last months of 2000 were re-imported in 2001 and kept the figure high for that year.

It seems reasonable to maintain that the fall in OPT with the CEEC does not mean a reduction in the extent of the production network with these countries. Indirect evidence that this is the correct interpretation of the decrease of OPT figures with the CEEC can be found examining the sub-division of the trade flows by industry: if the flows in the industries that are known to be mostly involved in the OPT have kept up in the last few years, it means that the de-localization of production is still taking place.

## Trade with Romania

Romanian imports have more than trebled from their lowest level, in the early 1990s. Before the change of regime, they reached more than US$8,500 million but they plummeted to little more than US$5,000 million in 1991. Since then, their growth has been remarkable (US$23,800 million in 2003) and mostly continuous.

The origin of Romanian imports has noticeably changed. In 1989, the former USSR covered almost 40 per cent of Romanian imports and the other Central and Eastern European countries took another 18 per cent. The EU share was very small (7 per cent), China was an important supplier (almost 5 per cent) and North Africa and the Near East took the bulk of the rest (20 per cent). Now the EU covers almost two thirds of Romanian imports (almost 40 per cent from Italy and Germany), Russia is in steady decrease, the CEEC are slowly regaining ground, and the rest of the world plays a very small role. Since 1999 Italy is the main exporter to Romania, while also Romanian exports to Italy have increased briskly (Table 10.2).

The composition of the trade between Italy and Romania sheds light on the characteristics of the Italian presence in that country. Table 10.3 gives the first ten products among Italian exports to Romania, in terms of value. Only three of them are not linked with either the leather and footwear or the textile and clothing industries, which reach 52.7 per cent of the value of Italian exports to Romania.

*Table 10.2* Trade between Italy and Romania (million Euros) and its trend (1995 = 100)

| | *1993* | *1995* | *1997* | *1999* | *2000* | *2002* | *2003* |
|---|---|---|---|---|---|---|---|
| Italian exports | 517 | 1,080 | 1,502 | 1,923 | 2,672 | 3,613 | 3,873 |
| Index of exports | 48 | 100 | 139 | 178 | 247 | 334 | 359 |
| Italian imports | 375 | 1,153 | 1,495 | 1,942 | 2,564 | 3,815 | 3,895 |
| Index of imports | 33 | 100 | 130 | 168 | 222 | 331 | 338 |

*Source*: Based on data supplied by ICE.

Despite the large role these industries play in Italian exports in general (in 2003 their exports amounted to 14.7 per cent of total exports), their preponderance among the exports to Romania is rather unusual. Within the first ten products exported from Romania to Italy, exports of products pertaining to the textiles, clothing, leather and footwear industries make up 60 per cent of total (Table 10.4). The great importance of these products, all linked to the

*Table 10.3* Main Italian exports to Romania, 2003 (000s Euros)

| *Products* | *Value* | *%* | *Change on 2002* |
|---|---|---|---|
| Footwear | 474,674 | 12.2 | 8.6 |
| Leather | 370,004 | 9.5 | −0.9 |
| Clothing and accessories thereof | 246,609 | 6.4 | −0.5 |
| Cotton yarns | 256,566 | 6.6 | 9.8 |
| Other yarns | 190,006 | 4.9 | 1.9 |
| Electrical household appliances | 134,312 | 3.5 | 28.3 |
| Machinery for textile and leather industries | 89,236 | 2.3 | −10.6 |
| Vehicles | 84,811 | 2.2 | 8.9 |
| Lingerie | 69,432 | 1.8 | −9.9 |
| Heathers and boilers for heathing | 70,919 | 1.8 | 31.9 |
| *Total exports to Romania* | 3,873,000 | 100.0 | 7.1 |

*Source*: Based on data supplied by the Istituto Italiano di Statistica.

*Table 10.4* Main Italian imports from Romania, 2003 (000s Euros)

| *Products* | *Value* | *%* | *Change on previous year* |
|---|---|---|---|
| Footwear | 996.144 | 25.6 | 4.7 |
| Clothes | 645.783 | 16.6 | −2.2 |
| Lingerie | 336.496 | 8.6 | 2.9 |
| Pullovers, cardigans and other knitted clothes | 246.732 | 6.3 | 11.0 |
| Steel | 114.944 | 2.9 | −12.5 |
| Clothing and accessories thereof | 100.076 | 2.6 | −2.1 |
| Electrical household appliances | 92.198 | 2.4 | 8.9 |
| Aluminium and aluminium semilavorati | 72.264 | 1.9 | −38.8 |
| Engines, generators and electric transformers | 60.659 | 1.6 | 11.4 |
| Furniture | 58.475 | 1.5 | 12.6 |
| *Total imports from Romania* | 3,895.000 | 100.0 | 13.2 |

*Source*: Author's elaboration on ISTAT data.

same industries that make up the largest part of Italian exports, lies in the de-localization policy of the Italian SMEs.

Among the most important Italian exports are goods, such as leather and yarns, which are upstream in the production process of the goods making up the bulk of Romanian exports to Italy. Thus, despite the lack of details, it is possible to maintain that also another condition necessary for having an international production network is satisfied, i.e. that export flows of intermediate goods is balanced by imports of products that are downstream in the production process.

Considering that the trade flows of goods in the leather and footwear and textile and clothing industries constitute such a large part of the trade between Italy and Romania, it is possible to maintain that also the third condition, that there are stronger flows along the *filière* in comparison with other flows, is satisfied and that an international production network is operating between Italy and Romania in these industries. The effects connection may be felt in the local development of Romanian areas that have been more involved in this process. There is where the prospects of the adaptation of the AS development model are more likely and where an SME-led development can take place.

## Small businesses de-localization in Romania and the adaptation of the AS model

The opening of CEEC economies stimulated a new phase in the internationalization process of Italian SMEs. The availability of a pool of relatively skilled, low cost labour within easy reach just at the moment when competitive pressure from low cost producers from East Asia became serious, presented them with an opportunity to regain a competitive advantage.[6] This they did by de-localizing their production, initially taking advantage of the OPT rules. The first countries to attract OPT were the ones closer to Italy. However, in these countries salaries soon moved to higher levels and the SMEs, in their quest for low labour costs moved to farther places. One of the most popular destinations was Romania. De-localization to Romania became very important and, since a large proportion of de-localizing SMEs belongs to an AS, where the relation network tends to stimulate imitation also in strategic choices, it is becoming the de-localization of the AS.

The importance of this 'migration' of the AS in the CEEC can be seen from data related to district de-localization. In 2001, de-localization processes to CEEC were taking place in 21 out of the 35 Italian provinces that have the highest 'district-ness'[7] (Farabullini and Ferri 2004). They involved 30 of the 64 district specializations of those 21 provinces. From this activity emerged 63 province-industry-country nodes in eight CEEC countries. The country with the greatest concentration is Romania, which has 25 nodes, followed by Poland (13). In terms of value, the prevalence of Romania is even greater, because it collects 59.5 per cent of the exports directed to those 63 nodes.[8] In the leather and footwear industry, nine nodes were identified, originating from only four provinces, two of them from Veneto (Treviso and Verona). All four provinces originated a node in Romania where 44 per cent of the nodes in this industry is concentrated. Romania is an important destination for most of the industries where district de-localization took place, and almost the only target for de-localization of leather and footwear: 75 per cent of the value of exports to this type of nodes goes there.

A much less intense internationalization of Italian banks is taking place towards the CEEC. The Italian banking system has traditionally been reluctant (or unable) to internationalize and only recently seems to have started supporting the district SMEs by penetrating in the countries where they have de-localized. In 1996 only one Italian banking group was present in only one of the CEEC, five years later there were six groups, for a total of 16 presences. Five out of six are present in Romania (Farabullini and Ferri 2004: 468–9).

Italian banks, whose role is vital for maintaining SMEs' competitiveness, then, are insufficiently present. Moreover, it must be noticed that, for the time being, the banks that have moved in the CEEC are the biggest banking groups, while local banks, so important in supplying financial resources to the district SMEs, have not yet moved. According to our interviews, some local banks are increasingly contributing to the de-localization of their SMEs clients, but without settling in the de-localized area themselves. This points to a danger for the local banks and perhaps for the district SMEs: if the former cannot follow the latter in the areas where they are de-localizing and starting to recreate a district, they risk losing those clients and their clients risk losing one of the planks that made the AS model so strong.

Although different strategies can be identified when looking at Italian firms de-localizing in CEEC (Majocchi 2004), for years most of those firms aimed only at reducing production costs and were ready to move farther away as soon as the costs increased. Nevertheless, the advantages of a consolidated relation with sub-contracting firms, in terms of more reliable production, better and more stable product quality, and the disadvantages linked to a switch to new and less experienced suppliers, started to outweigh the advantages of lower costs. It is certainly true that, as reported during our interviews, a number of firms, faced with an increase in labour costs in Romania, have moved to Moldova or Ukraine. They compete in the lower segments of the market, where competition is mainly on price. These firms, having little market power, could not remain competitive after the increase in labour costs. However, the high number of firms that have not moved show that they entered a new phase in their de-localization process (Turato 2001). Their footloose search of ever-lower labour costs has left place to a growing integration in those countries.

This change was made easier by the fact that most of those firms are SMEs from an AS. Their nature and operational practice require a constant exchange with the surrounding environment: a sort of osmosis with the local society.

Four main characteristics have been discerned in this process that has been called 'entrepreneurial re-localization':[9]

(a) the pursuit of *business strategies* resulting in *deeper contacts with the local economy;*
(b) the establishment of *close links with the local community;*
(c) the search for *structured relationships with local institutions;*
(d) the formulation of *comprehensive strategies for embedding the relationship* Italy–Romania.

(*a*) This is consequence of the reappraisal of the reasons for and the mode of de-localizing to Romania as well as the motivation for maintaining the activity therein. Many firms that moved to Romania because of lower costs have changed their competitive strategy. These firms were in a difficult situation, because their lack of visibility on the market made them vulnerable to strong competition, but grasped the chance to gain a more autonomous role within the network linking the home AS to the de-localized area. Also the leading AS companies, that have a proprietary brand name and direct access to the consumer market, are finding reasons to give a new meaning to their presence in Romania. This is attained by expanding the activity in three possible ways: *enlargement and diversification of production,* aimed at supplying the Italian business with cheaper components; *penetration in the local market* (the largest in the Balkans and slowly showing its potential); *use of the Romanian base as the staging point* for penetration in the Balkans and in larger markets to the East, through the *multi-brand strategy* discussed in relation to the Veronese district. For these firms stability and potential growth in the local market are more important than lower costs. Consequently they deeply changed their approach to the place where they de-localized.

(*b*) The de-localizing firms are an important component of the local society. As such, they are affected by the social problems of the community, linked to endemic poverty and crumbling of community feelings. This social decay spills over to the firm activity through human resource management problems that sometimes are closer to the problems a social worker has to face than to those of a firm's manager. Their position as an important local employer gives these SMEs a weighty role in helping to solve social problems.

(*c*) This is probably the least developed characteristics. The link with institutions of various types is a normal component of the AS SMEs, therefore they tend to recreate in the area where they settle this network of collaborative links. The design of the relational network of the Veneto SMEs in Romania shows as main component the local firms and the local entrepreneurial associations. The SMEs also pursue a continuous relationship with local administrations; but this was hampered and skewed by the bad shape of the local administration in various areas of Romania. The situation is now changing but 'administrative inefficiency is still seen as the main hurdle to economic activities' (Majocchi 2004: 10). Institutional support from Italian district institutions at the beginning was absent. However, lately the SMEs have been helped in their attempts to establish institutional links by the effort of their own institutional bodies, such as chambers of commerce or industrialists' associations. This appears to start helping to solve some of the problems mentioned above.

(*d*) Here the fact that the exogenous primers of local economic activity are SMEs from an AS appears in all its significance. The AS SMEs propensity to subcontract slowly helped the creation of a network of business links with Romanian counterparts, therefore promoting the diffusion of an entrepreneurial culture in the area. A number of entrepreneurs pointed out that there is a trend towards the enlargement of activities in the de-localized area, both from the de-localizing SMEs, which in larger numbers are moving an increased range of processing phases to Romania, and from the receiving regions, which are slowly acting to support the establishment of the connections that define an evolving industrial district.

The process that started as a 'simple' move in search of lower costs of a few SMEs pressed by stiffening competition is growing, without much institutional support either from Italy or Romania, into an unplanned example of SMEs-led local development. Despite their dimension, the de-localizing SMEs are becoming a force for change and development in the region where de-localization is directed. On the one hand, their presence helps economic growth and a generalized, albeit up to now small, increase in income, while the increase of the areas where the de-localization is taking place helps the diffusion of local economic development and the circulation of resources and income between different areas of the country. On the other hand, these SMEs are expressing a strong demand for services and infrastructures as well as for a local development policy conducive to the taking root of the district model.

## The Veneto SMEs and the Veronese footwear district in Romania

Italian trade with Romania is geographically very concentrated. Fourteen out of twenty Italian regions, export and import for less than 100 million Euros. The five most important regions in Italo-Romanian trade concentrate more than four-fifths of exports (81.3 per cent) and imports (82.3 per cent). Veneto is by far the most important Italian region in the trade with Romania, counting for almost one-third of exports and absorbing more than one third of imports.

The trade between Veneto and Romania shows, heightened, the same characteristics of the trade between Italy and Romania. Footwear and leather are the most important products, followed by clothing and textiles. Only special machinery (mainly for leather, clothing and textile industries) and domestic appliances among the eight most important products do not belong to those industries. Very clear is the mark of the international production network: higher Veneto exports in the upstream products and higher imports in the downstream ones (for example, leather exports are 221 million Euros and imports are 7 million Euros, while in footwear exports are 230 million Euros and imports 565 million Euros).

The intensity of this trade is linked to de-localization. The first cases of de-localization of production of Italian firms to Romania involved large companies, but in a relatively short time SMEs appeared and became the main actor of this process (Gomirato 2004: 72). In all the manufacturing industries, de-localization affects mostly products that are simple and/or easily programmable. Taking as an example the two footwear districts of Veneto, it has been noted (Turato 2001) that the Veronese one shows a more intense de-localization: it is characterized mainly by production of men's footwear which is relatively simpler and (since less affected by fashion's vagaries) more easily programmable than the high quality ladies' shoe, the main specialization of the Riviera del Brenta district, where SMEs have been less keen in following the de-localization strategy.

In 2002, in Romania there were 12,366 Italian firms of all industries, including trade and services. Firms from Veneto were 2,038, 16.5 per cent of the total. Veneto firms are concentrated in wholesale trade and services; the most represented manufacturing industries are textile and clothing, furniture and wood processing, food and beverages, and leather and footwear (Table 10.5).

The first de-localization moves of Veneto firms to Romania were directed towards the westernmost part of the country around the city of Timişoara. It expanded later in the neighbouring province of Arad, towards north to the

*Table 10.5* Veneto firms in Romania, by selected industries

| *Industry* | *No.* | *%* |
|---|---|---|
| Textile and clothing | 215 | 10.5 |
| Furniture and wood processing | 183 | 9.0 |
| Food and beverages, agribusiness | 180 | 8.8 |
| Leather and footwear | 142 | 7.0 |
| Mechanical products | 103 | 5.0 |
| Other manufacturing | 162 | 7.9 |
| Wholesale trade | 322 | 15.8 |
| Other and not specified | 731 | 35.9 |
| *Total firms* | 2,038 | 100.0 |

*Source*: Based on data Centro Estero Veneto (2003).

Maramureş County and to the south toward Bucharest. However, the largest concentration is still in the west. In the region of Banat-Crişana, which includes the Counties of Timiş and Arad, is clustered 52 per cent of the investments from Veneto in the country; and the Veneto investments are 30 per cent of the total Italian investments in the Region.

The presence of the Veronese footwear SMEs in Romania is the outcome of individual uncoordinated actions of AS SMEs. Only subsequently entrepreneurial organizations intervened, very much as followers of the pioneer entrepreneurs, to give some organizational structure to the presence of the SMEs. However, these institutional parties have not shown a great capacity to devise strategies and their activity consists mainly in lobbying Italian and Romanian government and local authorities in order to attain better operational conditions for their associated firms.

Also the banks moved, later, as followers of the leading entrepreneurs. They, up to a point and in an uncoordinated way, have taken upon themselves, by default of any other party, the role of strategic guidance of the firms operating in the area.

The Veronese footwear firms have moved to Romania in large numbers, but most of them through de-localization of production phases to Romanian firms. Few of them have established branches there; however, the relationship of these firms with their suppliers is much closer than just a buyer-seller link: some sort of close collaboration akin to supervision is common between them. All the firms interviewed that have de-localized, regardless of the type of de-localization, claim that their competitiveness was enhanced by the move. All say that they have de-localized in Romania because of the lower cost. The firms that have a branch in Romania said that the only activity carried out there is production and that the role of the branch, even in those very few cases where decision-making is decentralized, is to implement the strategies worked out by the headquarters in Italy.

The chance that the Veronese footwear firms act as an external primer for Romanian local development depends on the evolution of the situation, that is moving in such a direction, but also on the opinion the Veronese entrepreneurs have of the chances of development in Romania. In this regard there is a guarded attitude: most say that the country development potential is sufficient or good, but find that it is hampered by poor infrastructures. The competitive capacity of the country is considered sufficient, due to reliability and learning capacity of the workforce. However, its limited flexibility and poor industriousness lowers the evaluation of Romania's growth potential. Particularly bad in this regard is the low expectation that many Veronese entrepreneurs have of the entrepreneurial potential of the country: most of them rate it as poor, if not inexistent. There is still a long way before a footwear district can take shape in western Romania but, despite some scepticism, the simple fact that the footwear firms have strengthened the links with that part of Romania indicates that many consider it as a good potential base for their operations. If they remain linked to the area for a few more years, the simple fact of their continuous presence could be the primer for a significant local development.

Basically, the relation between the Veronese AS and the Timiş-Arad area is the sum of bilateral relations between an Italian firm and a Romanian one. Seldom there is a multilateral relation between an Italian firm and a number of Romanian ones and practically inexistent are star shaped relations among a number of firms, both Italian and Romanian.

For now, although the strengthening interaction points to such an evolution, it is difficult to see more than the embryonic shape of an AS. The Timiş-Arad area is the de-localization destination of SMEs from other AS, and of German companies, too, and is considered as a non-specialized district, still halfway 'between a non performing area and a successful district' (Majocchi 2004: 10).

## Notes

1. Many other remain at the simpler stages and can be considered as districts that are an AS in its *embryonic phase* (or, sometimes, an *aborted* AS). Similar concepts, albeit in a different classification of clusters, appear in Enright (2002), where *working, latent, potential, policy driven* and *wishful thinking* clusters are mentioned.
2. According to Marelli *et al.* (1992), if a large company moves in an area with poor entrepreneurial traditions, most often it becomes an almost useless (for local development purposes) white elephant.
3. See, for example, C. Tripodi (2000: 335), who said that 'in practical terms, the empirical evidence available up to now does not allow to express a solid opinion on the issue'. This was the general opinion a few years ago and it is still valid.
4. This is also a consequence of the history of the district. Most of the firms that produce and/or market the final product were established in order to take advantage of export potential, through supply to foreign retail chains. They have been and still are suppliers for private label lines of large retailers, mainly from Germany but also from France and Britain.
5. After Ascoli Piceno, Treviso – another of the district areas of Veneto-, and Macerata, in this order.
6. As it was emphasized during our interviews, between the Italian workforce and that of the CEEC there was and still is a significant differential in terms of productivity and quality of workmanship.
7. The *index of districtness* (*indice di distrettualità*) of a province measures the proportion of the total work force being employed in the industry or industries wherein the industrial district(s) of that province specialize.
8. The complete distribution of exports to the 63 nodes is as follows: Romania, 59.5 per cent; Hungary, 14.6 per cent; Poland, 10.5 per cent; Croatia, 7.2 per cent; Czech republic, 3 per cent; Bulgaria 2.8 per cent; Ukraine, 2.4 per cent Slovenia, 0.03 per cent. (Farabullini and Ferri 2004: 464).
9. Turato (2001) gives the results of a research carried out among Triveneto entrepreneurs, who de-localized in any Balkan country. The findings of this research are in line with and reinforce the findings of our interviews.

# 11
# The Balkans Viewed from Brussels: the Local Development in SEE

*Sandro Gozi*[1]

## Introduction

To view the Balkans from Brussels is not easy. In order to fully understand Balkan affairs, it is necessary to rid oneself of several preconceptions and make a particular effort, first of all cultural. An effort that should begin by getting rid of 'geo-cultural' analyses based on the model developed by Samuel Huntington, who explained the events of Bosnia and the former Yugoslavia through the paradigm of the 'clash of civilizations': Muslims against Christians, Catholics against Orthodox, along a 'frontier of civilization' that would separate the 'two Europes', the catholic and the protestant Europe from the orthodox one, passing through the Ukraine, divided by Catholics and Orthodox, and Bosnia (Huntigton 1996).[2] And to get over the attitude summarized by Winston Churchill's quote, 'the Balkans are a region that produces more history than it can consume'.

Based on such analysis, the Balkans, with the exception of Croatia, would remain an uncomfortable neighbour, to be controlled and kept at a safe distance. But it is more than obvious that such an idea is in sharp contrast to the multicultural nature of the Union and the historical reality of the region itself.

The EU welcomes different languages, cultures, and histories. And it is the plurality of these differences that encapsulates the extraordinary richness of the European plan, in which nothing and nobody is wiped out or denied.

Multiculturalism should never be a clash but an edifying factor, an opportunity for further dialogue to be exploited for improving and growing in the comparison to and the respect of other people's thought. In this context, local development is the key to the process of transition towards the ambitious project of integration.

The end of the bipolar system has placed the Balkans in a new and indefensible position, showing the inability of the States of the region to realize, on their own, a new security system, and highlighting the weak territorial integrity of Yugoslavia. After the communist lid was lifted, the disintegration factors which had matured in the period following the downfall of the great empires emerged again: artificial borders separating populations that lived together for long, the advent of a nationalism constructed on the concept of ethnos rather than citizenship, the emergence of new unsatisfied and threatened minorities (Nikiforos Diamandouros and Stephen Larrabee 2001).

Moreover, compared to others parts of Europe, a centre – periphery dynamic was not achieved, in which one state or a group of states was at the head of a new process of stabilization, creating a political, economic and cultural centre of gravity. In this case, the regional centres did not exist, while forms of ethno-nationalism reappeared in order to realize dreams of Great Albania or Great Serbia.

Generally speaking, the existence of a social rupture along ethnic lines is undoubtedly an 'element' that prevents the start of the areas local development. In the case of the Western Balkans, this type of rupture seems to persist and is closely connected to the heritage of the conflict, to the extended instability and, in particular, to the disarticulation of the social–economic context. The local development, therefore, should be more strategically targeted as a possible common point and an instrument able to transmit internationalization and integration processes of the region as a whole.

## Towards a stabilization process

The present Balkan conflicts started in a moment of European institutional, political and operational emptiness, just as it was very timidly acquiring the basic instruments of common foreign and security policy – CFSP (introduced by the treaty of Maastricht, in 1992) and still blocked by the debate 'to deepen integration or to enlarge the Union?' (Philip 1994).

With a confused European Community, some powers, such as France, Germany, Russia and Turkey, were strongly tempted to consolidate their own national positions, while religious and ethnic divisions and conflicts were reviving; the Americans considered at first that it was up to the Europeans to prevent the new tensions from degenerating into a conflict.

As a matter of fact, various European countries did not totally spot the ongoing disintegration process in Yugoslavia. Only after the direct intervention of the United States and the agreements of Dayton, did the European policies start to change. In particular, at the beginning of the nineties, France and Germany were bitterly divided over how to interpret several principles of international law that were at stake since the beginning of the conflict: self-determination of the people and inviolability of the frontiers, defence of the rights of minorities and not interference in the internal affairs of a sovereign state (Heimerl and Van Meurs 2002). The apex of the divergences between Paris and Bonn came with the issue of the independence of Slovenia and Croatia, proclaimed on 25 June 1991, and the firm intention of Germany to recognize the two new republics (Germany will recognize the two new republics on 23 December 1991, without taking into account the worries of other European partners). Whilst the Germans, in fact, identified Milosevic as the person responsible of the whole destabilization of the region, the French looked on with worry at the risk of an expansion of a civil war only justified by ethnic considerations. It was the age of the famous speech of the former president of the French Republic François Mitterand on the 'tribalization' of Europe. Subsequently, however, various episodes and decisions contributed to a reconciliation and the adoption of a more coherent role by the Europeans (for example, the constitution of a *contact group* or the constitution of *Ifor – Implementation Force,* subsequently transformed into *Sfor – Stabilisation Force* and finally into one mission totally managed by UE called *Altea,* in BiH).

From 1996 onwards, a progressive convergence among the policies of the European countries towards the Balkans has been reported and today it can be said that there are no basic divergences between the interests of several European governments in the Balkans, even though differences persist in respect of some aspects, such as the means and terms of implementation of the Union's new strategy, above all linked to the geographic position of several countries.

Moreover, the recent developments seem to point towards a sort of 'normalization' of the Balkans: the end of the Milosevic regime, the start of democratic and pluralistic processes in the region and the international medias shift of attention towards other issues and parts of the world since 11 September 2001.

Viewed from Brussels, the events in the Balkan, and above all the cases of BiH and Kosovo, have tested several political and legal certitudes but, at the same time, have indirectly confirmed some basic choices made by the Union.

The 'end of territories' (Badie 1995), which constituted the exclusive support of the social belongings and the space of political and legal control, was produced very strongly in the Balkans, that is, in the middle of the European continent, difficult to arrest with the instruments and the traditional policies. The territorial crisis in the Balkans takes on various aspects: the violation of the borders was justified by appealing to either 'ethnic' or more widespread religious ties. The reference to the *dar-al-Islam* and the belonging to the *Umma* were important factors during the negotiations which led to Dayton (Holbroke 1999), fuelling the notion of a Bosnian–Muslim 'territory' and encouraging the *Bosnians* ('Muslim ethnos') to resist and assert themselves against the Serbian and Croatian claims to Bosnia. In the Bosnian case a multi-ethnic state was invented in order to make war and peace, denying traditional levels of tolerance and tightly closing ranks.[3] In Dayton, probably there was no other choice, and it was essential to stop the conflict, but today it is necessary to go beyond Dayton.

If today the real problems of the region appear more structural, connected to the weakness of institutions and economic and social backwardness, the sentiments that triggered the last bloody conflicts still lurk in the background, especially in Kosovo: 'Why would you want me to be a minority in your State while you could be a minority in mine?' (Vernet 1999).

Here is then the confirmation for Europe. The confirmation of the revolutionary character of the European method for integration. The confirmation that only such method can offer long-lasting solutions in order to organize the reconciliation between the enemies of the past. The model of European integration is potentially exportable and theoretically applicable on a minor scale, as it is based on shared principles which maintain their value at any level of application. It should therefore be possible to extend the method at a local level.

In Bosnia, in particular, but more generally in the whole region, the European perspective seems in fact the only way out. This is not news for those who know the strength of the European integration process. In fact, in 1968, in the preface to the Italian version of Viktor E. Meier's work, *La rinascita del nazionalismo nei Balcani*,[4] Altiero Spinelli anticipated such an analysis with great lucidity.

Observing that the Balkan region had always been a frontier region, between at least two, even more, imperial systems, Spinelli found out that the Balkan resistances and rebellions had always been possible thanks to some external influence or support. Historically the former had always been the determining factor, but had also led to a strong mutual distrust between the governments and the people of the region. Therefore, every time they wanted to rebuild or obtain their independence, they did not do so based on the ideals of increased solidarity, strong interdependence or regional integration, but rather on a mere national model of independence encouraged and supported by external forces. The Balkan wars in 1912 and 1913 are examples which clearly illustrate the aggressive character of Balkan nationalism: since then, Balkan policies, clashes and sectarian incompatibilities have always been formulated in such a context (G. Voskopouos 2001).

So, viewed from Brussels, a third way and a new method are possible for a long-lasting stabilization and development of the region as a whole: the guidelines towards the European Union and the application of the experience acquired during half a century of European integration to reorganize the relationships between the several countries of the region.

As Altiero Spinelli pointed out, 'the progressive reduction of nationalism to internal policies aimed at cultivating the ethnic cultural peculiarities and the development of a supranational political conscience could not be given to our Balkan neighbours from the outside. . . . This maturity must take place in the Balkans'. Today, the presence of the European Union, quite different from the interventions of the great national powers of the past, can provide a new method and a new objective.

The same path was indicated by Romano Prodi:

> the European community has allowed to overcome the notion for which peace can be guaranteed from the frontier change, the redesigning of

borders, and the movement of people. There are too many wars and conflicts to actually believe that in this day and age the partnership between state and nation can guarantee peace and prosperity. Europe sees the borders with a sense of proportion and goes beyond them, favours the free circulation of people and ideas, the dialogue, the exchange, the comparison. It is not in fact the frontier, but the adhesion to fundamental common principles that guarantees national, communal, regional or local diversities and characteristics in the Union. A Union of diversities, therefore: an alliance of minorities. In Europe we are all in fact a 'minority' and it is from our Union that we can draw the strength to guarantee order, peace and prosperity for our people and to contribute to the government of world-wide events.

The supranational Union, therefore, and the political and administrative decentralization are the alternative to the fragmentation and 'tribalization' to which a conception and an absolute application of the principle of the self-determination would lead. Self-determination is not 'the' value, but 'a' fundamental value that must be protected and guaranteed together with others, but that cannot be demanded in a situation of democratic respect and tolerance guaranteed in an open and pluralistic society.

Are not perhaps these some of the essential elements for the clashes and conflicts in the Balkans? Is not it perhaps in the light of these principles that we must assure the reconstruction of this part of Europe?

(Prodi 2002)

After all, the crisis of the nation-state model which, in its ethnic deformation, was one of the main causes of the Balkan tragedies, should favour the reconciliation and the relaunch of the whole region. In fact, as Konrad Adenauer pointed out: 'the age of the nation state has come to an end, and everyone must realize this change; an age is over and another one is starting, where people will look beyond the frontiers of their countries and work in a brotherly cooperation with other nations . . .'.

The importance of political and administrative decentralization is more needed where a strongly dirigiste tendency was reported in the past. This is exactly the case of the Balkan area, where the dirigiste tendency was accompanied by a close connection between economy and power, by cosy relations and regimes of semi-monopoly in various externally closed economic area and protectionism.

Today, the Balkans are slowly proceeding their march towards Europe. But it is a road full of obstacles.[5] After not even a month from Croatia's application for Membership in March 2003, the Serbian Prime Minister Djindjic was shot dead by two sharpshooters. These signs are only apparently conflicting, confirming instead the necessity to accelerate the ongoing change of European policies in the Balkans. Therefore, the choice must originate from the region;

it must be felt and shared by the majority of the populations, but it should be undoubtedly encouraged, favoured and supported firmly by the Union.

The process of reform and stabilization is a choice that the region should deeply feel as its own, as well as the completion of the adjustment process, fiscal consolidation, and trade liberalization, which represent a pre-condition needed to defeat the reluctance of the foreign investors to operate in small and highly risky markets. The structural reforms should be perceived and conceived as an instrument of local development and, consequently, a relaunching of the whole region.

In the recent past, rather than carrying out the role of political and moral authority the Balkans desperately needs, Europe carried out a limited political role, in which it did not always succeed in translating unprecedented economic aid into political capital and it saw the regional approach reduced to a series of selective parallel relationships which prevented it from developing a real regional strategy.

During the negotiations of Rambouillet, the Union began to show a real will to carry out a role of political authority in the Balkans in order to stop the spiral of violence. This was an important political fact which had been absent at the negotiations in Dayton. From January 1999, the Europeans showed greater coherence and unity, especially when the reaction to the conflict in Kosovo is compared to the diplomatic acknowledgment of Slovenia and Croatia in 1992. The Europeans carried out a significant role within the contact group in defining the political parameters for negotiation. Moreover, the relationship with Russia during the North Atlantic Treaty Organization (NATO) bombings was managed differently by Europeans and Americans. The Europeans wanted to resort to mechanisms and structures which assured the participation of the Russians, namely the contact group in Rambouillet, the Organization on Security and Cooperation in Europe (OSCE), the Stability Pact for SEE (Gozi 2000: 31).

The EU is therefore becoming the guarantor of a restructuring process for SEE that should be founded on new political outlets and new forms of regional and social solidarity, replacing the role of mediation of the tensions and conflicts carried out in the past from the territorial principle.

The guidelines and the decisions of the Union in the next few years will be vital in determining the degree of stability or instability of the region. As Chris Patten, Commissioner for external relations in Prodi's Commission, stated: 'the choice is very clear: we can export stability to the Balkans or they will export instability towards us: I know what I prefer. There is a lesson I learnt from the Balkans today: never, never never give up' (Patten 2002).

The Union must instead offer, in a credible and tangible way, a true perspective of European integration and new forms of political cooperation to the region as a whole. That implies brave choices and full acceptance of the leadership of such a process. It is, in fact, impossible even counter-productive, to think or to hope of having a real impact on the Balkan process through a rigid, contractual approach, closely related to the conditionality and reduced to a logic such as '*do ut des*' in which some pretend to progress in the reform process and others pretend they cannot see the structural weaknesses of the new states.

Also from Brussels a need is emerging to pass to a new political phase, a phase of full, convinced and convincing 'Europeanization' of the Balkans.

## From Zagreb to Thessalonica: a new impetus to the Eurobalkan policy or a missed opportunity?

At the Zagreb Summit, the first summit that gathered all the leaders of the Union and the Balkans, held under the French presidency of the Union, in autumn 2000, the prospect of accession had been offered on the basis of fulfilment of the criteria defined at the Copenhagen European Council in June 1993 and the progress made in implementing the Stabilisation and Association Agreements, in particular those on regional cooperation. Another step forward was made at the European Council of Thessalonica and at the Balkans Summit, in June 2003. On this occasion, seated around the same table, the leaders of the Union and the Balkans approved the document *The Thessalonica Agenda for Western Balkans: Moving towards European Integration*,[6] which gives a very clear and unequivocal political sign on the future of the Balkans: 'the future of the Balkans is within the Union'.[7]

At Thessalonica, the new bilateral '*European partnerships*' were launched, with the twofold purpose to stimulate the regional cooperation and to strengthen the political dimension of the relations between the Union and the Balkans.

The Western Balkans were invited to align themselves with the *demarche*, the declarations and the common positions of the Union relating to issues of common foreign policy and security, and the possibility to create joint parliamentary committees called 'Parliamentary Committees of Stabilization and Association' was suggested. Moreover, the states of the region could create a Balkan Conference of the Committees of European affairs whose representatives could participate in the conference of bodies concerned with Community affairs (COSAC), which has played a long and active role within the Union and which unites parliamentary representatives from all Member States.

Subsequently, it was decided to enrich the process of stabilization and association with the most characteristic elements of the enlargement, to strengthen the political dialogue (extended also to S&M and BiH), to increase the commitment against organized crime and the cooperation in the field of justice and internal affairs, and to favour the economic development starting with the transport, energy and telecommunication infrastructures.

The introduction of some elements of the enlargement strategy in the process of stabilization and association can really mark the beginning of the turning point in the Union's 'Balkan strategy'. In particular, the application of the principle of differentiation between countries, which in the Balkan context meant each region would be judged and compensated on their own merits, a policy which was instead neglected during the first phase of the enlargement strategy towards the countries of Eastern and Central Europe.

Real '*European partnerships*' will be elaborated for each country, inspired by the accession partnerships (used for the enlargement) and specifically adapted to the process of stabilization and association, which will have to reflect, in a dynamic and evolutionary way, the state of the relationships between the Union and the single countries, identifying the priorities and the efforts necessary in order to approach the European Union. The objective of such partnerships is to identify a number of reforms in the short and the medium term that should serve as a reference in order to guide community assistance.[8] The priorities would have to be strategic and political, identified by the Commission in its annual evaluation reports of the individual countries, taking into account the criteria of Copenhagen and the conditionality elaborated in 1997.[9] Such a political picture will be accompanied also by instruments used for the enlargement strategy, like the *partnerships* between public administrations of the Member States of the Union and the Balkans, the strategy of the Technical Assistance Information Exchange Office (TAIEX), which will inform the Balkan countries on the state and the evolution of the European legislation and will verify the compatibility of the local legislation with the European standards. In addition to Tempus and the research framework programme, the Balkans could be invited to take part to other Community programme, in particular in the fields of education, training and culture, research, energy, environment, civil society, support to the SMEs and coordination against fraud.

A High School for Training on the Reform of the Public Administration could also be created. The European leaders have then insisted on the fight against organized crime and cooperation in fields such as the trafficking of people, illegal immigration and the readmission agreements.

Finally, the Union encourages further progress in favour of the return of refugees and evacuees, in particular through the regional initiative Migration, Asylum and Regional Initiative for Refugees (MARRI), and demands the Balkan governments continue to develop their regional cooperation, above all for the realization of an area of free regional exchange, and regional markets for electricity and gas, in order to establish the full freedom of movement for the people in the area (the so-called 'mini Balkan Schengen'), for the control of the light weapons and for the cross-border water management.

In the economic field, the European Union asks the governments of the region to maintain and expand the results obtained in terms of macroeconomic stability and emphasizes the importance of the priorities identified by the Stability Pact in the fields of transportation, energy and telecommunications. There is also the need to face up the environmental challenges through strategies closer to the environment law of the Union.

A fringe summit called 'Zagreb II' was held during the European Council gathering at Thessalonica. It brought together all the leaders of the Member States of the Union, the candidate countries and the Balkans. Its statement confirmed that 'the future of the Western Balkans is in Europe' and that the recent enlargement of the Union 'encourages the countries of the Western Balkans to follow the same road to success' but 'the speed is in the hands of the countries of the region'. The declaration adds that the States of the region will have to overcome through dialogue 'the fragmentations along ethnic lines . . . incompatible with the European perspective . . . the European perspective should act as a catalyst in order to face the problems of the region'. These are significant statements and objectives, which can contribute to that qualitative jump we wish for Euro-Balkan relations. Assertions that are however insufficient, because they are not followed by more operational decisions, like an agenda for accession, new financial instruments and a stronger will to act jointly by the Union. We believe that the five leaders of the region referred to this point when, in their letter to Romano Prodi asked that the document of Thessalonica should contain 'a reference to the accession perspectives of our countries, as a strong message and an impetus to continue on our way towards European integration',[10] a request taken up by Romano Prodi in his letter in January 2003 to the first Greek Minister, Costas Simitis and to the Italian Minister, Silvio Berlusconi (presidents in charge of the Union in 2003) with whom he emphasized the importance of confirming the support of the Union to the region by using the accession perspective as a powerful factor of change inside these societies. The path remains therefore full of obstacles.

One of the key points of Europeanization of the Balkans, on which substantial steps forward have not been accomplished, is undoubtedly the free circulation of people and the abolition of the visa requirements in order to enter the common space. Disappointing are also the decisions on the financial aspects. The European Council had only committed to maintaining the recent level of assistance to the Balkans, for which however a progressive decrease was foreseen: 200 million Euros have been allocated for the CARDS programme until 2006. The framework of this programme gave great importance to the field of civil society at local level, specifically through calls for proposals for partnerships, and activities aimed at strengthening the democratic local structures and improving the capabilities of civil society organizations.

Encouraging a fair participation of ethnic groups, minorities and women in the democratic process; increasing the level of responsibility of local administrations; establishing sustainable consultancy offices for the citizens; informing local minorities and ethnic groups of their civil rights and their access to the services distributed by local authorities; thematic seminars, workshops and conferences; campaigns to awaken the new role of the local government; measures designed to promote the transparency of the local administrations. These are only some of the activities that the programme CARDS promotes.

The Union has undoubtedly invested huge sums for the stabilization and the development of the Balkans, a total of 4.65 billion Euros for 2000–2006 (La Repubblica 20 June 2003). But it is clear that also from a financial viewpoint, after 2006, the Union will have to show much more courage, in order to avoid giving the Balkans the feeling of 'stepping into a full bus in which new passengers could think that there is no more room for them', to quote the comment of the Serbian Minister of foreign policies, Goran Svilanovic, in Thessalonica.[11]

## For a Europeanization of the Balkans

The Union is slowly abandoning an approach based on a number of selective and bilateral relationships with several countries of SEE favouring a strategy that considers the region as a whole.

With the Stabilization and Association process, the European Union for the first time gave a long-term vision for integration for all the countries of the region, while the Pact of Stability constitutes the greatest attempt by the international Community to use economic assistance and European perspective to stabilize the entire region in a long-lasting way.[12]

Such process remains a base for the relationships between the Union and the Balkans, but it should be considered in a new political context in which the Union and the Balkan countries elaborate a real common agenda and mutually engage to complete all the necessary efforts to realize it.

The region offers mixed results. There are important developments, like the conciliation of Bosnia, a beginning of reconciliation in Macedonia, and some important engagements and plans at regional level. But there are also signs of instability and insecurity: the difficult Serbian transition, the unsolved Albanian issue, the difficult functioning of the institutional order of Dayton, the insistence of some groups on an old idea of 'territoriality' and borders.

The success of the infrastructures to the fight of organized crime, the monetary policy, trade and investments, all depend on the real will of regional cooperation of the Balkan governments and people (see Gozi 2000). And it is a difficult process.

In order to cooperate effectively, an advanced level of mutual trust is a *conditio sine qua non*. In the Balkans, such trust is not sufficient. The lack of trust, amongst the population, in the rhetoric of some political powers and in some concrete examples (the street signs),[13] is tangible.

In the new context of the enlarged Union, it is now possible to start new processes and recognize particular statuses. As the Union grows and proposes a new type of international relationship to its neighbours, it must give a proof of foresight and courage in its policies towards the Balkans. Today, in fact, there is already a remarkable variety of relationships between the Union and European countries not members of the Union: from the status of candidate with negotiations in progress (Romania and Bulgaria), to pre-accession strategies without negotiations (Turkey), to the imminent start of negotiations with Croatia, to the candidacy of Macedonia and new regional processes like neighbourhood policy, in particular for Ukraine, Moldova and the countries of Caucasus.

In such a context, it becomes possible to make a step forward also in the Balkans, giving the status of 'candidates to accession' to all the countries of the region, without opening negotiations until the necessary reforms are completed and sufficient progress is made. Therefore, as with the other candidate countries, it would become possible to totally exploit all the external potential of the several Community policies and, if necessary, to create new specific instruments of regional and local development, inspired by the existing programs inside the Union. The Union's assistance would be placed in a wider and more stable political context, something in between the internal policy and the external action of the Union.

More generally, the Union must demonstrate it has the courage to totally engage itself in the politics, assuming its responsibilities without hiding behind technical requirements. In particular, the Union should not only aim to be a model to imitate but also an ally with whom to develop common strategies in order to pursue common objectives. Strategies adapted to specific conditions and circumstances, which should not be one-off cases but part of an overall objective common to both the Union and the Balkan countries, namely accession.

The situation in the Balkans should be reinterpreted through the paradigm of social modernization and a greater emphasis on the real fears and worries of the people of the region. There is inevitably little time for SEE. A balance must be struck between the eagerness to build and the frustration of unfulfilled expectations. Other forms of immediate integration should be introduced in order to keep the countries of the region on the right path, especially in event in which full integration cannot be an immediate option.

The basic conditions stated in the Helsinki Paper and the Copenhagen criteria have been partially fulfilled. But the Copenhagen criteria can be applied in several ways – political or technical – in the annual evaluation the Union undertakes for every candidate country. Moreover, their application is remarkably more difficult today compared to ten years ago in CEE. In fact, while in this region the economic indicators were already heading in a positive direction as the criteria was being evaluated, the present situation in the Balkans in terms of unemployment, inflation and de-industrialization has reached levels much lower than the starting points of countries like Poland or Slovakia (Van Meurs and Weiss 2003).

The targets should be realistic and achievable. At Thessalonica, for example, two road maps were drawn solely to avoid increasing the gap between the ten new countries members and Romania and Bulgaria, leading these two countries along the European path towards the accession (probably in 2007), with a 40 per cent increase in assistance from 2006 and the possibility of participating in several Community programs, and the activities of agencies and committees of the Union.

A new balance between urgency and patience in helping the region will have also to be found (Van Meurs and Weiss 2003). Urgency is required due to the problems relating to a backward economy and organized crime. At the same time, an immediate solution does not exist and only a long term engagement can lead to the final desired result.

A renewed strategy towards the region will add impetus to the security cooperation in the region and a gradual integration into NATO, as well as for the European security model which is being constructed.

The Union must also consider the need to prevent the Balkans from becoming a 'black hole' on the map of a unified Europe and from creating failed states or uncontrolled territories characterized by the presence of organized crime, terrorism and poverty linked to a lack of opportunities, which in turn would aggravate the emigration problems. Without stable partners in SEE, it will be very difficult to tackle the challenges that the EU faces in areas such as Caucasus, Central Asia and also the Mediterranean. The region can play a multiple role – it could be the last to join the EU's enlargement process, and represent the first step within the strategy of a 'larger Europe' almost acting as a bridge between these two processes and facilitating the performance of the neighbourhood strategy of the Union for a special relationship with all the neighbouring countries, from Russia to the Mediterranean, passing through Belarus, Moldova and Ukraine.

After all, the credibility of the EU depends on the stability and development of the Balkans. How could attention be paid to an actor who wants to be a peace and stability promoter at world level and who does not succeed in resolving even the existing problems in the European continent?

From this point of view, the Balkans become a mirror of Europe, of its ability to reform itself in order to act more effectively and of its real political will to become a real political player. It goes without saying that the Union is making a very important contribution to overcome the divisions and to encourage agreements between the countries of the region. Examples are the new constitutional solution for S&M, the agreement of Ohrid between Slavs and Albanians in Macedonia, military troops and police in several countries of the region, and finally, the important military presence in Macedonia and Bosnia. But all this, although necessary, is not enough. It is not enough because the Union is not exploiting all its potential nor is it pursuing all the channels of communication at its disposal. In fact, compared to other international actors in the region the Union has greater means. Europe does not mean only cooperation with the international Court of the Hague and economic assistance. Europe means even more: a new model of society, a new perspective of democratic consolidation and economic development. But to do this, it must approach the governments and the Balkan people, it must develop joint initiatives and not merely limit itself to indicating the path to take.

## Conclusion

The Euro-Balkanic policy was developed around a model based on the close cooperation and collaboration between the various international actors and the several local authorities of the region. However, this collaboration, today, must be translated in a more detailed local development policy that bears in mind the specific idiosyncrasies of the territory. In fact, often in the international and national institutions strategic programming documents there is no precise reference to the concept of local development.

Economic development and local development: the first meaning structural macro-reforms and flows of investment, the second support to governance and administrative strengthening, are instead absolutely connected. Therefore, an approach able to integrate measures and initiatives ranging from local development to structural reform policies would be sufficient to compensate for the limited level of intervention carried out so far.

The support for local development, aimed at appreciating the resources and values shared by territorially identified communities, can start important cohesion processes. Local development fosters a general sense of belonging, as well as rules and practices typical of local economic development (for example, strategic alliances between enterprises, and amongst individuals and public organizations). The mobilization of all local potential (natural, human, economic, financial, organizational, and cultural) could create the necessary synergies between territory, environment and production that still are missing.

It is necessary therefore to accelerate and to strengthen the entire process of stabilization and association, by placing it in a framework similar to the one used for the enlargement process. The same international context must push Europe to immediately apply, without hesitation, its new strategic proposal for the whole continent. It is necessary to lay the foundations for a new regional political construction, which will become a balanced and farsighted contribution to a new world governance. The mobilization of all local potential (natural, human, economic, financial, organizational, and cultural) could create the necessary synergies between territory, environment and production that still are missing.

It is necessary therefore to accelerate and to strengthen the entire process of stabilization and association, by placing it in a framework similar to the one used for the enlargement process. The same international context must push Europe to immediately apply, without hesitation, its new strategic proposal for the whole continent. It is necessary to lay the foundations for a new regional political construction, which will become a balanced and farsighted contribution to a new world governance.

## Notes

1. A personal note by Sandro Gozi, political adviser of the President of the European Commission. The theses supported and the opinions expressed are personal and do not concern the institution the author belongs to. The author thanks Luciano Gaudio and Adam Nyman for the assistance in drawing up the present work.
2. For a criticism on this thesis applied to the Balkans' case, see, *inter alia*, A. del Valle (2000).

3. See R. Ivekovic (1999), pp. 147 and followings.
4. V.E. Meier, (1968).
5. The literature on the Balkans is huge. For a general overview to more or less recent Balkan facts, see P. Garde (2001).
6. This document was adopted by the Council, based on the communication from the Commission to the Council and the European Parliament – *The Western Balkans and European Integration*, 21 May 2003.
7. See Declaration of Thessalonica at the EU–Balkans Summit, p. 1.
8. See Communication from the Commission to the Council and the European Parliament – *The Western Balkans and European Integration*, Brussels, 21 May 2003.
9. Conclusions of the Council 'General Affairs' of 29 and 30 April 1997.
10. The letter of the Presidents of Albania, Alfred Moisu, Bosnia-Herzegovina, Mirko Sarovic, Croatia, Stipe Mesic, Macedonia, Boris Trajkovski and Yugoslavia, Vojislav Kostunica, to Romano Prodi, 5 December 2002.
11. Quoted in *Les Echos*, 23 June 2003, 'Balkans: des promesses, des étapes mais pas de calendrier'.
12. Communication from the Commission to the Council and the European Parliament on the Stabilization and Association process for countries of SEE, COM (99) 235, 26 May 1999.
13. As Jadranko Prlic (2003: 204) explains, there are no street signs in the East of Lipovac, in Croatia, which should indicate Belgrade and, more generally, Serbia.

# References

AAVV (1995) 'Il traffico di perfezionamento passivo nel settore tessile-abbigliamento italiano', *Sinergie*, Rapporto di Ricerca n. 1, Verona, Cueim.

Abramowitz, M. and H. Hurlburt 'Can the EU Hack the Balkans? – a Proving Ground for Brussels' in *Foreign Affairs*, September–October 2002.

Adam, F. and M. Tomsic (2002) 'Elite (Re)Configuration and Politico-economic Performance in Post-socialist Countries; Europe–Asia Studies', 54/3: 435–54.

Allen, D. (2000) 'Cohesion and the Structural Funds', in H. Wallace and W. Wallace (eds.), *Policy-Making in the European Union*, 4th edn, Oxford: University Press.

Amin, A (1998) 'Una prospettiva neo-istituzionalista dello sviluppo locale', *Sviluppo locale*, Vol. V, n. 8: 75–94.

Anastasia, B. and G. Corò (1993) *I distretti industriali in Veneto*, Venezia: Nuova Dimensione.

Anderson, J. (1991) 'Skeptical Reflections on a Europe of Regions: Britain, Germany and the ERDF', *Journal of Public Policy*, 10, 4: 417–44.

Anderson, J.E. and D. Marcouiller (1999) 'Trade, Insecurity, and Home Bias: an Empirical Investigation', NBER Working Papers, 7000.

Anderson, J.E. and E. van Wincoop (2004) 'Trade Costs', *Journal of Economic Literature*, XLII (September), 691–751.

Andor, L. and M. Summers (1998) *Market Failure: Eastern Europe's 'Economic Miracle'*, London: Pluto Press.

Ansell, C.K., C.A. Parsons and K.A. Daarden (1997) 'Dual Networks in European Regional Development Policy', *Journal of Common Market Studies*, 35, 3: 347–75.

Armstrong, H.W. (1995) 'The Role and Evolution of European Community Regional Policy' in B. Jones and M. Keating (eds.), *The European Union and the Regions*, Oxford: Clarendon Press.

ASME (2003) *Regular Report on SMEs 2002*, Sofia: Agency for SMEs.

Bache, I. (1998) *The Politics of European Union Regional Policy. Multi-level Governance or Flexible Gatekeeping?*, Sheffield: Sheffield Academic Press.

Bache, I. and M. Flinders (2004) (eds.), *Multi-level Governance*, Oxford: Oxford University Press.

Badie, B. (1995) *La fin des territoires – Essai sur le désordre international et sur l'utilité sociale du respect*, Paris: Fayard.

Bagella, M. and C. Pietrobelli (1995) 'Distretti industriali e internazionalizzazione. Presupposti teorici ed evidenza empirica dall' America Latina', *Economia e Politica Industriale*, 86: 69–93.

Balawyder, A.(1980) (ed.) *Co-operative Movements in Eastern Europe*, London: Macmillan.

Baldersheim *et al.* (1996) *Local Democracy and the Process of Transformation in East–Central Europe*, Oxford: Westview Press.

Baldwin, R. (1989) 'Measurable Dynamic Gains from Trade', NBER Working Papers, 3147.

Baldwin, R., Forslid R, Martin P. and G. Ottaviano (2003) *Economic Geography and Public Policy*, Princeton: Princeton University Press.

Baragani, M (1996) 'I distretti industriali: indicatori per l'internazionalizzazione', *Politica Internazionale*, 24.

Barratt-Brown, M. (1996) *The Yugoslav Tragedy: Lessons for Socialists*, Nottingham: Spokesman Books.

Barro, R. (2000) 'Inequality and Growth in a Panel of Countries', *Journal of Economic Growth*, 5, 1: 5–32.

Bartlett, W. (2003) *Croatia: Between Europe and the Balkans*, London: Routledge.

Bartlett, W. and G. Pridham (1991) 'Co-operative Enterprises in Italy, Portugal and Spain: History and Development', *International Journal of Interdisciplinary Economics*, 4: 33–59.

Bateman, M. (2003) ' "New Wave" Micro-finance institutions in South-East Europe: Towards a More Realistic Assessment of Impact', *Small Enterprise Development*, 14, 3.

—— (2004a) 'Imposing Ideology as "Best Practise": the Problematic Role of the International Financial Institutions in the Reconstruction and Development of South-East Europe', in LeBarre F and Jureković P (eds.), *Regional Stability in South East Europe: Through Economy to Democracy and Security? an Integrated Approach to Stability in South East Europe*, Vienna: National Defence Academy.

—— (2004b) *Institutional Assessment: Croatia*, Consultants report prepared for the World Bank, (Grant No TF050513), April. Zagreb: IMC Consulting Ltd.

—— (2004c) *Formalising the Informal Sector Economy in the Western Balkans: Policy Recommendations and Economic and Social Effects*, European Union Strategic Studies in the CARDS Region, March, Brussels: Commission of the European Communities.

—— (2005) *Sustainable Local Economic Development in Croatia and the Role of Social Capital: Disentangling Lofty Rhetoric from the Emerging Reality*, paper presented at the 5th International Conference 'Economic Integration, Competition and Co-operation', 22–23 April, 2005, Lovran, Croatia.

Bateman, M. and S. Maleković (2003) *The National Co-operative Development Strategy for Croatia* (Final Report, November), Brussels: ECODES Consortium.

Batt, J. (ed.), (2004) 'The Western Balkans moving on', *Chaillot Paper* n. 70, Paris: EU Institute for Security Studies, October.

Baumol, W.J. (1990) 'Entrepreneurship: Productive, Unproductive, and Destructive', *Journal of Political Economy*, 98, 5: 893–921.

—— (1993) *Entrepreneurship, Management, and the Structure of Payoffs*, Cambridge MA: MIT Press.

—— (2004) 'Entrepreneurial Enterprises, Large Established Firms and Other Components of the Free-Market Growth Machine', *Small Business Economics*, 23: 9–21.

Becattini, G. (1987) (ed.), *Mercato e forze locali: il distretto industriale*, Bologna: il Mulino.

—— (1990) 'The Marshallian Industrial District as a Socioeconomic Notion' in F. Pyke, G. Becattini and W. Sengenberger (eds.), *Small Firms and Industrial Districts in Italy*, Geneva, International Institute for Labour Studies.

—— (1998), *Distretti industriali e Made in Italy: le basi socioculturali del nostro sviluppo economico*, Torino: Bollati Boringhieri.

—— (2002) 'From Marshallian to Italian "Industrial Districts": a Brief Critical Reconstruction', in A. Quadrio Curzio and M. Fortis (eds.), *Complexity and Industrial Clusters: Dynamics and Models in Theory and Practice*, Heidelberg: Physica Verlag.

—— (2004) *Industrial Districts: a New Approach to Industrial Change*, Cheltenham: Edward Elgar Publishing.

Becattini, G. and E. Rullani (1993) 'Sistema locale e mercato globale', *Economia e Politica Industriale*, 80: 25–47.

Bellandi, M. (1996) 'Innovation and Change in the Marshallian Industrial District', *European Economic Planning*, 3: 357–68.

Bellandi, M. and M. Russo (eds.) (1994), *Distretti industriali e cambiamento economico locale*, Torino: Rosenberg & Sellier.

Beninski, S. (2000) 'Training of Institutions Employees Engaged in Various Spheres and Units of the European Integration Process in Bulgaria – Case Study of the Local Expert Facility Training Activity,' in E. Vatchkova (ed.), *Varna 2000. Human Resource Management*, Sofia: International Business School 'Transbusiness-E'.

Berloffa, G. and M.L. Segnana (2004) *Trade, Inequality and Growth: Two perspectives, One Message?*, GRADE WP, Dept. of Economics, Trento.

Berman, E. and S. Machin (2000) *'Skill-biased Technology Transfer: Evidence of Factor Based Technological Change in Developing Countries'*, Mimeo: Boston University.

Bernard, A.B. and J.B. Jensen (2004) 'Exceptional Exporter Performance: Cause, Effect, or Both?', NBER WP 6272.

Bianchi, Miller and Bertini, (1997) *The Italian SME Experience and Possible Lessons for Emerging Countries*, Wien, UNIDO.

Bianchini, S. and G. Schopflin (1998) *State-building in the Balkans – Dilemmas on the Eve of the 21st century*, Ravenna: Longo.

Bieber, F. (2003) 'Montenegrin politics since the disintegration of Yugoslavia', in F. Bieber (ed.), *Montenegro in Transition: Problems of Identity and Statehood*, Baden-Baden: Nomos Verlagsgesellschaft.

Birchall, J. (1997) *The International Co-operative Movement*, Manchester: Manchester University Press.

—— (2001) *Organizing Workers in the Informal Sector: a Strategy for Trade Union-Cooperative Action*, Cooperative Working paper No 01–1, Geneva: Co-operatives Branch, ILO.

—— (2003) *Rediscovering the Co-operative Advantage: Poverty Reduction through Self-Help*, Geneva: ILO.

Birchmore, J. *et al.* (2002) *'Proposed Strategy for the Revitalisation of the Wood Processing Industry in Montenegro: Final Report'*, Podgorica: European Agency for Reconstruction.

Bird, R.R., R. Ebel and C. Wallich (1995) *Decentralisation of the Socialist State*, Washington, DC: World Bank.

Bleaney, M. and I. Filatotchev and K. Wakelin (2000) *Learning by Exporting: Evidence from Three Transition Economies*. Research Paper No. 6, Centre for Research on Globalisation and Labour Market.

Blinder, A. (ed.) (1990) *Paying for Productivity*, Oxford: Oxford University Press.

Bomberg, E. and A. Stubb (ed.) (2003) *The European Union: How Does It Work?*, Oxford: Oxford University Press.

Boone, P. (1996), 'Politics and the Effectiveness of Foreign Aid', *European Economic Review*, 40, 2: 289–329.

Börzel, T. (2002) *States and Regions in the European Union: Institutional Adaptation in Germany and Spain*, Cambridge: Cambridge University Press.

Bourguignon, F. (2002) 'The Distributional Effects of Growth: Case Studies vs. Cross-country regressions', DELTA WP 2002–23.

Bradley, F. (1991) *International Marketing Strategy*, Cambridge: University Press.

Broadman, H.G., J. Anderson, Constantijn A., Claessens, R. Ryterman, S. Slavova, M. Vagliasindi and G.A. Vincelette (2004) 'Building Market Institutions in South Eastern Europe', in *Comparative Prospects for Investment and Private Sector Development*, Washington, DC: World Bank.

Brunazzo, M. and S. Piattoni (2004a) 'Redrawing the Solidarity Map: Structural Funds in an Enlarged Union' in P. Messina (ed.), *EU Enlargement. Borders, Boundaries and Constraints*, Padua: Cleup.

—— (2004b) 'Negotiating the Regulation of the Structural Funds: Italian Actors in EU Regional Policy-making', *Modern Italy*, 9, 2: 159–72.

Brunetti, F. (1995) 'Una ricognizione sul traffico di perfezionamento passivo', in AAVV, *Il traffico di perfezionamento passivo nel settore tessile-abbigliamento italiano*, Sinergie, Rapporto di Ricerca n.1, Verona, Cueim.

Brusco, S. (1994), 'Sistemi globali e sistemi locali', *Economia e politica industriale*, 84.

Brusco, S. and M. Pezzini (1990) 'Small-scale Enterprise and the Ideology of the Italian Left', in Pyke F, Becattini G, Sengenberger W (eds.), *Industrial Districts and Inter-firm Cooperation in Italy*, Geneva: ILO.

Burnside, C. and D. Dollar (2000) 'Aid, Policies and Growth', *The American Economic Review*, 90, 4: 847–68.

Camiah, N. and G. Hollinshead (2003) 'Assessing the potential for effective cross-cultural working between "new" Russian managers and Western expatriates,' *Journal of World Business*, 38: 245–61.

CCIAA (Chamber of Commerce) VR, Servizio Studi e Ricerche (2004), *I distretti produttivi di Verona*, CCIAA, Verona.

CEC (2002) *Federal Republic of Yugoslavia: Country Strategy Paper 2002–2006*, European Commission, External Relations Directorate General, Directorate Western Balkans.

—— (2004) *Proposal for a Council Decision on the Principles, Priorities and Conditions Contained in the European Partnership with Serbia and Montenegro Including Kosovo as Defined by the United Nations Security Council Resolution 1244 of 10 June 1999*, Commission of the European Communities, COM(2004) yyy final.

Centro Estero Veneto (2003) *Indagine sulla presenza imprenditoriale veneta in Romania*, Venezia, Centro Estero Veneto, Antenna Romania.

CFER (Council on Foreign Economic Relations) (2000) *Promoting Sustainable Economies in the Balkans: Report of an Independent Task Force Sponsored by the Council on Foreign Economic Relations*, Washington, DC: Council on Foreign Economic Relations.

Chang, H.-J. (2003) *Globalisation, Economic Development and the Role of the State*, London: Zed Books.

Collier, P. and Dollar, D. (2002) 'Aid Allocation and Poverty Reduction', *European Economic Review*, 85, 1: 46; 8: 1475–500.

—— (2004) 'Development Effectiveness: What Have We Learnt?', *The Economic Journal*, 114: F244–F271.

Collier, P. and A. Hoeffler (2004) 'Aid, Policy and Growth in Post-conflict Societies', *European Economic Review*, 48, 5: 1125–45.

Commission of the European Communities (2004) *The Stabilisation and Association Process for South East Europe*, Third Annual Report, Brussels, 30 March 2004.

Commission Staff Working Papers (2002) *Federal Republic of Yugoslavia – Stabilisation & Association Report 2002*, Brussels, April 4, SEC343.

—— (2003) *Serbia and Montenegro – Stabilisation & Association Report 2003*, Brussels, March 26, SEC(2003) – 43.

—— (2004) *Serbia and Montenegro: Country Report – Stabilisation and Association Report 2004*, Brussels, 30 March, SEC-yyy final.

Co-operative College (2005) *Making a Difference: Co-operative Solutions to Global Poverty*, Manchester: The Co-operative College.

Cornia, G.A. (2003) 'The Distribution of Income Over the Last Twenty Years in the developing and Transitional Economies', paper pres. at SIE, 44° Meeting, Salerno, 24–25 October.

Corò, G. and R. Grandinetti (1999) 'Strategie di delocalizzazione e processi evolutivi nei distretti industriali', *L'industria*, 20: 897–924.

Crescini, M. Mistri (1996) 'Il Veneto e il Traffico di Perfezionamento Passivo nel settore Tessile-Abbigliamento-Calzaturiero', *Economia e Società regionale*, 24–48.

Csaba, L. (2003) 'The Role of Financing in the Growth of the SME Sector: the Case of Hungary, in R.J. McIntyre and B. Dallago (eds.), *Small and Medium Enterprises in Transformational Economies*, Helsinki and Hondmills, Basingstoke: WIDER and Palgrave Macmillan.

Crosby, Lawrence A. and Nancy Stephens (1987) 'Effects of Relationship Marketing on Satisfaction, Retention, and Prices in the Life Insurance Industry', *Journal of Marketing Research*, 24: 204–11.

Čuješ, R. (1980) 'The Co-operative Movement in Slovenia' in Balawyder A. (ed.), *Co-operative Movements in Eastern Europe*, London: Macmillan.

Dalgaard, C.J. and H. Hansen (2001) 'On aid, growth and good policies', *Journal of Development Studies*, 37, 6.

Dallago, B. (1996) 'Investment, Systemic Efficiency and Distribution', *Kyklos*, 49, 4: 615–41.

—— (2003) 'Sme Development in Hungary: Legacy, Transformation and Policy', in R.J. McIntyre and B. Dallago (eds.), *Small and Medium Enterprises in Transformational Economies*, Basingstoke: Palgrave Macmillan.

Dallago, B. and M. Uvalic (1996) 'The Distributive Consequences of Nationalism: the Case of Former Yugoslavia', *Europe–Asia Studies*, No. 1, 1998: 71–90.

Dallago, B. and R.J. McIntyre (2003) 'Conclusions: The Role of Public Policy in SME Development', in R.J. McIntyre and B. Dallago (eds.), *Small and Medium Enterprises in Transformational Economies*, Basingstoke: Palgrave Macmillan.

Dallago, Bruno and Milica Uvalic (1998) 'The Distributive Consequences of Nationalism: The Case of Former Yugoslavia', Europe–Asia Studies, No. 1; 71–90.

Danis, Wade M. (2003) 'Differences in Values, Practices, and Systems Among Hungarian Managers and Western Expatriates: an Organizing Framework and Typology,' *Journal of World Business*, 38: 234–44.

Davis, P. (1999) *Managing the Co-operative Difference: A Survey of the Application of Modern Management Practises in the Co-operative Context*, Geneva: ILO.

de Vergottini, G.(1998) *Le transizioni costituzionali* (Bologna: il Mulino).

Dei Ottati, G. (1995) *Tra mercato e comunità: aspetti concettuali e ricerche empiriche sul distretto industriale*, Milano: Angeli.

del Valle, A. (2000) *Guerres contre l'Europe*, Paris: Syrtes.

'Development Fund of the Republic of Montenegro' (2002) *Annual Report*.

DfID (2004) *Regional Assistance Plan for the Western Balkans 2004/5 to 2008/9*, London: Department for International Development.

Di Matteo, M. and P. Piacentini (eds.) (2003) *The Italian Economy at the Dawn of the 21st Century*, Ashgate: Aldershot.

Dimitrijevic, N. and P. Kovacs (eds.) (2004) *Managing Hatred and Distrust: the Prognosis for Post-Conflict Settlement in Multiethnic Communities in the Former Yugoslavia*, Budapest: LGI Books.

Djurić, D. (2003) 'The Economic Development of Montenegro', in Bieber, F. (ed.), *Montenegro in Transition: Problems of Identity and Statehood*, Baden-Baden: Nomos Verlagsgesellschaft.

Djurović, G. *et al.* (2002) *Alternative Development Concepts of Economy of Montenegro*, Economics Faculty Podgorica.

Doina Catana and Gh.A. Catana (2002) 'A Framework for Management Development Through Market-oriented Learning,' *JEEMS*, 3: 298–315.

Dollar, D. and A. Kray (2001) 'Growth is Good for the Poor', World Bank Policy Research Department, WP. no. 2587, Washington.

Dolowitz, D.P. and D. Marsh (1996) 'Who Learns What from Whom? A Review of the Policy Transfer Literature', *Political Studies*, 44: 343–57.

—— (2000), 'Learning from Abroad: the Role of Policy Transfer in Contemporary Policy-making', *Governance*, 13, 1: 5–24.

Easterly, W. (2003) 'Can Foreign Aid Buy Growth?', *Journal of Economic Perspectives*, 17, 3: 23–48.

—— *et al.* (2004) 'Aid, Policies and Growth: Comment', *The American Economic Review*, 94, 3: 774–80.

EBRD (2000) *Transition Report 2000*, London: EBRD.

—— (2003) *Transition Report 2003*, London: EBRD.

—— (2004a) *Strategy for Serbia and Montenegro*, London: European Bank for Reconstruction and Development.

—— (2004b) *Spotlight on South-eastern Europe*, London: EBRD.

EC (1973) 'Proposals for a Community Regional Policy,' *Official Journal of the European Communities* (October).

—— (1975) 'Regulations Establishing a Community Regional Policy', *Official Journal of the European Communities* (March).

—— (1999) *Agenda 2000. Vol. I: for a Stronger and Wider Union. Vol II: the Challenges of Enlargement.* Luxembourg: Office for Official Publication of the European Communities.

—— (2000) European Commission External Relations Directorate General: *CARDs Assistance Programme to the Western Balkans: Regional Strategy Paper 2000–2006.* <http://europa.eu.int/comm/europeaid/projects/cards/pdf/regional_strategy_paper.pdf>

—— (2001a) *Unity, Solidarity, Diversity for Europe, Its People, Its Territory: Second Cohesion Report on Economic and Social Cohesion*, Luxembourg: Office for Official Publication of the European Communities.

—— (2001b) *Co-operatives in Enterprise Europe*, Draft Consultation paper, December, Brussels: Commission of the European Communities.

—— (2002a) *First Progress Report on Economic and Social Cohesion*, Brussels, 30.1.2002. COM (2002) 46 final.

—— (2002b) *First Annual Report of the EU Commission on the Stabilization and Association Process for South-East Europe,'* Document COM(2002), April.

—— (2003) *Second Progress Report on Economic and Social Cohesion*, Brussels, 30.1.2003. COM(2003) 34 final.

—— (2004) *A New Partnership for Europe: Convergence, Competitiveness, Cooperation. Third Report on Economic and Social Cohesion*, Luxembourg: Office for Official Publication of the European Communities.

Ellerman, D. (1990) *The Democratic Worker-Owned Firm: a New model for East and West*, London: Unwin Hyman.

Enright (2002) *Regional Clusters: What We Know and What We Should Know*, Kiel Institute International Workshop on Innovative Clusters and Interregional Competition, 12–13 November 2001; quoted in A. *Majocchi (2004).*

Estrin, S. (1983) *Self-Management: Economic Theory and Yugoslav Practice*, Cambridge: Cambridge University Press.

—— (1991) 'Some Reflections on Self-Management, Social Choice, and Reform in Eastern Europe', *Journal of Comparative Economics*, 15: 349–66.

European Commission and the World Bank (2004) *Report on Activities of the European Commission/World Bank Office for South-East Europe 2003*, Brussels: Office for South-East Europe.

European Commission for Democracy through Law (Venice Commission) (2004) *Opinion on the Draft Amendments to the Constitution of the Federation of Bosnia and*

*Herzegovina Concerning Local Government*, Opinion no. 276/2004, CDL-AD(2004)014, adopted at Venice, 29 March 2004.
—— (2004) *Opinion on the New Draft Amendments to the Constitution of the Federation of Bosnia and Herzegovina Concerning Local Government*, Opinion no. 276/2004, CDL-AD(2004)032, adopted at Venice, 8–9 October 2004.
European Training Foundation (2002) *A Management Tool Kit on Training Needs Assessment and Program Design: an Integrated Resource for Management Development in Transition Countries*, Torino.
Eyal, G. and E. Townsley (1995) 'The Social Composition of the Communist Nomenklatura: a Comparison of Russia, Poland, and Hungary,' *Theory and Society*, 24, 5: 723–50.
Eyal, G., I. Szeleny and E. Towsley (2000) *Making Capitalism Without Capitalists: The New Ruling Elites in Eastern Europe*, London: Verso.
Facchini, G. and M.L. Segnana (2003) 'Growth at the EU Periphery: the Next Enlargement', *The Quartely Review of Economics and Finance*, 43: 827–62.
Farabullini, F. and G. Ferri (2003) ' "Passaggi ad Est" per le banche italiane e i distretti industriali: collegati o indipendenti', in *Economie locali, modelli di agglomerazione e apertura internazionale: Nuove ricerche della Banca d'Italia sullo sviluppo territoriale*. Atti del convegno. Bologna, 20 November 2003, 453–83.
Farrell, H. and A. Heritier (2003) 'Formal and Informal Institutions Under Codecision: Continuous Constitution-Building in Europe', *Governance: an International Journal of Policy, Administration, and Institutions*, Vol. 16, 4 October: 577–600.
Fedderke, J.R., De Kadt and J. Luiz (1999) 'Economic Growth and Social Capital: A Critical Reflection', *Theory and Society*, 5: 710–45.
Federation of Danish Co-operatives and Agricultural Council (1993) *Danish Farmers and Their Co-operatives*, Copenhagen: FDC and Agricultural Council.
Feenstra, R.C. (1998) 'Integration of Trade and Disintegration of Production in the Global Economy', *Journal of Economic Perspectives*, 12, 4: 31–50.
Feenstra, R.C. and G.H. Hanson (1996a) 'Globalization, Outsourcing, and Wage Inequality' *American Economic Review Papers and Proceedings*, 86, 2: 240–5.
—— (1996b) 'Foreign Investment, Outsourcing, and Relative Wages', in Feenstra, R.C., Grossman, G.M. and Irwin, D.A. (eds.), *Political Economy of Trade Policy: Essays in Honor of Jagdish Bhagwati*, Cambridge, Mass.: MIT Press.
Foglio (1995) *Marketing Globale e mercato 2000: Prodotti, alleanze, strategie per il mercato globale*, II ed., Milano: Angeli.
Foote-Whyte, W. and K. Foote-Whyte (1988) *Making Mondragon: The Growth and Dynamics of the Mondragon Co-operative Complex*, Ithaca: Cornell University Press.
Foster, J. and M. Székely (2001) 'Is Economic Growth Good for the Poor?: Tracking Low Incomes Using General Means', Inter-American Development Bank, Working Paper, 453.
Frane, A. and Matvesz Tomšič (2002) 'Elite (re)Configuration and politico-economic Performance in Post-socialist Countries,' *Europe–Asia Studies*, 54, 3: 435–54.
Frankel, J.A. and D. Romer (1999) 'Does Trade Cause Growth?', *American Economic Review*, 89, 3: 379–39.
Fries, S., T. Lysenko and S. Polanec (2003) 'The 2002 Business Environment and Enterprise Performance Survey: Results from a Survey of 6,100 Firms', London: European Bank for Reconstruction and Development, *Working Paper No 84*, November.
Gandolfi, V. (1988) *Aree sistema: internazionalizzazione e reti telematiche*, Milano: Angeli.
Garde, P. (2001) *Fin de siècle dans les Balkans*, Paris: Jacob.

Garner, T.I. and K. Terrell (1998) 'A Gini Decomposition Analysis of Inequality in the Czech and Slovak Republics during the Transition', CEPR Discussion Paper Series Number 1897.

Garofoli, G. (1983) 'Le aree sistema in Italia', *Politica ed Economia*, 11.

Girardin, E. and X. Ping (1997) *Urban Credit Co-operatives in China*, OECD Development Centre Technical Paper No 125, Paris: OECD.

Gisolo, E. and P. Iodice (2004) 'I processi di internazionalizzazione delle imprese venete', *Economia e Politica regionale*, 1.

Gomirato, E. (2004) 'La delocalizzazione dell'abbigliamento in Romania: il caso Stefanel', *Economia e Società Regionale*, 3.

Gozi, S. (2000) 'Il futuro europeo dei Balcani' in *Europa/Europe*, 2.

Grancelli, B. (1997) 'Il management post-sovietico', *Sviluppo & Organizzazione*, 149: 24–42.

—— (1988) *Soviet Management and Labor Relations,* Boston: Allen & Uniwin.

—— (2002) 'Local Problems and Foreign Solution: Issues of Management Training in Russian and NIS', in M. Kelemen and M. Kostera (eds.), *Critical Management Research in Eastern Europe: Managing the Transitio,* London: Palgrave.

Granovetter, M. (1985) 'Economic Action and Social Structure: the Problem of Embeddedness', *American Journal of Sociology*, Vol. 91, 3: 481–510.

Green Cowles, M., J. Caporaso and T. Risse (eds.) (2001) *Transforming Europe. Europeanization and Domestic Change*, Ithaca, NY: Cornell University Press.

Grootaert, C. (1997) 'Social capital: "The Missing Link" ', in: *Expanding the Measure of Wealth: Indicators of Environmentally Sustainable Development*, Washington, DC: World Bank.

Grossman, G. (1983) 'The Party as Manager and Entrepreneur', in Gregory Guroff and Fred V. Carstensen (eds.), *Entrepreneurship in Imperial Russia and the Soviet Union*, Princeton: Princeton University Press.

Gunn, C. (2004) *Third-Sector Development: Making up for the Market*, Ithaca: Cornell University Press.

Hankiss, E. (1990) *East European Alternatives*, Oxford: Clarendon Press.

Hanley, E., N. Yershova, and R. Anderson (1995) 'Russia – Old Wine in a New bottle?: the circulation and Reproduction of Russia elites, 1983–1993,' *Theory and Society*, 24, 5: 639–68.

Hansen, H. and F. Tarp (2001) 'Aid and Growth Regressions', *Journal of Development Economics*, 64, 2: 547–70.

Harper, M. (1991) *Producers' Small-scale Industrial Co-operatives: Some Case Studies from Developing Countries*, Geneva: ILO.

Harper, M. and A.K. Roy (2000) *Co-operative Success: What Makes Group Entrepreneurs Succeed*, London: ITDG Publications.

Harrison, A. (1996) 'Openness and Growth: a Time Series, Cross Country Analysis for Developing Countries', *Journal of Development Economics*, 48: 419–47.

Hass, J. (1999) 'The Great Transition: The Dynamics of Market Transition and the Case of Russia, 1991–1995', *Theory and Society*, 3: 383–424.

Heimerl, D. and W. Van Meurs (2002) 'La France, l'Allemagne et les Balkans – Divergences et consensus', *Le courrier des pays de l'Est*, 1023, March.

Heinelt, H. (1996) 'Multi-Level Governance in the European Union and the Structural Funds' in H. Heinelt and R. Smith (eds.) *Policy Networks and European Structural Funds*, Aldershot: Avebury.

Henderson, S. (2002) 'Selling Civil Society. Western Aid and Nongovernmental Organization Sector in Russia,' *Comparative Political Studies*, 2: 139–67.

Higley, J., J. Pakulski and W. Wesolowski (eds.) (1998) *Postcommunist Elites and Democracy in Eastern Europe*, London: Macmillan.

Hirschman, A.O. (1985) *Getting Ahead Collectively: Grassroots Experiences in Latin America*, London: Pergamon Press.

Höcker-Weyand, C. (1980) *Die Rechtsinstitute und Rechtsinstitutionen des jugoslawischen Selbstverwaltungssystems*, Osteuropa Institut Berlin, vol. 9 (Berlin: Nomos).

Hodgson, G.M. (1988) *Economics and Institutions: A Manifesto for a Modern Institutional Economics*, Cambridge: Polity Press.

—— (1993) *Economics and Evolution: Bringing Life Back into Economics*, Cambridge: Polity Press.

Holbrooke, R. (1999) *To End a War*, New York: Knopf.

Holstrom, M. (1989) *Industrial Democracy in Italy*, Aldershot: Avebury.

Hooghe, L. (1996) 'Introduction: Reconciling EU-wide Policy and National Diversity' in L. Hooghe (ed.), *Cohesion Policy and European Integration: Building Multilevel Governance*, Oxford: Oxford University Press.

—— (2002) 'The Mobilization of Collective Interests and Multi-level Governance' in R. Balme, D. Chabanet and V. Wright (eds.), *L'action collective en Europe*, Paris: Presses de Sciences Po.

Hooghe, L. and G. Marks (2001) *Multi-Level Governance and European Integration*, Lanham: Rowman & Littlefield.

Horvat, A. (2004) 'Absorption Problems in the EU Structural Funds', paper presented at the 2004 Conference on Structural Funds in the EU as shown on www.sigov.si/umor/conference/2004/papers/Horvat.pdf

Horvat, B. (1976) *The Yugoslav Economic System*, New York: M.E. Sharpe.

—— (1982) *The Political Economy of Socialism*, Oxford: Martin Robertson.

—— (2000) 'Transition and Restoration: the Two Alternative Strategies', in N. Ostojić and N. Scott (eds.), *Proceedings of the 3rd ECPD International Round-Table*, Belgrade: European Centre for Peace and Development.

Huntigton, S.(1996) *The Clash of Civilizations and the Remake of the World Order*, New York: Simon & Schuster.

ICA (1996) *Statement on the Co-operative Identity*, Geneva: ICA.

Ilic, M. (2002) 'A Critical Review on the New Solutions in the New Law on Local Self-Government in the Republic of Serbia', in *Facta Universitatis*, Series Law and Politics vol. 1, No. 6, pp. 711–18.

ILO (1981) *Workers' Participation in Decisions Within Undertakings*, Geneva: ILO.

—— (2002) *Promotion of Co-operatives Recommendation 193*, Geneva: ILO.

Innocenti (2003) *Production Outsourcing in Italian Manufacturing Industry*, in M. Di Matteo and P. Piacentini (eds.), *The Italian Economy at the Dawn of the 21st Century*, Ashgate: Aldershot.

Ivanisevic S., I. Kopric, J. Omejec and J. Simovic (2001) 'Local Government in Croatia', in E. Kandeva (ed.), *Stabilization of Local Governments* Budapest: OSI/LGI.

Ivaschenko, O. (2003) 'Growth and Inequality: Evidence from Transitional Economies', CESifo Working Paper Series n. 746.

Ivekovic, R. (1999) *Autopsia dei Balcani. Saggio di psico politica*, Milano: Cortina.

Jeffery, C. (2000) 'Sub-National Mobilization and European Integration: Does It Make Any Difference?', *Journal of Common Market Studies*, 38, 1: 1–23.

Jeter, J. (2003) 'For Argentines, a Sweet Resolve: Co-operatives step in when factories fail', *Washington Post Foreign Service*, 24 February, 2003, p. A15.

Jokay, C. (2001) 'Local Government in Bosnia and Herzegovina', in E. Kandeva (ed.), *Stabilization of Local Governments*, Budapest: OSI/LGI.

Jones, C.I. (2002) *Introduction to Economic Growth*, 2nd edn., New York: W.W. Norton & Co.

Jonită, S. (2003a) 'Catching up: the Development Gap and Its Causes', Policy *Warning Report, Romania*, UNDP – Romanian Academic Society, May.

—— (2003b) 'Failures of the Romanian Institutional Reform and the Role of International Assistance', Romanian Academic Society (SAR), Crisis papers series, 3: 1–9.

Jonită, S. and C. Fortusnic (2002) 'Grassroots Government. Strategies, Attitudes and Effectiveness in the Romanian Local Administration', *SOCO Project Paper,* Wien: Institut für Wissenschaften vom Menschen, 80: 1–21.

Kakwani, N., S. Khandker and H. Son (2003) 'Poverty Equivalent Growth Rate: with Applications to Korea and Thailand', paper presented at Inequality, Poverty and Human well-being, WIDER Conference, Helsinky, Finland, 30–31 May. Available at: http://www.wider.unu.edu/conference/conference-2003-2/conference2003-2.htm

Kaminski, B. and M. de la Rocha (2003) 'Policy-induced Integration in Balkans: Policy Options and Their Assessment, *Trade Policies and Institutions in the Countries of South Eastern Europe in the EU Stabilization and Association Process,* Regional Report, 28 March, 2003, Document of the World Bank Report No. 24460.

Kandeva, E. (2001) 'Introduction to Comparative Local Government in Central and Eastern Europe: a Balkan Perspective', in E. Kandeva (ed.), *Stabilization of Local Governments,* Budapest: OSI/LGI.

Karshenas, M. (2001) 'Measurement and Nature of Absolute Poverty in Least Developed Countries', background report for The Least Developed Countries Report 2002, UNCTAD, Geneva.

Kaufmann (2003) 'Rethinking Governance. Empirical Lessons Challenge Ortodoxy', Global Competitiveness Report by the World Economic Forum, February.

Kaufmann, D., A. Kraay and P. Zoido-Lobaton (2002). *Governance Matters II; Updated Indicators for 2001,* The World Bank and Stanford University.

Kaufmann, D. and A. Kraay, (2002) 'Growth Without Governance', *Economia,* 3, 1: 169–229.

Keane, M.P. and E.S. Prasad (2000), 'Inequality, Transfers and Growth: New Evidence from the Economic Transition in Poland', IMF Working Paper WP/00/117.

Keating, M. (1995) 'Europeanism and Regionalism' in B. Jones and M. Keating (eds.), *The European Union and the Regions,* Oxford: Clarendon Press.

Knack, S. (2001) 'Aid Dependence and the Quality of Governance: Cross-country Empirical Tests', *Southern Economic Journal,* 68, 2: 310–39.

Knemayer, F.-L. (ed.) (2003) *Kommunale Selbstverwaltung in Ost und West,* Baden-Baden: Nomos.

Knowles, S. (2001) 'Inequality and Economic Growth: the Empirical Relationship Reconsidered in the Light of Comparable Data', CREDIT Research Paper, No. 01/03, University of Nottingham.

Konrad, G. and I. Szeleny (1979) *The Intellectuals on the Road to Class Power,* New York: Harcourt-Brace.

Kornai, János (1992) *The Socialist System,* Princeton: Princeton University Press.

Koubek, J. (2000) 'Human Resource Management in Transforming Economies – Convergence or divergence? (The example of Czech Republic), in E. Vatchkova (ed.), VARNA 2000, Sofia.

Krugman, P. (1991) *Geography and Trade,* Cambridge, Mass.: MIT Press.

Krugman, P. and A. Venables (1993) 'Integration, Specialization, and the Adjustment', NBER Working Papers 4559.

Kryshtanovskaya, O. and S. White (1996) 'From Soviet Nomenklatura to Russian Elite,' Europe–Asia Studies, 5: 711–33.

Laffan, B. and Mi. Shackleton (2000) '[The EU] Budget: Who Gets What, When and How', in H. and W. Wallace (eds.), *Policy-Making in the European Union,* Oxford: University Press.

Lampe, J. (1996) *Yugoslavia as History: Twice There Was a Country*, Cambridge: Cambridge University Press.

Lampe, J. and M. Jackson (1982) *Balkan Economic History 1550–1950*, Bloomington: Indiana University Press.

Lane, D. and C. Ross (1997) 'Russian Political Elites, 1991–1995: Recruitment and Renewal', *International Politics*, 34: 169–92.

Lazic, M. (2000) 'The Adaptive Reconstruction of Elites, in Higley, J. and G. Lengyel (eds.), *Elites after State Socialism*, Lanham: Rowman & Littlefield.

Leonardi, R. (1998) *Coesione, convergenza e integrazione nell'Unione europea*, Bologna: Il Mulino.

Leonardi, R. and R. Nanetti (2001) 'L'innovazione dei QCS. Il processo interattivo fra Stato, Regioni e Unione europea', *Le istituzioni del federalismo*, 22, 2: 325–60.

Lewer, J.J. and H. van den Berg (2003) 'How Large is International Trade's Effect on Economic Growth?', *Journal of Economic Surveys*, 17, 3: 363–96.

Lustig, N., O. Arias and J. Rigolini, (2002) 'Poverty Reduction and Economic Growth: A Two-Way Causality', *Inter-American Development Bank*, Sustainable Development Department Technical Papers Series, Washington, DC, March.

MacEwan, A. (1999) *Neo-liberalism or Democracy?: Economic Strategy, Markets, and Alternatives for the 21st Century*, London: Zed Books.

Maiocchi, A. (2000) *Are Industrial Clusters Going International?: the Case of Italian SMEs in Romania*, Working Paper n. 12, Facoltà di Economia, Università dell'Insubria.

—— (2004) 'Developing a Favourable Business Environment: Lessons from the Experience of Italian Firms in the Region of Timişoara, Romania', OECD–LEED conference on '*Cluster of enterprises and the internationalisation of SMEs: the case of the Romanian region of Timişoara'*, 24 May 2004.

Majocchi and A. Zucchella (2003) 'Internationalisation and Performance: Findings from a Set of Italian SMEs', *International Small Business Journal*, 21, 3: 249–66.

Marelli, M. *et al.* (1992) *Continuità e cambiamento nella vita delle imprese*, Milano: Angeli.

Marks, G. (1992) 'Structural Policy in the European Community' in A. Sbragia (ed.), *Europolitics. Institutions and Policy-Making in the 'New' European Community*, Washington, DC: The Brookings Institute.

—— (1993) 'Structural Policy and Multilevel Governance in the EC', in A.W. Cafruny and G. Rosenthal (eds.), *The State of the European Community, Vol. 2: The Maastricht Debates and Beyond*, Boulder, CO: Lynnie Riener Pub.

Martins, B. *et al.* (2003) *The Institutions of Economic Aid*, Cambridge: Cambridge University Press.

McIntyre, R. (2003) 'The Complex Ecology of Small Enterprise Systems', in R. McIntyre and B. Dallago (eds.), *Small and Medium Enterprises in Transitional Economies*, London: Palgrave Macmillan in association with the United Nations University.

Meier, V.E. (1968) *La rinascita del nazionalismo nei Balcani*, Bologna: Il Mulino.

Mele, G. (2002) 'Allargamento dell'Unione europea e riforma della politica regionale e di coesione', *Rivista Economica del Mezzogiorno*, 16, 4: 877–952.

Mencinger, J. (1996) 'Privatisation Experiences in Slovenia,' Annals of Public and Co-operative Economics, 67, 3.

Mezzetti, L. (2003) *Teoria e prassi delle transizioni costituzionali e del consolidamento costituzionale*, Padova: Cedam.

Michalopoulos, C. (2003) 'The Western Balkans in World Trade', in World Bank (2003e), p. 1–21.

Mikl-Horke, G. (2004) 'Globalization, Transformation and the Diffusion of Management Innovations', *JEEMS*, 2: 98–122.

Milanovic, B. (1999) 'Explaining the Increase in Inequality During Transition', *Economics of Transition* 7, 2: 299–343.

Minkov, M. (2000) 'Culturally-determined Attitudes Affecting Business Behaviour in Bulgaria, and Implications for Human Potential Development', in E. Vatchova (ed.), *Varna 2000: Human Resource Management*, Sofia.

Mistri, M. (1998) *Saggi su internazionalizzazione della piccola impresa*, Padova: Cedam.

Morata, F. (2002) 'La politica di coesione' in S. Fabbrini and F. Morata (eds.), *L'Unione europea. Le politiche pubbliche*, Roma/Bari: Laterza.

Müller, K. (1999) *The Political Economy of Pension Reform In Central–Eastern Europe*, Cheltenham: Edward Elgar.

Musso, F. (2000) *Economie distrettuali e canali di distribuzione all'estero*, Urbino and Genova, ASPI/INS-EDIT.

Nikiforos Diamandouros, P. and F. Stephen Larrabee (2001) 'La democratizzazione dell'Europa Sud-Orientale', *Rivista Italiana di Scienza Politica*, 1, April.

North, D.C. (1990) *Institutions: Institutional Change and Economic Performance*. Cambridge: Cambridge University Press.

OECD (2003) *Entrepreneurship and Local Economic Development: Programme and Policy Recommendations*, Paris.

OECD/LEED (2003) *L'Asset Building e l'uscita dalla povertà*, Paris: OECD.

OECD–EBRD (2002a) *Entrepreneurship and Enterprise Development: Romania*, Paris and London, March.

—— (2002b) *Bulgaria. Enterprise Policy Performance Assessment*, Paris and London, December.

—— (2003a) *Croatia: Enterprise Policy Performance Assessment*, Paris and London, May.

—— (2003b) *Moldova: Enterprise Policy Performance Assessment*, Paris and London, May.

—— (2003c) *Albania: Enterprise Policy Performance Assessment*, Paris and London, June.

—— (2003d) *Bosnia and Herzegovina. Enterprise Policy Performance Assessment*, Paris and London, September.

—— (2003e) *Montenegro: Enterprise Policy Performance Assessment (Serbia and Montenegro)*, Paris and London, September.

—— (2003f) *FYR Macedonia: Enterprise Policy Performance Assessment*, Paris and London, September.

—— (2003g) *South East Europe Region. Enterprise Policy Performance: a Regional Assessment*, Paris and London, October.

Ottolenghi, D. and A. Steinherr (1993) Yugoslavia: Was It a Winner's Curse? *Economics of Transition*, 1, 2.

Panati, G. (1980) *Politiche di ristrutturazione industriale e decentramento produttivo*, Padova: Cedam.

Paraskevopoulos, C. and R. Leonardi (eds.) (2004) 'Learning from Abroad: Regionalization and Local Institutional Infrastructure in Cohesion and Accession Countries', *Regional and Federal Studies*, special issue, 14, 3.

Parayil, G. (ed.) (2000) *Kerala – The Development Experience: Reflections on Sustainability and Replicability*, London: Zed Books.

Parnell, E. (2001) The Role of Co-operatives and Other Self-Help Organisations in Crisis Resolution and Socio-Economic Recovery, Geneva: ILO.

Patten, C. 'Western Balkans Democracy Forum', Thessaloniki, 11 April 2002.

Pejovich, S. (1998) *Economic Analysis of Institutions and Systems*, Rev. 2nd edn, Dordrecht: Kluwer Academic Publishers.

Péteri, G. (2001) 'Foreword', in E. Kandeva (ed.), *Stabilization of Local Governments*, Budapest: OSI/LGI.
Philip, L. (1994) 'European Security: from Europhoria to Confusion', *European Security*, 3, 2.
Piattoni, S. (2003) 'Il Comitato delle Regioni' in S. Fabbrini (ed.), *L'Unione europea: Le istituzioni e gli attori di un sistema sopranazionale*, Roma/Bari: Editori Laterza.
Pinto, R. (2004) 'Key SME Policy Trends and Issues in South East Europe', paper presented to First Meeting of the Advisory Group of the OECD LEED Trento Centre for Local Development.
Pleština, D. (1992) *Regional Development in Communist Yugoslavia: Success, Failure and Consequences*, Boulder, Co: Westview Press.
Porter, M.E. (1990) *The 'Competitive Advantage' of Nations*, New York: Macmillan.
—— (1998) *On Competition*, Boston: Harvard Business School Press.
Prlic, J. (2003) 'Possible Strategies for Europeisation of South-Eastern Europe' in G. Gozzi (ed.), *Le prospettive europee di apertura all'Europa orientale e ai paesi del Mediterraneo*, Ravenna: Longo editore.
Prodi, R. (2002) *Moja Evropa*, Belgrade: BMG.
Pryor, F.L. (2005a) 'Market economic systems', *Journal of Comparative Economics*, 33: 25–46.
—— (2005b) *Economic Systems of Foraging, Agricultural, and Industrial Societies*, Cambridge: Cambridge University Press.
Pučko, Danijel and Tomasz Cater. (2001) 'Business Annual Planning and Controlling in Slovenian Managerial Practice', *JEEMS*, 4: 355–65.
Putnam, R. (1993) *Making Democracy Work: Civic Traditions in Modern Italy*, Princeton: Princeton University Press.
Pyke, F., G. Becattini and W. Sengenberger (eds.) (1990) *Small Firms and Industrial Districts in Italy*, Geneva, International Institute for Labour Studies.
Quadrio, C. and M. Fortis (eds.) (2002) *Complexity and Industrial Clusters: Dynamics and Models in Theory and Practice*, Heidelberg: Physica Verlag.
Querimi, Q. 'South-East Europe's EU integration: Dreams and Realities', *South-East Europe Review*.
Radaelli, C. (1999) 'The Public Policy of the European Union: Whither the Politics of expertise?' *Journal of European Public Policy*, 6, 5: 757–74.
—— (2003) 'The Europeanization of Public Policy' in K. Featherstone and C.M. Radaelli (eds.), *The Politics of Europeanization*, Oxford: Oxford University Press.
Radevic, D. and K. Beegle (2002) *Living Standards and Poverty in Montenegro in 2002*, Podgorica: Institute for Strategic Studies and Prognoses.
Radosevic, S. (2002), 'Regional Innovation Systems in Central and Eastern Europe: Determinants, Organizers and Alignments', *Journal of Technology Transfer*, 27: 87–96.
Raiser, M. and A. Rousso and F. Steves (2003) 'Trust in Transformation: Cross-Country and Firm Evidence, Working paper No. 82, London: European Bank for Reconstruction and Development, October.
Ramljak, M. (1989) 'Local Self-Government in Yugoslavia', in J. Kregar, I. Šimonović (eds.), *Yugoslavia: Legal Framework, Social, Political and Economic Aspects*, Zagreb: Narodne Novine.
Ranis, G. and F. Stewart (1993) 'Rural Non-agricultural Activities in Development: Theory and Application', *Journal of Development Economics*, 40: 75–101.
Ravallion, M. (2001) 'Growth, Inequality and Poverty: Looking Beyond Averages, *World Development*, 29, 11: 1803–15.
Ravallion, M. and G. Datt (2002) 'Why Has Economic Growth Been More Pro-Poor in Some States of India than Others?', *Journal of Development Economics*, 68: 381–400.

Rinella, A. (1997) *La forma di governo semi-presidenziale. Profili metodologici e 'circolazione' del modello francese in Europa centro orientale*, Torino: Giappichelli.
Roberts, M.J. and J.R. Tybout (1996) *Industrial Evolution in Developing Countries: Micro Patterns of Turnover, Productivity, and Market Structure*, Oxford University Press: New York.
Rodriguez, F. and D. Rodrik (2000) 'Trade Policy and Economic Growth: a Skeptic's Guide to the Cross-National Evidence', in Bernanke B.S. and Rogoff K. (eds.), *NBER Macroeconomics Annual*, Cambridge: MIT Press.
Rodrik, D., A. Subrimaniane and F. Trebbi (2002) 'Institutions Rule: the Primacy of Institutions Over Geography and Integration in Economic Development', *IMF Working Paper* 02/189.
RoM (2000) *Montenegro Regional Development*, Government Secretariat for Development, Podgorica.
Rose, R. (1993), *Lesson Drawing in Public Policy: a Guide to Learning Across Time and Space*, Chatham NJ: Chatham House.
Rosefielde, S. (2005) 'An Abnormal Country', *The European Journal of Comparative Economics*, 2, 1: 3–16.
Sacco, R. (1992) *Introduzione al diritto comparato*, Torino: Giappichelli.
Sachs, J. (1990) '*What Is To Be Done?*', The Economist (January 13), London.
Sanguigni, V. (1995) 'Una survey sul traffico di perfezionamento passivo', in AAVV (1995), *Il traffico di perfezionamento passivo nel settore tessile-abbigliamento italiano*, Sinergie, Rapporto di Ricerca n.1, Verona, Cueim.
Sapir, A. *et al.* (2004) *An Agenda for a Growing Europe: the Sapir Report*, Oxford: University Press.
SAPRIN (Structural Adjustment Participatory Reviews International Network) (2001) *The Policy Roots of Economic Crisis and Poverty*, Washington, DC: SAPRIN.
Savitt, R. (1998), 'Evolving Management Practices in the Czech Republic: Restructuring and Market Orientation', JEEMS, 4: 339–54.
Scarciglia, R. (2001) 'Nuove tendenze dell'ordinamento locale', in R. Scarciglia and M. Gobbo (eds.), *Nuove tendenze dell'ordinamento locale. Fonti del diritto e forme di governo nell'esperienza comparata*, Trieste: E.U.T.
Scase, R. (2003) 'Entrepreneurship and Proprietorship in Transformation: Policy implications for the SME sector, in R.J. McIntyre and B. Dallago (eds.), *Small and Medium Enterprises in Transformational Economies*, Basingstoke and New York: Palgrave Macmillan.
Schiattarella, R. (1999) 'La delocalizzazione internazionale della produzione: problemi di definizione e misurazione: Un'analisi per il comparto del Made in Italy', *Economia e Politica Industriale*, 103: 207–39.
—— (2002) 'Gli effetti della delocalizzaazione internazionale nei Paesi Terzi Mediterranei. Un'analisi per il comparto del made in Italy', *Argomenti*, 6: 35–56.
Schneider, Friedrich (2002) 'The Development of the Shadow Economies and Shadow Labor Force of 22 Transition and 21 OECD Countries', *12A Discussion Paper*, No. 514.
Sevic, Z. (2001) 'Local Government in Yugoslavia', in E. Kandeva (ed.), *Stabilization of Local Governments*, Budapest: OSI/LGI.
Shuman, M. (2000) *Going Local: Creating Self-Reliant Communities in a Global Age*, New York: Routledge.
Simon, H.A. (1976) 'From Substantive to Procedural Rationality', in Spiro J. Latsis (ed.), *Method and Appraisal in Economics*, Cambridge: Cambridge University Press, pp. 129–48.
Singleton, F. (1985) *A Short History of the Yugoslav Peoples*, Cambridge: Cambridge University Press.

Sistek, F. and B. Dimitrovova (2003) 'National Minorities in Montenegro After the Break-up of Yugoslavia', in F. Bieber (ed.), *Montenegro in Transition: Problems of Identity and Statehood*, Baden-Baden: Nomos Verlagsgesellschaft.

Skurbaty, Z. (ed.) (2005) *Beyond a One-Dimensional State: an Emerging Right to Autonomy?*, Leiden: Martinus Nijhoff.

Smallbone, D. (2005) 'Institutions, Governance and the Development of Entrepreneurship: The Experience of Central and East Europe', paper presented at the International Conference on *'Local Development and Governance in Central, East and South-East Europe'*, OECD LEED Centre for Local Development, Trento, 6–8 June.

Smallbone, D. and $$ F.W. (2001) 'The Distinctiveness of Entrepreneurship in Transition Economies', *Small Business Economics*, 16: 249–62.

Smerdel, B. (1989) 'The Constitutional Developments of Socialist Yugoslavia', in J. Kregar, and I. Šimonović (eds.), *Yugoslavia – Institutional Framework*, Zagreb.

Sorrente, G. (2002) 'La politica di coesione dell'Unione europea per il periodo 2007–2013. Lo stato dei lavori', *Le istituzioni del federalismo*, 23, 6: 1083–112.

Sperling, V. (1998) *Foreign Funding of Social Movements in Russia*, Cambridge: Harvard University Press.

Spoor (2003) 'Inequality, Rural Poverty and Conflict in Transition Economies', CESTRAD and ISS working paper, The Hague, The Netherlands.

Staniszkis, J. (1991) 'Political Capitalism in Poland', *East European Politics and Society* 1: 127–41.

Stark, D. (1996) 'Recombinant Property in East European Capitalism', *American Journal of Sociology*, 101, 4: 993–1027.

Steen, A. and V. Gel'man (2003) *Elites and Democratic Government in Russia*, London: Routledge.

Steering Committee On Local And Regional Democracy (CDLR), (2001) *Relationship Between the Size of Local and Regional Authorities and Their Effectiveness and Economy of Their Action* (Strasbourg: Council of Europe, December 2001).

Steger, T. and R. Lang (2003) 'Career Paths of the Elite of Former GDR Combinates During the Postsocialist Transformation Process,' *Journal of World Business*, 38: 168–81.

Steves, F. and A. Rousso (2003) 'Anti-corruption Programmes in post-communist Transformation Countries and Changes in the Business Environment, 1999–2002', Working paper No. 85, London: European Bank for Reconstruction and Development, October.

Stiglitz, J. (2002) *Globalisation and Its Discontents*, London: Allen Lane.

—— (1998) 'More Instruments and Broader Goals: Moving toward the Post-Washington Consensus', *WIDER Annual Lectures 2*, Helsinki: UNU/WIDER.

—— (2004) 'The Role of Co-operatives in Globalization', paper presented at the LegaCoop International Conference 'The Culture of Development, Globalization, Co-operative Enterprises', Genoa, Italy, 2–3 July.

Stone, D. (2004) 'Transfer Agents and Global Networks in the "Transnationalization" of Policy', *Journal of European Public Policy*, 11, 3: 545–66.

Storper, M. (2000) 'Globalization, Localization and Trade', in Clark, Gordon L., Maryann P. Feldman, and Meric S. Gertler (eds.), *The Oxford Handbook of Economic Geography*, Oxford: Oxford University Press.

Suttcliffe, J.B. (2000) 'The 1999 Reform of the Structural Regulations: Multi-level Governance or Re-nationalization?', *Journal of European Public Policy*, 7, 2: 290–309.

Swianiewicz, P. (ed.) (2002) *Consolidation or Fragmentation? the Size of Local Governments in Central and Eastern Europe*, Budapest: OSI/LGI.

Szeleny, I. and S. Szeleny (1995) 'Circulation or Reproduction of Elites During the Postcommunist Transformation in Eastern Europe: Introduction', *Theory and Society*, 5: 615–38.

Szeleny, S., I. Szeleny and I. Kovach (1995) 'The Making of the Hungarian Postcommunist Elite: Circulation in Politics, Reproduction in the Economy,' *Theory and Society*, 24, 5: 697–722.

Sztaniszkis (1991) *The Dynamics of Breakthroughs in Eastern Europe: The Polish Experience*, Berkeley: University of California Press.

Todeva, E. (1996) 'Dynamics of Management Practices in Eastern Europe: the Case of Bulgaria,' *Journal of East European Management Studies* (JEEMS), 4: 47–70.

Todorovski (2001) 'Local Government in the Macedonia', in E. Kandeva (ed.), *Stabilization of Local Governments*, Budapest: OSI/LGI.

Tomašević, S. (1955) *Peasants, Politics and Economic Change in Yugoslavia*, Stanford, CL.: Stanford University Press.

Trefler, D. and S.C. Zhu (2004) 'Trade and Inequality in Developing Countries: an Empirical Assessment', Society for Economic Dynamics, Meeting papers, 535.

Tripodi, C. (2000) 'I sistemi locali di imprese: alcune riflessioni sulla riproducibilità del modello', *Sinergie*, 52: 333–51.

Turato, F. (2001) 'Da delocalizzazione a ricollocazione. Le PMI del Nord Est nei Balcani', *Nord Est 2001: rapporto sulla società e sull'economia*, Venezia, Fondazione Nord Est.

Tybout, James R. (2001) *'Plant and Firm-level Evidence on New Trade Theory', NBER*, wp no. 8418, August.

UN FAO and MAF (Ministry of Agriculture and Forestry) (2003), *Rural Development Strategy for Croatia*, Zagreb: MAF.

UNDP (1999) *Human Development Report for Central and Eastern Europe and the CIS*, Bratislava: UNDP.

Uvalić, M. (2004) 'Trade Liberalization in the Balkans: a Blessing in Disguise?', presented at XIV Convegno biennale AISSEC, 27–28 febbraio, Napoli.

Uvalić, M. and D. Vaughn-Whitehead (1997) (eds.) *Privatisation Surprises in Transition Economies: Employee Ownership in Central and Eastern Europe*, Cheltenham: ILO and Edward Elgar.

Van Meurs, W. and S. Weiss (2003) *The Next Europe: Southeastern Europe After Thessaloniki*, CAP, Bertelsmann Stiftung, June in www.bertelsman-stiftung.de

Vandelli, L. (2001) 'Fonti del diritto e forme di governo locale dell'esperienza locale', in R. Scarciglia and M. Gobbo (eds.), *Nuove tendenze dell'ordinamento locale: Fonti del diritto e forme di governo nell'esperienza comparata*, Trieste: EUT.

Verheijen, T. (2001) 'Public Administration Reform: a Mixed Picture', in A.-M. Bíró and P. Kovács (eds.), *Diversity in Action: Local Public Management of Multi-ethnic Communities*, Budapest: LGI Books.

Vernet, D. (1999) 'Le malheur des Serbes', *Revue Politique étrangère*, 3.

Viesti, G. (2000) *Come nascono i distretti industriali*, Bari: Laterza.

Viesti, G. and F. Prota (2001) 'Le prospettive della politica di coesione comunitaria in un'Europa allargata', *Stato e Mercato*, 1, April, pp. 49–87.

Vitosha Research (2004) *The Hidden Economy in Bulgaria*, Sofia, November.

Volz, U. (2004) 'European financial integration and the financing of local businesses in the new EU member states', Working paper No 89, London: EBRD, October.

Voskopouos, G. (2001) 'Western Europe and the Balkans: a Geo-Cultural Approach of International Relations?', *Perspectives*, 17.

Vujacic, V. (2001) 'The Challenges of Ethnic Federalism: Experiences and Lessons of the Former Yugoslavia', in J. Rose and J.C. Traut (eds.), *Federalism and Decentralization. Perspectives for the Transformation Process in Eastern and Central Europe* (George

Marshall European Centre for Security Studies vol. 2, Hamburg, LIT Verlag), pp. 259–70.
Vukadinovic, R. (2002) 'Southeastern Europe and European Security Architecture' in D. Sotiropoulos, and T. Veremis (eds.), *Is Southeastern Europe Doomed to Instability?*, London: Cass.
Wacziarg, R. (2001) 'Measuring the Dynamic Gains from Trade', *World Bank Economic Review*, 15, 3: 393–429.
Waterston, A. (1962) *Planning in Yugoslavia: Organisation and Implementation*, The Economic Development Institute, International Bank for Reconstruction and Development, Baltimore: Johns Hopkins Press.
Watson, J. (2002), *Romania. a Case Study*, Report, OECD–DAC Task Force on Donors Practices.
Windolf, P. (1998) 'Privatization and Elite Reproduction in Eastern Europe', *Archives Europeennes de Sociologie*, 2: 335–75.
Winters, L.A., N. McCulloch and McKay (2004) 'Trade Liberalization and Poverty: The Evidence So Far', *Journal of Economic Literature*, 62, 1: 72–115.
Woodward, S. (1995) *Balkan Tragedy: Chaos and Dissolution After the Cold War*, Washington, DC: Brookings Institution.
World Bank (1975) *Yugoslavia: Development with Decentralisation*, Washington, DC: Johns Hopkins Press for the World Bank.
—— (1991) *Industrial Restructuring Study: Overview, Issues, and Strategy for Restructuring*, Washington, DC: World Bank.
—— (1997) *Bosnia and Herzegovina: From Recovery to Sustainable Growth*, Washington DC: World Bank.
—— (2000a) *The Road to Stability and Prosperity in South Eastern Europe*, Washington, DC: World Bank.
—— (2000b) *Making Transition Work for Everyone: Poverty and Inequality in Europe and Central Asia.*
—— (2001) *World Development Report*, Washington, DC: World Bank.
—— (2002) *Transition – The First Ten Years: Analysis and Lessons for Eastern Europe and the former Soviet Union.*
—— (2003a), Romania: *Poverty Assessment*, vols 1 and 2.
—— (2003b), *Serbia and Montenegro Poverty Assessment*, vol. 1 and 2.
—— (2003c), *Bosnia and Herzegovina Poverty Assessment*, vol. 1 and 2.
—— (2003d), Albania: *Poverty Assessment.*
—— (2003e), *Trade Policies and institutions in the Countries of South Eastern Europe in the EU Stabilization and Association Process*, 28 March 2003.
—— (2004) *Local Economic Development Agencies*, Washington, DC: World Bank Local Economic Development.
World Bank, European Commission and EBRD (1996) *Bosnia and Herzegovina: Towards Economic Recovery*, Discussion paper no. 1, prepared for the Second Donors Conference.
Yin, R. K. (2003) *Case Study Research: Design and Methods*, Thousand Oaks: Sage.
Žagar, M. (2004) 'The Collapse of the Yugoslav Federation and the Viability of Asymmetrical Federalism', in S. Ortino, V. Mastny, and M. Žagar (eds.), *Changing Faces of Federalism*, Manchester: Manchester University Press.

# Index